CRUISING TO DESOLATION SOUND

Howe Sound, the Sunshine Coast, Desolation Sound and the Discovery Islands

Destinations, Passages, Marinas, Marine Parks and Anchorages

Other books by the same author
Mariner Artist John M. Horton
Gulf Islands Cruising Guide
North of Desolation Sound
Docks and Destinations
Anchorages and Marine Parks
Antiques Afloat

PETER VASSILOPOULOS

www.marineguides.com

Contents copyright © 2009 Peter Vassilopoulos.
Pacific Marine Publishing, Canada.
PO Box 1312 Stn A, Delta, BC V4M 3Y8
In the USA: PO Box 984, Point Roberts WA 98281-0984
Prepress graphics and production Pacific Marine Publishing.

Photographs and illustrations by the author unless indicated otherwise.
All information and illustrations in this book are provided without guarantee and it is up to
the boat operator to ensure the proper use of navigational charts and other aids to navigation.
Use of charts, depth sounders, BC Sailing Directions, Small Craft Guide and other sources
is recommended. Hydrographic Charts and tide and current tables should be used at all times
when navigating waterways, bays, coves, harbours and marinas.
The publisher and author is not liable for marine operations leading to accident, damage or
injury in any way connected with reference to this book.

Waypoints included were taken by the author at the point of reading, using a marine GPS unit.
Every effort has been made to ensure accuracy but this is subject to transposition and final
information cannot be guaranteed.

Printed in Canada

Library and Archives Canada Cataloguing in Publication

Vassilopoulos, Peter, 1940-
Cruising to Desolation Sound : Howe Sound, the Sunshine
Coast, Desolation Sound and the Discovery Islands of British
Columbia / Peter Vassilopoulos.
(Western waters cruising guide v. 3)
Includes bibliographical references and index.
ISBN 978-0-919317-45-1

1. Boats and boating--British Columbia--Howe Sound Region--
Guidebooks. 2. Boats and boating--British Columbia--Sunshine
Coast--Guidebooks. 3. Boats and boating--British Columbia--Desolation
Sound--Guidebooks. 4. Boats and boating--British Columbia--Discovery
Islands--Guidebooks. 5. Howe Sound Region (B.C.)--Guidebooks.
6. Sunshine Coast (B.C.)--Guidebooks. 7. Desolation Sound (B.C.)--
Guidebooks. 8. Discovery Islands (B.C.)--Guidebooks. I. Title. II. Series.
III. Series: Vassilopoulos, Peter, 1940- . Western waters cruising guide.

GV776.15.B7V363 2009   797.1'0971131   C2008-906376-7

Copies available from marine stores, marinas and book stores.
Distribution and acquisition enquiries to
Pacific Marine Publishing. Phone (604) 943-4618.
website: *www.marineguides.com* email: *boating@dccnet.com*

*The author and the boat he and his wife,
Carla, use for cruising the BC coast.
Below:* Balladeer II *at the Okeover dock.*

Peter Vassilopoulos is a veteran boater of over 35 years in the
Pacific Northwest and British Columbia waters. He and Carla are
well known in western waters where they spend their time main-
taining this and their other marine guides:
**The Gulf Islands Cruising Guide, North of Desolation Sound,
Docks and Destinations** and **Anchorages and Marine Parks.**

The author wishes to express gratitude to those who assisted in the acquisition of material for this book.
Thanks to friends Sharon Allman and Iz Goto, Norman
Elliott and Justin Taylor. A special tribute to the memory
of Henry Karcz who enthusiastically assisted with the acquisition of earlier aerial photos. Special thanks to my wife
Carla and to Chris Fraser for ther input and assistance in
editing and proof reading. Also Robin Battley and charter
operators, marina owners and tenants for their input.

Cover: Sailing down Sutil Channel towards the entrance
of Von Donop Inlet in Desolation Sound.

CRUISING TO
DESOLATION SOUND
FEATURING
DESOLATION SOUND
AND THE SUNSHINE COAST

PETER VASSILOPOULOS

Pacific Marine Publishing

This spectacular waterfall is a short distance north of the mouth of Toba Inlet near Walsh Cove.

DESTINATIONS

Popular anchorages and havens

Throughout this guide icons are used to indicate anchoring locations, compass bearings, waterways, ferry landings and park facilities. These are added for graphic embellishment of illustrations and are not necessarily precise.
Use official CHS nautical charts to determine depths and hazards.
Shown to the right are some examples of the icons used in the unofficial, hand-drawn diagrams.
Sailboat icons and anchor icons are used interchangeably as space allows.
Red dots marinas, blue dots communities.
R: Launch Ramps. K: Kayak launching.

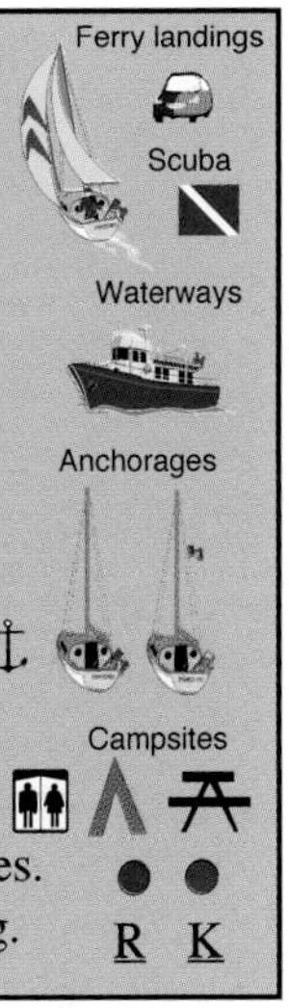

Ferry landings

Scuba

Waterways

Anchorages

Campsites

R   K

CONTENTS

Vancouver Harbour to Howe Sound

The Sunshine Coast

The Discovery Islands

Beyond Desolation Sound

Preface

This third book in the series of cruising guides to popular British Columbia destinations completes the series that I began with my books *North of Desolation Sound* and *The Gulf Islands Cruising Guide*. I have chosen to include Indian Arm, Howe Sound, the Sunshine Coast and reference to Vancouver Harbour as part of this book. It takes in the popular destinations and overnight stops along the way to Desolation Sound as well as the famed Princess Louisa Inlet.

Desolation Sound, for the purposes of this book, includes the Discovery Islands, lying to the west of the sound. The inclusion of the Discovery Islands and Campbell River in this volume, extends the area covered in the *Gulf Islands Cruising Guide*, which includes the east coast of Vancouver Island to Comox. In the three books I have been able to cover all of the coast where the most popular cruising destinations are located.

The Gulf Islands book includes Lasqueti Island as part of the northern Gulf Islands and this book has Texada Island, which although lying closely adjacent to Lasqueti, is considered more as part of the Sunshine Coast than a northern Gulf Island. There are those who felt a separate book on the Sunshine Coast would be appropriate, but in an attempt to keep a vessel's inventory of guidebooks under control, the idea of three rather than four prevailed. The first in the series, *North of Desolation Sound*, continues beyond this guide to include Johnstone Strait and the Broughton Islands.

While I have included information about services available at marinas, in blue type, far more comprehensive coverage to those facilities can be found in my guide/directory *Docks and Destinations*. I have included as much detail as possible on anchorages in the areas covered. A less detailed but wider ranging look at anchorages beyond the the scope of this book can be found in my guide *Anchorages and Marine Parks*.

—*Peter Vassilopoulos*

Anchorages, waterways and places of interest referenced in this book are based on the explorations and findings of the author. Some suggestions included in this guide have been made by other mariners, authors and friends familiar with the area. There are many tiny nooks and coves in which to anchor, or places of interest to visit that are the personal findings or choices of some mariners who have visited the Islands or who will do so in the future. Due to space limitations every one of these places cannot be included in this guide. The author welcomes suggestions from mariners for future editions. Correspondence to PO Box 1312 Delta BC V4M 3Y8. Email: boating@dccnet.com

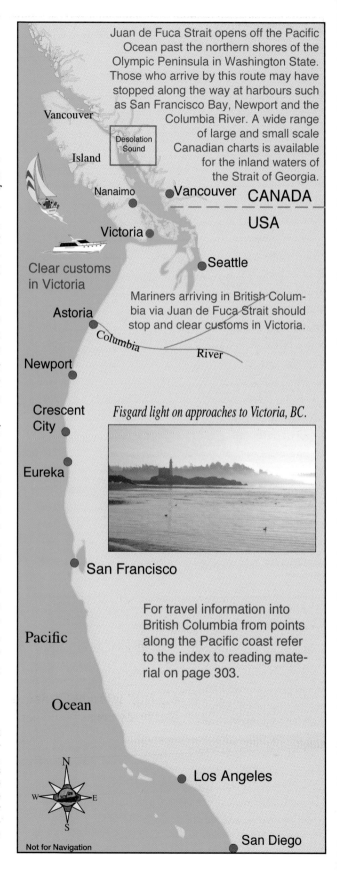

Juan de Fuca Strait opens off the Pacific Ocean past the northern shores of the Olympic Peninsula in Washington State. Those who arrive by this route may have stopped along the way at harbours such as San Francisco Bay, Newport and the Columbia River. A wide range of large and small scale Canadian charts is available for the inland waters of the Strait of Georgia.

Vancouver

Island

Desolation Sound

Nanaimo

Vancouver CANADA

USA

Victoria

Seattle

Clear customs in Victoria

Mariners arriving in British Columbia via Juan de Fuca Strait should stop and clear customs in Victoria.

Astoria

Columbia River

Newport

Crescent City

Fisgard light on approaches to Victoria, BC.

Eureka

San Francisco

For travel information into British Columbia from points along the Pacific coast refer to the index to reading material on page 303.

Pacific

Ocean

Los Angeles

San Diego

Not for Navigation

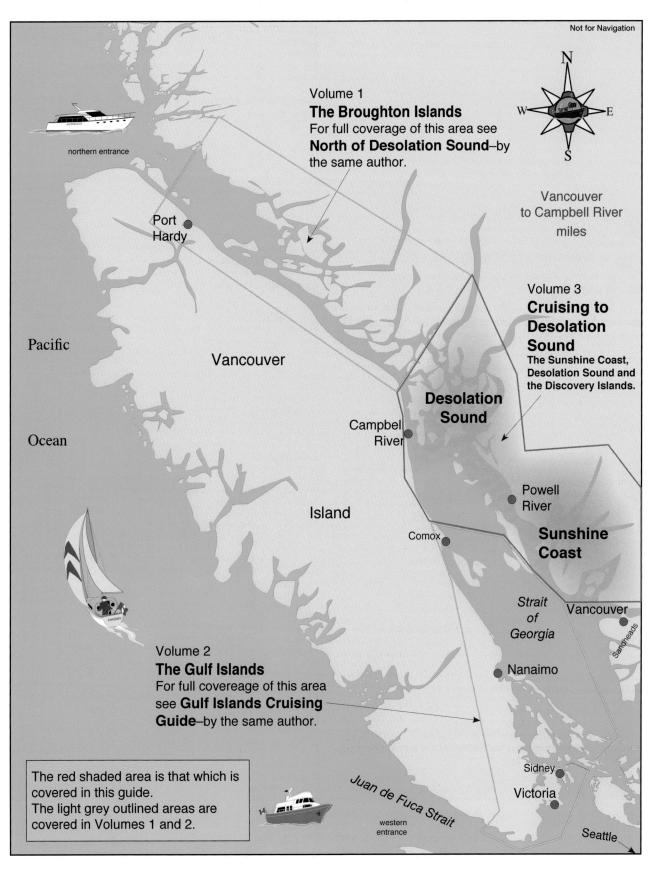

northern entrance

Volume 1
The Broughton Islands
For full coverage of this area see
North of Desolation Sound–by
the same author.

N
W   E
S

Vancouver
to Campbell River
miles

Port
Hardy

Volume 3
Cruising to
Desolation
Sound
The Sunshine Coast,
Desolation Sound and
the Discovery Islands.

Pacific

Vancouver

Desolation
Sound

Campbel
River

Ocean

Powell
River

Island

Sunshine
Coast

Comox

Strait
of
Georgia   Vancouver

Volume 2
The Gulf Islands
For full covereage of this area
see **Gulf Islands Cruising**
Guide–by the same author.

Sandheads

Nanaimo

The red shaded area is that which is
covered in this guide.
The light grey outlined areas are
covered in Volumes 1 and 2.

Sidney

Juan de Fuca Strait

Victoria

western
entrance

Seattle

A painting by marine artist John M. Horton depicting Captain George Vancouver's ships in Desolation Sound in 1792.
This and many more of Horton's paintings are included in the book **Mariner Artist John M. Horton** *(Heritage House 2007).*

Introduction

Since arriving in Canada, I have had the pleasure of working and cruising on one of he loveliest coastlines in the world. The Sunshine Coast, Desolation Sound and the Discovery Islands are but one part of the coast worthy of exploration. And I have had the pleasure of enjoying these areas along with many others in my years of cruising on the British Columbia coast.

Rugged, wild and sometimes peaceful, blessed with a natural beauty of abundant wildlife, for the mariner new and unknown places can be frightening yet fantastic. I have always carried a library of books aboard my own vessel to inform me of the navigational hazards and dangers that I might encounter as well as the fascinating history of the Pacific Northwest.

Included in my collection are all of the beautifully produced and well written cruising guides by Peter Vassilopoulos. They are all in constant use and the fact that they are updated regularly keeps me abreast of our ever changing coastal installations.

Peter Vassilopoulos is an enthusiastic mariner and knows the coast and its people well. The friendships he has developed over the years in villages, towns and out-of-the-way settlements make his books more interesting, valuable and accurate.

I look forward to adding this book to the shelf over my chart table.

–John M. Horton

Ports and Passes tidal advice

The tides and currents have a huge impact on our boating experiences. We have to plan departures, transit of narrows, arrivals, and activities based on the tides and currents. Along the entire west coast of North America, it is accepted that the tidal current floods to the North.

This flow of water continues to the east in the Northern latitudes and then floods to the south along the eastern coast of North America. Vancouver Island creates an obstruction for the currents to wrap themselves around. At the southern end of the island, Juan de Fuca funnels the flooding ocean into the straits and southward to Puget Sound, while at the same time filling the Strait of Georgia. As the flood of ocean water on the west coast of Vancouver Island reaches Cape Scott in the north, it curls around and floods southward, filling the fjords on the east side of Vancouver Island until he flood of water meets with the northwesterly flowing current from the south near the aptly named Mitlenatch Island. These two opposing forces often generate violent turbulence when they meet, which can be amplified by winds. Be wary of travelling through this area during periods of maximum flood. Desolation Sound is close to this meeting place and tucked away behind peninsulas and islands, and the water is almost similar to a tidal pool. Okeover Inlet and the lagoon-like Theodosia Inlet stay warm all summer. The waters surrounding Gifford Peninsula and Prideaux Haven are not troubled by extreme currents or tricky passages. This, along with the natural beauty and number of secluded gunk holes, makes it easy to understand why there are so many favourite spots for anchoring in Desolation Sound. When dropping your anchor for an overnight stay, pay attention to the current height of tide.

We recently heard the story of a novice boater who excitedly found the perfect corner to spend the night in a quiet anchorage and dropped the hook in a little over twelve feet of water. He believed that he had plenty of allowance for his 5 foot draft. In his haste, he neglected to consult his tide book (**Ports and Passes** is a popular choice) or notice the tree boughs within reach of the water surface. Twelve feet is not enough water beneath your keel on a falling fourteen foot tide, regardless of your draft. Always anchor with caution and only after consulting your charts, tide book and surroundings. —*Norm and Jodi Brochno*, **Ports and Passes**.

Conversion Tables

**1 nautical mile = 6,067.11 feet (1 land mile = 5,280 feet).
1 metre = 3' 3.7"**

Measures:

1 US gallon	0.833 Imperial gallon
1 US gallon	3.785 litres
1 Imperial gallon	1.201 US gallons
1 Imperial gallon	4.546 litres
1 litre	0.264 US gallon
2 pints	1 quart
4 quarts	1 gallon
1 litre	1.0567 quarts
1 quart	0.9463 litre

Mariners' Measures:

6 feet	1 fathom
120 fathoms	1 cable (length)
5,280 feet	1 statute mile
6,067.11 feet	1 nautical mile

Linear Measure:

1 metre	39.37 inches (1.0936 yards)
(1 metre	3'.3.7")
1 kilometre	0.621 mile
1 mile	1.609 kilometres

Temperatures:
A Fahrenheit is smaller than a Centigrade (Celsius) degree. It is 5/9 of a Celsius degree.
Conversion method
To convert Celsius to Fahrenheit multiply by 9, divide by 5 and add 32.
To convert Fahrenheit to Celsius, subtract 32, multiply by 5 and divide by 9.

A simple variation for an approximate conversion:
Celsius to Fahrenheit–Multiply by two and add 32.
Fahrenheit to Celsius–Subtract 32 and divide by two.
For example:
Fahrenheit–72° minus 32 = 40 divided by 2 = 20°C.
Celsius–10° multiplied by 2 = 20 plus 32 = 52°F

METRIC: Throughout this guide chart distance references have been made in nautical miles and depths in metres. Tides affect depths and therefore all suggested anchoring depths are approximate. More precise measurements, if needed, can be calculated with the use of your nautical charts or taken from official publications such as the BC Sailing Directions. The above suggested method of conversion is intended as a quick way for the mariner to convert measures and distances to their preferred standard.

Customs information

The master of any pleasure boat must report to Customs immediately after arriving in Canada or the United States and must report any foreign merchandise that is subject to duty. The report should include the name of the boat, its nationality, name of the master, place of docking and arrival time. If an inspection is required, the Customs officer will direct the vessel to an inspection area. The vessel must make formal entry with Customs within 48 hours.

It is now required that passports be carried when crossing the border in either direction.

Vessels entering the USA that are 30 feet or longer in length must pay an annual fee to enter the USA. Vessels under 30 feet with nothing to declare are not subject to the fee. The fee may be paid annually, by credit card over the phone, and a decal will be issued.

The I-68 or NEXUS programs allows small craft entry to the USA. Anyone seeking entry to the United States must report their arrivals. Boaters participating in the I-68 or NEXUS programs must report but may do so by phone at a designated point of entry (telephones are available at ports of entry or use your cellular phone when you have docked).

Call 1-800-562-5943. Provide the following information to the customs officer: • Vessel name and length • Registration Number • User fee decal number (if applicable) • Date of your intended departure.

You will be given a release number which you should enter in your logbook along with the time of clearance and place of reporting.

In Canada the Automated Customs Information Service (ACIS) system now called Border Information Service (BIS) is reflected on the Internet, intranet, and in CBSA publications. The Border Information Service On-line, or BIS Online, provides access to all the recorded phone information from the BIS telephone system in a convenient, navigable format. Use one of the categories below and follow the links to answer many basic border services questions:

For in-depth enquiries, call the BIS phone service during regular business hours - Monday to Friday (except holidays) from 8:00-16:00 local time, and press 0 to speak to an agent: From within Canada, call: 1 800-461-9999 (toll free). From outside Canada, call: 204-983-3500 or 506-636-5064 (long-distance charges apply).

U.S Customs and Border Protection

U.S. citizens are required to carry proof of citizenship such as a valid passport. Canadian citizens should present proof of Canadian citizenship (passport).

If your boat has anchored or tied up, you are considered to have entered the United States. No one may board or leave the boat without first completing customs processing, unless permission to do so is granted by the Customs officer in charge. The only exception to this requirement is for the captain to report arrival.

If it is necessary for someone to leave the boat to report arrival to U.S. Customs, he or she must return to the boat after reporting and remain on board. No one who arrived in that boat may leave until the Customs officer grants permission to go ashore. Violations may result in substantial penalties and forfeiture of the boat. Reporting is required after having been at any foreign port or place and/or having had contact with any hovering vessel.

Canada Customs

All vessels arriving in Canada from across the border must clear customs immediately after docking. The master or his designated representative must report in person or by telephone. No one else may leave the vessel and no merchandise or luggage may be removed until it has been cleared.

The master may call at 1-888-226-7277 or from a Customs Direct line phone. Canpass members phone 1-888-CANPASS (226-7277). Canpass or Nexus may be used only if all on board are members. You will still have to stop at a Canpass or Nexus designated reporting station, but processing is quick.

It is required that you have a passport. US citizens must also have a passport. Citizens of other countries need passports and sometimes visas, and birth certificates for minors on board. Documentation for non-related children is required for crossing the border.

When you report by telephone you may be directed to a customs port where an officer is present and able to conduct an inspection of your vessel.

You may be asked for all or some of the following:
• Vessel Name, length and registration numbers
• Names, birth dates, addresses and citizenship of everyone on board.
• Estimated time of departure (boats returning to the US).

You will be given a clearance number which should be posted in a side window. Keep a logged record of this number, with the date, place and time of clearance.

Designated US Ports of Entry

Report your arrival in the United States to U.S. Customs nearest your point of entry.
Call 800-562-5943
Weekday Phone Numbers:

Anacortes	360-532-2030
Bellingham	360-734-5463
Blaine	360-332-6318
Everett	425-259-0246
Friday/Roche Hbr	360-378-2080
Longview	360-425-3710
Neah Bay	206-645-2311
Olympia	253-593-6338
Point Roberts	360-945-2314
Port Angeles	360-457-4311

Designated BC Ports of Entry (for central coast waters destinations)

Report your arrival in Canada at the following ports of entry:

Victoria:	Royal Victoria Yacht Club (Cadboro Bay), Victoria Inner Harbour customs dock, Oak Bay Marina. Canadian Forces Sailing Association (Members only)
Sidney:	Angler's Anchorage Marina, Canoe Cove Marina, Port Sidney Marina, Royal Victoria Yacht Club (Tsehum Harbour), Van Isle Marina.
Nanaimo:	Nanaimo Port Authority Basin, Brechin Point Marina. Townsite Marina–permit holders only.
Vancouver:	Steveston gas dock, Coal Harbour, Burrard Inlet. False Creek public dock.
Campbell River:	Discovery Harbour Marina.

Contact Canada Customs toll free at 1-888-226-7277
Vancouver: Call 604-278-1825 or 604-278-7422   www.cbsa.gc.ca
Reporting by phone could still require inspection.

Foreword

The popular routes to Desolation Sound from the south include following the Sunshine Coast north from Vancouver or taking a course along the east coast of Vancouver Island. Some mariners arriving from offshore, Puget Sound or southern parts of Vancouver Island cross the Strait of Georgia from Gabriola Pass, Nanaimo or north of Nanaimo to follow all or part of the Sunshine Coast. Those crossing the Strait should be cognisant of the restricted area WG which is a miltary firing and testing area. It may be crossed when there is no activity. This can be determined by listening for notices on VHF channel 16 or CB channel 9. Or by contacting the marine operator on channel 10.

Once safely en route to Desolation Sound many travellers with available time stop in at Secret Cove, Smuggler Cove, Pender Harbour or Princess Louisa Inlet. Some make this beautiful deep fjord their final destination or include a side trip through Skookumchuck Narrows into Sechelt Inlet.

For those familiar with Desolation Sound, its features draw them back time and again, looking for the majestic beauty of the surrounding mountains, the cosy nooks that afford protected anchorage and the warm waters for swimming. These extend beyond the confines of Desolation Sound to the adjacent islands and waterways of the Discovery Islands which lie to the immediate west of the sound.

This book encompasses the routes to Desolation Sound, with an extensive coverage of the Sunshine Coast and the Discovery Islands. The adjacent cruising areas are destinations in their own right. They have been bundled in with this work on Desolation Sound to enable the pleasure boating community to refer, in one book, to the destination of their choice within easy reach of those routes.

In this third book of the series of cruising guides, I have used a larger graphic format, allowing photographs to be bigger and more plentiful. I have chosen more aerial photographs and reduced the number of diagrams of dock layouts, feeling that the clear, close-up photographs are more useful. The inclusion of drawings of sailboats at anchor is intended to show the approximate location of suitable spots in which to drop the hook.

Where space has tended to not allow the insertion of a large enough icon of this sailboat I have used the emblem of an anchor. Duplication of diagrams is intended to help the reader easily refer to location of places without having to page back and forth. The use of other icons is for the purpose of illustrating coastal features such as campsites, ferry terminals and popular scuba diving spots. The boat icons used throughout are simply embellishments to the graphics, but they also help indicate the waterways as opposed to land mass.

Reminder: Transmit on low range when using VHF if you are near the vessel or facility you are trying to contact. Reserve high frequency for longer distances.

There is no point transmitting five miles on high power when you are trying to reach a station within sight. It not only uses a lot of battery energy but also interferes with vessels communicating well beyond the range of your needs.

Local weather reports

When cruising between Vancouver and Desolation Sound along the Sunshine Coast, monitor weather on your vessel's VHF radio. If you wish to avoid rough water in open passages, such as along Malaspina Strait, use the reports of wind conditions from the various weather reporting stations. Take note of wind strength and wave heights to assess whether to continue or wait at a safe anchorage or marina.

The weather stations providing information are located at the following locations:

Jericho (English Bay)
Pam Rocks (Howe Sound)
Grief Point (Malaspina Strait)
Cape Mudge (Campbell River)
Chatham Point (Discovery Passage)

Northern Strait of Georgia:
Sentry Shoal (Buoy position: 49.92N 125.00W)

Southern Strait of Georgia:
Halibut Bank (Buoy position: 49.34N 123.72W)

*At a tranquil anchorage, in the lee of Mink Island
in Desolation Sound.*

Vancouver
Gateway to the Sunshine Coast

Charts 3311, 3481, 3493, 3494, 3495, 3463

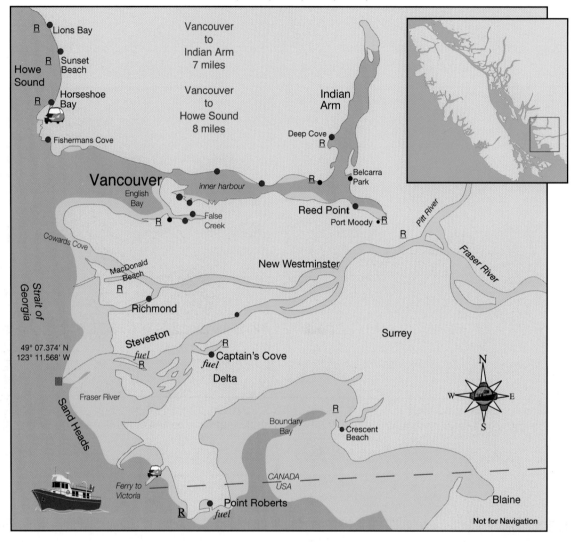

Mariners arriving in Canada from offshore proceed to Victoria to clear customs. Phone 1 888-226-7277

Vancouver to Indian Arm

Any trip to the Sunshine Coast, Desolation Sound and the Discovery Islands from points south should include a visit to Vancouver. It is this city that was named for the famous Captain George Vancouver, who explored and charted the inside passage in his vessels *Discovery* and *Chatham*. In Vancouver, mariners will find a host of opportunities to enjoy the many cultures and the maritime nature of British Columbia.

The city sits on a small peninsula that juts into the Strait of Georgia. It is lapped by the waters of English Bay on the one side of the peninsula and Vancouver Harbour in Burrard Inlet on the other.

The Sunshine Coast, where this book commences, has its beginnings on the North Shore of Burrard Inlet. Hence this area, from Indian Arm, through Burrard Inlet and into Howe Sound, is included as the first section of the guide. Cross the Burrard Inlet and visit Vancouver, stopping in Coal Harbour and the tourist melting pot of False Creek, taking in Granville Island as part of your voyage.

Motoring out of Vancouver's downtown Coal Harbour.

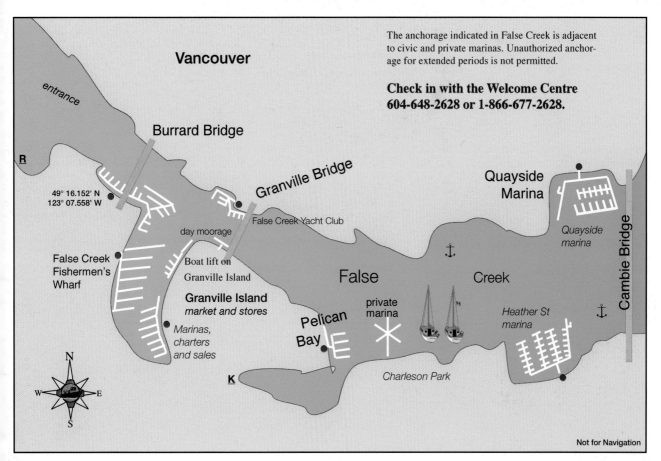

The anchorage indicated in False Creek is adjacent to civic and private marinas. Unauthorized anchorage for extended periods is not permitted.

Check in with the Welcome Centre 604-648-2628 or 1-866-677-2628.

Vancouver

Burrard Bridge

Granville Bridge

Quayside Marina

49° 16.152' N
123° 07.558' W

False Creek Yacht Club

day moorage

Quayside marina

False Creek Fishermen's Wharf

Boat lift on Granville Island

False Creek

Creek

Cambie Bridge

Granville Island *market and stores*

Marinas, charters and sales

Pelican Bay

private marina

Heather St marina

Charleson Park

Not for Navigation

False Creek

This is a waterway that opens off English Bay, leading to the renowned Granville Island, an essential stop for any visitor to Vancouver. **Granville Island** is a man-made island but with a causeway linking it to the city. At one time an industrial site, the island now hosts an eclectic selection of vendors, restaurants and art and craft stores as well as a large indoor market selling fresh produce, meats, specialty foods, baked goods and delicacies. Several marinas along the shores of False Creek are home to private vessels. Visiting boats should enquire about overnight moorage. And for some, anchoring is an option. Check with the welcome centre at 604-648-2628 or call them on VHF channel 66A for transient moorage or anchoring information. Refer also to the author's marine guide and directory ***Docks and Destinations***.

Coal Harbour

Most larger vessels visiting Vancouver stay overnight at Coal Harbour Marina in Burrard Inlet, phone 604-681-2628. The marina is located on the waterfront of downtown Vancouver, and affords quick and easy access to the city centre.

Vancouver attracts tourists from all over the world for its dramatic scenery and outdoor recreation, such as skiing on the

Opposite: False Creek is a mostly sheltered body of water. Check in with the visitor centre for moorage or anchorage space allocation. At the entrance (top) is the large civic marina to starboard, followed by an arm of water leading to the fishermen's wharf and the south side of Granville Island. Continuing into False Creek there is a dock on the north side of Granville Island and one at the east end, for temporary stops, and a marina on the opposite shore. Anchoring is possible inside False Creek where it opens up (bottom photograph). More marinas are located beyond this point.

slopes of the tall mountains on the north shore, hiking their trails or chartering a boat and cruising off to places such as Desolation Sound. It is known also, of course, for its historic heritage, its culture, entertainment and arts. The science centre on the east shore of False Creek and the adjacent Chinatown are busy with visitors year round. The maritime museum and the museum of anthropology give the visiting mariner a taste of the coast they are about to explore and are worth the taxi or bus trip to get to them.

Voyaging around Burrard Inlet requires entering the harbour beneath the Lions Gate Bridge and navigating the tidal

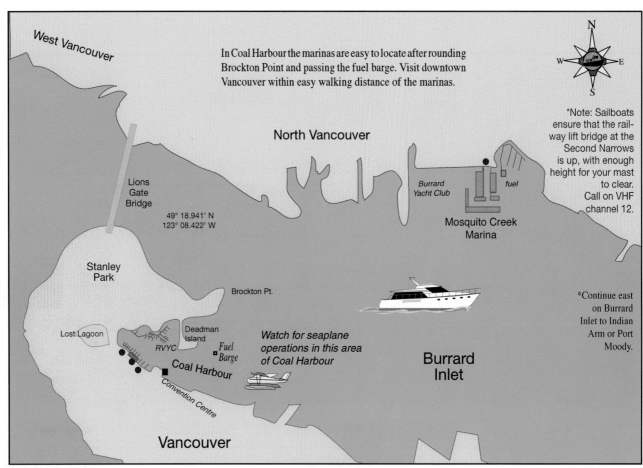

West Vancouver

North Vancouver

In Coal Harbour the marinas are easy to locate after rounding Brockton Point and passing the fuel barge. Visit downtown Vancouver within easy walking distance of the marinas.

N
W E
S

*Note: Sailboats ensure that the railway lift bridge at the Second Narrows is up, with enough height for your mast to clear. Call on VHF channel 12.

Lions Gate Bridge

49° 18.941' N
123° 08.422' W

Burrard Yacht Club

fuel

Mosquito Creek Marina

Stanley Park

Brockton Pt.

*Continue east on Burrard Inlet to Indian Arm or Port Moody.

Lost Lagoon

Deadman Island

RVYC

Fuel Barge

Watch for seaplane operations in this area of Coal Harbour

Burrard Inlet

Coal Harbour

Convention Centre

Vancouver

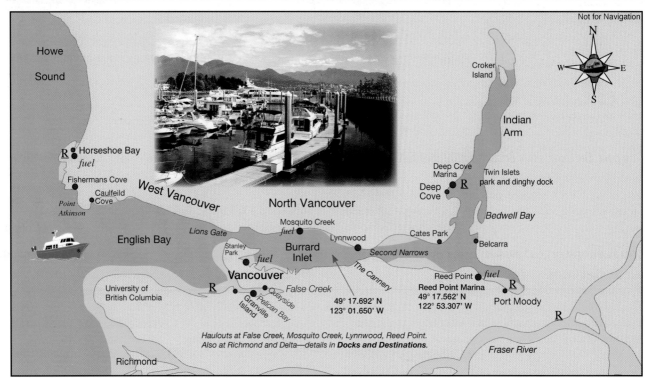

Not for Navigation

N
W E
S

Howe
Sound

Croker Island

Indian Arm

R Horseshoe Bay
fuel

Fishermans Cove

Caulfeild Cove

Point Atkinson

West Vancouver

North Vancouver

Deep Cove Marina

Twin Islets park and dinghy dock

Deep Cove R

English Bay

Lions Gate

Mosquito Creek
fuel

Lynnwood

Cates Park

Bedwell Bay

Belcarra

Stanley Park

fuel

Burrard Inlet

Second Narrows

Vancouver

The Cannery

University of British Columbia

R

False Creek

Quayside

Granville Island

Pelican Bay

49° 17.692' N
123° 01.650' W

Reed Point
fuel

Reed Point Marina
49° 17.562' N
122° 53.307' W

R

Port Moody

R

Richmond

Fraser River

Haulouts at False Creek, Mosquito Creek, Lynnwood, Reed Point.
Also at Richmond and Delta—details in **Docks and Destinations**.

Top: Coal Harbour, Vancouver. The city waterfront is on the north side of a peninsula that protrudes into English Bay and Burrard Inlet. The fuel dock is on a floating barge in the harbour. Off to the right is Deadman Island, home of HMCS Discovery Naval Reserve base. Marinas line the city's shoreline and Stanley Park is to the right. The University of British Columbia is on the point in the background.

Right: The big, busy Coal Harbour Marina, which is seen also in the top photograph, beyond Deadman Island. It accommodates mariners looking for overnight moorage in Vancouver.

First Narrows. Use of tide and current charts will enable the mariner to do so safely and with ease. Pass Brockton Point and the floating fuel barge to reach the marinas and yacht clubs' docks.

The dramatic sail-like roof of the convention centre looms prominently as you approach the city. The Royal Vancouver Yacht Club and the Vancouver Rowing Club have their facilities in the western nook of Coal Harbour just beyond the convention centre. Beyond Coal Harbour Marina, Bayshore West Marina and adjacent marinas accommodate mostly permanent resident boats. Watch for the operations of float planes, as the harbour waterways include an official floatplane aerodrome. On the opposite shore of the harbour, alongside Burrard Yacht Club, **Mosquito Creek Marina** is a good fuel stop with possible overnight moorage.

Continuing east in Burrard Inlet, approach the second narrows with its Ironworkers Memorial (Second Narrows Crossing) bridge spanning another tidal passage. To the south before reaching the narrows, *The Cannery* dock accommodates a few boats stopping in for lunch or dinner. They offer a superb take-out picnic basket. The location of this restaurant will be changed in 2010, but the new address was not known at the time of publication. On the north shore, immediately adjacent to the bridge is **Lynnwood Marina** where haulouts, repairs and services are possible.

Pass through the narrows and you are on your way to

Port Moody and Indian Arm. Many local mariners who keep their boats in Burrard Inlet, use Indian Arm as their frequent getaway destination. In summer it is well protected from weather conditions, although the occasional wind picks up a light to moderate chop. In winter the waters are not quite as hospitable.

A launch ramp at Port Moody and another at Cates Park, keep the waterways of Burrard Inet and Indian Arm quite busy with small craft. Reed Point Marina on the approaches to Port Moody is a well-known fuel stop.

Reed Point Marina

850 Barnet Hwy
Port Moody BC V3H 1V6
Phone 604-937-1600
office@reedpoint.com
www.reedpoint.com

This is a major service centre with gas and diesel fuels available at the fuel barge. It is a full service yard with many services including boat haulouts, repairs, boat tops and canvas repairs, engine servicing, and overhauls. There is a well-equipped marine chandlery for supplies.

The marina has a travelift and a major workyard and offers dry storage for boats. There is short and long term moorage for boats of all sizes. Facilities include 30 amp shore power and washrooms.

Top: The view west over Burrard Inlet, Vancouver Harbour. Atop the hill to the left is Simon Fraser University. The city lies to the left in the distance with Stanley Park occupying the land to its right. The harbour entrance is to the right of Stanley Park under the Lions Gate Bridge (First Narrows). Entrance to the eastern portion of the inlet is by way of the Second Narrows under the Ironworkers Memorial Bridge (Second Narrows Crossing), at left of centre. Inset: Another vew of Second Narrows Bridge above Lynnwood Marina. Bottom: Reed Point Marina in Port Moody. It is not shown in the photograph, centre, but is located to the left beyond the bottom of the picture. The small marina on the opposite shore is private. Opposite page: A busy Coal Harbour Marina in downtown Vancouver.

Above: Looking up Indian Arm from above Roche Point and the launch ramp at Cates Park. The building on the distant shore is the power station at Buntzen Bay.

Left: A view over Port Moody showing the fuel tanks at Ioco and the launch ramp near Reed Point. Reed Point Marina can be seen partially, at the right side of the waterway.

Bottom: The launch ramp at Port Moody, showing the large restaurant in the former boat trailer parking lot. Note the approaches to this launch ramp, which are marked to keep vessels off the shallows at the head of the inlet.

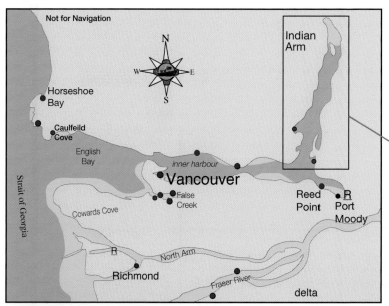

Not for Navigation

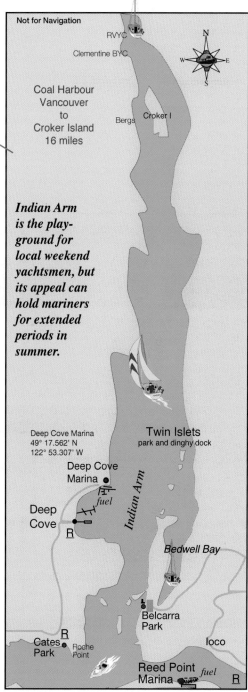

Not for Navigation

Coal Harbour
Vancouver
to
Croker Island
16 miles

*Indian Arm
is the play-
ground for
local weekend
yachtsmen, but
its appeal can
hold mariners
for extended
periods in
summer.*

The entrance to Indian Arm with Belcarra Park public dock to the right.

Indian Arm
Vancouver's adjacent waterway

Charts 3311, 3495, 3463

Indian Arm

Just before entering Indian Arm, pass **Cates Park** on the north shore. This is a busy launching spot where a dock accommodates boats being launched or ready to be loaded. Into Indian Arm, **Belcarra Park** on the eastern shore has a dinghy dock and nearby temporary anchorage in 5 to 10 metres. At this park, there is a large expanse of lawn, and a kiosk that sells hamburgers and refreshments. On a summer weekend you will find lots of people fishing off the dock.

This is true also of the dock at **Deep Cove**, a little farther up the Arm and on the western shore. Moorage is available at Deep Cove public dock. Alongside the public dock is the Deep Cove Yacht Club. The Deep Cove public dock is located at the foot of the main street in Deep Cove Village. It is 44 metres in length and handles boats to 12 metres by way of a pay machine. The dock is for day use only. Walk up into the village and enjoy some of its many delights. Cafes, restaurants, novelty stores and shops abound.

Following the sweep of the shore you arrive at Deep Cove

Top: Bedwell Bay, Indian Arm. Note the Buntzen Power Station in the distance. Above, left: Deep Cove Marina. Above: Looking into Deep Cove.

Left: A tranquil temporary anchorage at the head of Belcarra Bay off Belcarra Park. Passage around Hamber Island leads into Indian Arm and around to the anchorage at Bedwell Bay, or to the opposite shore and the entrance to Deep Cove.

Opposite page: The dock at Deep Cove allows short stops to visit the stores in the village. Boats anchored out should check wind forecasts.

Best overnight anchorage, in summer, is on the east side of Indian Arm in Bedwell Bay.

Marina at the entrance to the bay, where some overnight moorage may be found for smaller boats and where fuel and some supplies are available.

Bedwell Bay

On the eastern shore of Indian Arm, opposite Deep Cove is the opening to Bedwell Bay, the major anchorage of the area. It is generally well protected but is open to northeasterly winds, which are not frequent in summer. **Twin Islets** and **Racoon Island Marine Park** lie a short distance north of the entrance to Bedwell Bay.

The park is served by a small dinghy dock in the narrow passage between Twin Islands and the mainland. It is possible to anchor temporarily in this passage, particularly in the nook on the opposite shore. The island, above the landing, has a short but good trail, and camping facilities.

The beach on Racoon Island is a good place to land a small boat and wander its sandy shore. It is possible to anchor temporarily in a nook formed by the north end of the island and a reef indicated by two protruding rocks. We used to scuba dive for Dungeness crabs on Black Shoal, a very shallow stretch of water to the south of the islands.

A cruise to the head of Indian Arm ends with a passage around **Croker Island**. Anchorage may be taken in shallow water off **Bergs** at the Bishop Creek mouth. The reef off the south end of Croker Island is a popular scuba diving site.

The Burrard Yacht Club has an outstation facility at the mouth of **Clementine Creek**, on the west shore near the head of the arm. The nearby former **Wigwam Inn** building and adjacent floats belong to the Royal Vancouver Yacht Club. It is private but very picturesque and is worth cruising by just for the photographic possibilities.

It is possible to anchor off the northeast shore at the head of Indian Arm in fair weather. Also picturesque are Granite Falls on the opposite shore and Silver Falls south of Croker Island on the west shore.

The huge structure on the waterfront at Buntzen Bay on the opposite shore is the Buntzen Power Plant, the first powerhouse to provide Vancouver with electricity. It was built below Buntzen Lake in the first decade of the 20th century. There is no public access to the powerhouse.

Deep Cove North Shore Marina

2890 Panorama Drive, North Vancouver BC V7G 1V6
Phone 604-929-1251
www.deepcovemarina.com

Call ahead for moorage. The fuel dock offers gas and diesel fuels as well as water and 15, 20, and 30 amp power. It has a pumpout, washrooms and a chandlery with bait, fishing supplies, ice and snacks. The marina also offers boat rentals, repairs and servicing. It is within walking distance of the restaurants and stores at Deep Cove village.

Leaving Burrard Inlet for Howe Sound, cruise through First Narrows at or near slack and follow the West Vancouver shoreline around Point Atkinson to Howe Sound. It is best not to attempt Point Atkinson if a strong northwesterly is blowing against a receding tide, as seas become short and steep off the point. If conditions are rough, consider waiting at anchor temporarily in one of the coves along the West Vancouver shoreline.

A small dock at **Caulfeild Cove** will accommodate a boat or two and provide walking access to the nearby park at the point, where it is possible to get close-up views of the old Point Atkinson lighthouse, built in 1874, and of the prevailing sea conditions from its vantage point. Anchoring is also possible inside Caulfeild Cove, but monitor southeasterly winds.

Queen Charlotte Channel, Howe Sound. To the Right is Boyer Island, to the left, the tip of Bowen Island and in the centre distance is Anvil Island.

Coastal British Columbia is a rugged, mountainous region. Cruise it and enjoy the best of boating. This photograph was taken from 1,525 metres above Hotham Sound looking west towards Texada Island and the mountains of Vancouver Island. Khartoum Lake and Lois Lake are in the foreground.

dra Island events

ng Festival, Community
—April/May. Canada
elebrations and Fire-
Rebecca Spit—July.
online at
iscoveryislander.com

Top: The harbour and public docks at Quathiaski Cove.
Left and above: The harbour master offices, and shops in the adjacent parking lot.

Beyond Desolation Sound
Cape Mudge, Mitlenatch Island
Southbound, Northbound
Charts 3311, 3312. 3513

Above: Small boats run across Wilby Shoal off Cape Mudge at high tide. Medium to larger vessels keep well clear, rounding the red buoy P60 and the black can P61. The area can be extremely rough in windy conditions. This is when shallow areas are particularly dangerous. Note the diminutive Mitlenatch Island in the near distance. Below: The launch ramp at Campbell River. It is exposed and there is no adjacent dock.

Cape Mudge

Here Captain Vancouver, going ashore with Archibald Menzies, the ship's botanist, made an excursion to Tsqulotn, a First Nations village at the top of the cliff. They found 12 typical wood slat houses and a population of about 350 people. The Salish, original occupants of the area, were forced out of their elevated village by members of the Lekwiltok band of the Kwakiutl tribe from the north. The settlement of Yuculta on the west shore of Quadra Island, just north of Cape Mudge, is where they established a village as it stands today. Vancouver named the cape after Zachary Mudge, first lieutenant aboard his ship *Discovery*.

Some historians erroneously believe that Captain Vancouver's encounter with the First Nations people of British Columbia marked the beginning of the changes to their way of life. However, it was not Vancouver but the traders and missionaries who did so. Captain Vancouver was intent only on surveying the coast in keeping with his mandate. He was known for establishing good relations with the natives as well as explorers (Spanish) and traders already surveying and working on the coast.

Chief Billy Assu was a notable character in local history. He was instrumental in helping modernize the native settlement of Yaculta at Cape Mudge. An edition of the Canadian

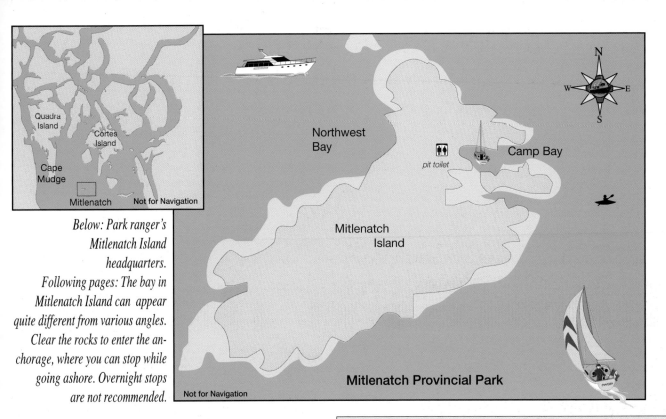

Quadra
Island

Cortes
Island

Cape
Mudge

Mitlenatch   Not for Navigation

Northwest
Bay

pit toilet

Camp Bay

Mitlenatch
Island

Mitlenatch Provincial Park

Not for Navigation

*Below: Park ranger's
Mitlenatch Island
headquarters.
Following pages: The bay in
Mitlenatch Island can appear
quite different from various angles.
Clear the rocks to enter the anchorage, where you can stop while
going ashore. Overnight stops
are not recommended.*

five-dollar bill issued in the 1970s had an engraving of his son Harry's fishing boat at Ripple Rock in 1958 during the historic sockeye run of that year.

Visit the museum at Cape Mudge. On display are items the government confiscated from those ignoring the potlatch ruling, and that have since been returned by the National Museum after the repealing of the law. You may have to get there by road. If you do, there is a First Nations operated RV park and a popular restaurant nearby.

Cape Mudge public dock (Yaculta)
Quadra Island Harbour Authority
Ph: 250-285-3622
The float is north of the tip of Cape Mudge, on First Nations land. It is used extensively by local residents.

Mitlenatch Island
Located at the north end of the Strait of Georgia, Mitlenatch Island is an often bypassed destination. However, it is under-standable that it is missed by many because it is isolated from regular lanes used by pleasure craft travelling to and from Desolation Sound. It does lie in the way of those travelling from Gorge Harbour, south towards Sabine Channel between Texada Island and Lasqueti. Or north in the opposite direction. The northern and southern flowing tides meet at Mitlenatch, producing surprisingly warm water suitable for swimming.

Frequently when we have travelled that route, weather has influenced us to keep going to avoid worsening sea conditions.

But on a calm day and with time available, it is a worthwhile destination, even if for a short visit. The island is accessible only by boat (or float plane), with a small sometimes unsettled anchorage in the northeast side. This provincial nature park encompasses 36 hectares of land and 119 hectares of water, and contains the largest seabird colony in the Strait of Georgia. Sealions are often seen basking in the sun on the island shores. There is a 300 metre park boundary extending from the shoreline, that protects all marine life within the area. It is an ecologically sensitive area and visitors are not allowed to leave the trails. Bikes and pets are not permitted.

Looking northwest, Mitlenatch Island sits isolated off the south perimeter of the Discovery Islands. It is located to the south of Cortes Island, east of Cape Mudge and west of Hernando and Savary Islands at the north end of the Strait of Georgia.

Campbell River to Comox

From Campbell River along the east coast of Vancouver Island to Comox is a fairly exposed stretch of water. On a calm day it is a nice cruise. With a gentle breeze, sailboats have little trouble covering the distance. On stormy days a cautious attitude should prevail as huge seas can build up off Cape Mudge. There is some shelter available at two resorts along this coast. They are not easy to enter when it is stormy, or if it is a very low tide. They are Salmon Point Resort and Pacific Playgrounds Resort. Both have shallow entrances requiring careful navigation at the best of times. All vessels, and especially larger ones, should call ahead to verify depths in the entrances, as well as availability of space.

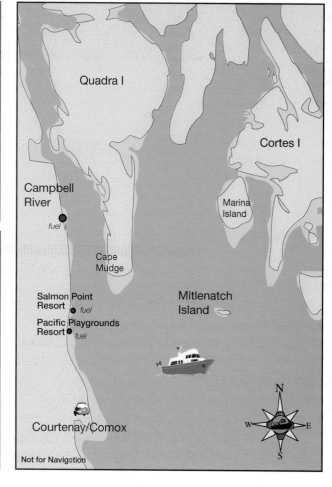

286

Above: Pacific Playgrounds Resort and Marina at the Oyster River mouth.
Right: Salmon Point Marina not far from the south end of Campbell River. Boats entering need a minimum of a 1.52 metre tide.
Opposite page: Two views of the anchorage in Camp Bay on Mitlenatch Island.

Beyond Desolation Sound–Southbound.

The shore south of Campbell River has a sloping shallow shelf with a fairly straight coastline. It is broken by several river mouths, one of which provides shelter and moorage at an adjacent marina, albeit mostly for smaller craft. The other marina is close by, also accessible across a shallow bank with a channel that provides limited access. These two marinas are not far from one another, one at Salmon Point and the other at the Oyster River mouth.

Salmon Point Resort and Marina

2176 Salmon Point Road, Campbell River BC V9H 1E5
Phone 250-923-6605
sales@salmonpoint.com   www.salmonpoint.com
This facility is very busy in summer and overnight moorage is for resort guests only. It has gasoline at the fuel dock. There is water and 30 and 50 amp power at the docks. An RV park and cabins keep the place busy. If you have a trailerable boat, this is a good place to know about. Book well ahead.

*Above: The coast south to Comox has shallows that extend offshore at places, and limited possible shelter. The BC Ferries terminal, seen in the centre right of the photograph, is located just north of Cape Lazo and Comox. See the **Gulf Islands Cruising Guide** by this author.*
Opposite page: Looking up Discovery Passage past Seymour Narrows. Inset: Chatham Point where Discovery Passage meets Johnstone Strait.

There is a restaurant and seasonal grocery store on site as well as a heated pool and hot tub. The resort offers propane, laundry, washrooms and showers. It is set up for fishing guides and charters. Fish freezing is available and the facility has internet access. This is a place to stop for nature walks, golf, tennis and bird watching. There is a launch ramp at the marina.

Pacific Playgrounds Resort and Marina

9082 Clarkson Drive, Black Creek BC V9J 1B3
Phone 250-337-5600
info@pacificplaygrounds.com   www.pacificplaygrounds.com
This marina is on the banks of the Oyster River. Like Salmon

Point, it has limited guest moorage and is also very busy in summer. Slips are available to 40 feet.
Reservations are recommended. There is water and 30 amp power at the docks. It also has a large RV park. The resort offers laundry, washrooms and showers. It has a small store with fishing gear and marine supplies as well as a heated pool and a grassy playground. There is a restaurant and grocery store nearby as well as access to golf, tennis and bird watching.

Salmon Point and Pacific Playground resorts have narrow, shallow entrances. Salmon Point marina needs a 1.5m tide to enter. Pacific Playground marina entrance dries at zero tide.

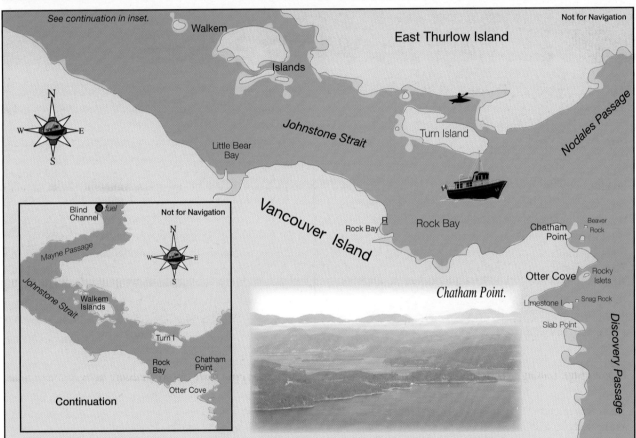

Chatham Point.

Northbound

Travelling north of Desolation Sound and on to the Broughton Islands, because of strong currents and tide rips, mariners must plan their passage carefully through Seymour Narrows, around Chatham Point, past Kelsey Bay and into Johnstone Strait. An alternative route is to go north of the Discovery Islands, by way of the famous Yaculta Rapids, Dent Rapids, Green Point Rapids and Whirlpool Rapids.

Slower boats would do well to plan stops through the waterways in which these rapids lie so as to take advantage of the best tidal currents. High water slack is usually best and it is particularly easier when the tidal changes are minimal. Stopping at places along the way, rather than rushing through as many of the current-swept passages as possible in one leg, allows for interesting meetings with local residents. Stop at the marinas along the Cordero Channel route to Port Neville in Johnstone Strait. Take advantage of the facilities provided

Above: Rock Bay in Johnstone Strait, near Discovery Passage.

at the various marinas and resorts and make that an integral part of your trip, if not your actual destination. More on this area can be found in the cruising guide, ***North of Desolation Sound***, by this author.

Rock Bay

This small landing was once a busy settlement. It had a school, post office, hotels and stores. Today it is not much more than an RV park, campsite and launch ramp at the end of a long unpaved road that leads off the main island highway north of Campbell River. It serves as a landing for marina and resort owners in the Discovery Islands and beyond. And obviates the need for them to travel by boat to Campbell River through the swift waters of Seymour Narrows.

Thurston Marine Park

The marine park lies along parts of the shoreline of Cameleon Harbour and Thurston Bay. It is located on the northwest side of Sonora Island and should be entered from Nodales Channel which runs into Discovery Passage and the extreme south end of Johnstone Strait. From Stuart Island use Cordero Channel to Nodales Channel.

A lovely spot to anchor is just off Cameleon Harbour in **Handfield Bay**. A small islet forms a protective breakwater but care should be taken when entering and anchoring, and allow for tide changes and swinging of your boat. The anchorage behind Block Island is the most protected in Thurston Bay. The island is covered in second growth timber for the most part and similar landscape covers the adjacent shore. It is an undeveloped park. **Anchorage Lagoon** should be entered and used with caution due to its shallows as well as rocks near the entrance. Across Nodales Channel, **Hemming Bay** is an alternative but less frequented anchorage. At the north end of Nodales Channel is Cordero Channel leading to Green Point Rapids and Big Bay.

A short distance to the north, consider **Blind Channel** on West Thurlow Island as a destination. There is a marina with fuel, groceries and liquor, post office, restaurant and facilities for mariners. To the south, Johnstone Strait and Discovery Passage lead to Campbell River.

Bute Inlet and Ramsay Arm

If you are heading for Stuart Island from Desolation Sound and the Toba Inlet area, continue west along Pryce Channel to Raza Island. An excursion into Ramsay Arm opposite this island will produce little more than a sightseeing turnaround. The only notable feature of the arm is the logging operation at the Quatam River mouth. Adjacent to the log dump is a set of company floats and ashore there is an airfield. It is also the site of the Deep Valley First Nations Reserve. **Frances Bay** is a suitable anchorage, despite it being wide open at its entrance. The Downie Range rises between Frances Bay and Bute Inlet. This is another, long, deep fjord cutting into the British Columbia mainland.

Northbound from Raza Island to Stuart Island turn north in Calm Channel and pass Church House. Here Bute Inlet opens to the northeast and the Yucaltas to the northwest. Church House was a thriving, but small, Homalco First Nations community not long ago. Today it is abandoned with the buildings, including a picturesque church, decaying with time and weather. There is good prawning and fishing in the area. The native people have been fighting to prevent the establishment of a fish farm off the reserve lands. Anchor for a brief stay, in the lee of **Bartlett Island**.

Top: Thurston Bay on Sonora Island from the southeast. Handfield Bay is seen at the upper edge of the large basin. In the distance is Hemming Bay on East Thurlow Island. This area is a popular destination when travelling north of Desolation Sound.

Below: Church House, an historic First Nations site at the north end of Calm Channel, en route north to Big Bay. This photograph was taken recently, and shows how the buildings are succumbing to the ravages of weather and time since being abandoned. The inset photographs show the village as it appeared in its heyday and more recently as a working community with fishing nets draped on the docks (circa 1983).

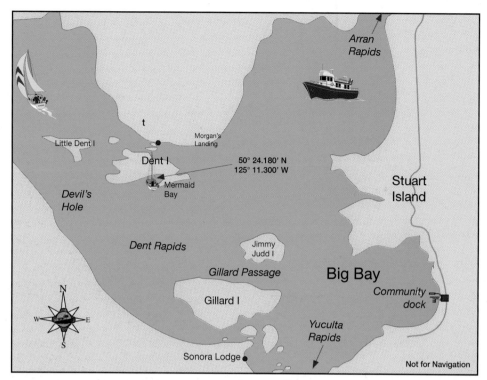

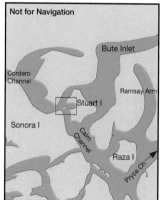

Opposite page, top: Big Bay, looking southeast, from above Gillard Island. The passage northbound is to its left. The smaller island, to the left of Gillard Passage, is Jimmy Judd Island. Opposite, bottom: The community marina, flanked by private docks, at Big Bay on Stuart Island. Bute Inlet can be seen beyond the island.

Bute Inlet is a long exposed waterway. It is considered one of the grandest fjords in the world. The scenery is spectacular, with tall mountains rising from the water's edge. It is 75 kilometres long and it is deep. The depth sounder could record up to more than 650 metres. A Calgary businessman and fellow-contributor to *Pacific Yachting Magazine*, Arthur Child, once said there was no point going part way up Bute Inlet, because the best of it was the view of the mountains and estuary of the Homathko River as you come into sight of Waddington Harbour at the head of the inlet.

Bute Inlet is fed by the Homathko Glacier, which is one of the biggest icefields south of the Arctic Circle. Nearby, in the Coast Range, are the tall Mount Queen Bess and Mount Grenville and in the distance BC's tallest mountain, Mount Waddington. A trip up the inlet could be worthwhile, with viewing of cascading waterfalls as well as bears, otters, sea lions and even killer and minke whales, Pacific white-sided dolphins and porpoises. Fishing is outstanding, especially off the Southgate and Homathko rivers, which run into the head of the inlet in Waddington Harbour. This is not a harbour as such. It is exposed and the waters are either too deep or too shallow. The river can be explored in a shallow draft boat.

At one time, in the mid 1800s, there was an attempt made by Alfred Waddington, a Canadian entrepreneur and promoter, to have this estuary become the west coast terminus of the Trans-Canada railway line. The project never reached fruition when, in 1864, some of the 14 men constructing a road to the interior were killed by Chilcotin natives.

There is no significant long-term anchorage in Bute Inlet.

Temporary stops can be made in several coves, where small, shallow shelves protrude from the steep shores. One of the better places is at **Orford Bay**, site of a First Nations Reserve where anchorage can be taken at the north side off the drying shallows of the Orford River mouth.

If you are in Big Bay and want to venture into Bute Inlet, passage can be taken through Arran Rapids. But be mindful of the tides, as strong currents to nearly eight knots run through this passage. It is often busy with sports fishing boats.

Big Bay

Big Bay, Stuart Island, at the northern extremity of Desolation Sound, is a waiting place for tide changes enabling safe passage through the tidal waters of Dent and Yuculta Rapids. Travelling south or north along the BC waterways, Big Bay is a major focal point for all mariners. It is the gateway from Desolation Sound to areas north via Johnstone Strait, and it is a popular stop on the route south from the narrow northern passages with their intimidating rapids and whirlpools.

At Big Bay, anchor at **Mermaid's Cove** on Dent Island, or better yet sit at the community dock and watch the passage of fishing boats and tugs with their barges under tow, slow moving pleasure craft and a variety of small vessels, making their run through the tidal waters during slack periods.

Because of their heavy, deep draft, and restricted manoeuverabilty, large commercial vessels and luxury cruise ships use Seymour Narrows, rather than the Stuart Island route, to travel more directly between Johnstone Strait and Discovery Passage.

Looking north from Stuart Island and Big Bay. The luxurious Sonora Lodge lies
on the Sonora Island shore adjacent to the Gillard Islands and Gillard Passage.
Cordero Channel, beyond, leads to Mayne Passage and Blind Channel.

Above: Looking south from Big Bay, the Yuculta Rapids with Gillard Island and Gillard Passage in the foreground, Stuart Island is to the left. Bottom: Blind Channel Resort and Marina is the nearest place for fuel and supplies when travelling to or beyond the northern perimeter of the Discovery Islands. A smiling welcome from Laura and Eliot Richter awaits those who venture north and stop at Blind Channel Resort.

Big Bay is a more tranquil place, though, than Seymour Narrows and Campbell River. As a destination, it attracts a large number of visiting sport fishermen annually, who stay at the local lodges, and charter the small fishing boats to go out in quest of the big salmon.

A short distance north of Big Bay is **Blind Channel** where supplies and fuel are available. The resort at Blind Channel offers moorage, post office, a store and fine dining. This stop marks the beginning of the way north to the Broughton Islands. See the cruising guide, ***North of Desolation Sound***, by this author, for full details on navigating the waterways to that remote and extraordinary destination.

Opposite page, top and inset: Arran Rapids. This waterway should be navigated at slack tide, as it reaches speeds of nearly 8 knots in either direction. Bottom: Carla and Lianne watch the fast flowing stream at Arran Rapids connecting Big Bay with Bute Inlet on the north side of Stuart Island.

Howe Sound
Bowen Island, Gambier Island, Squamish, Keats Island

Charts 3311, 3534, 3526, 3512

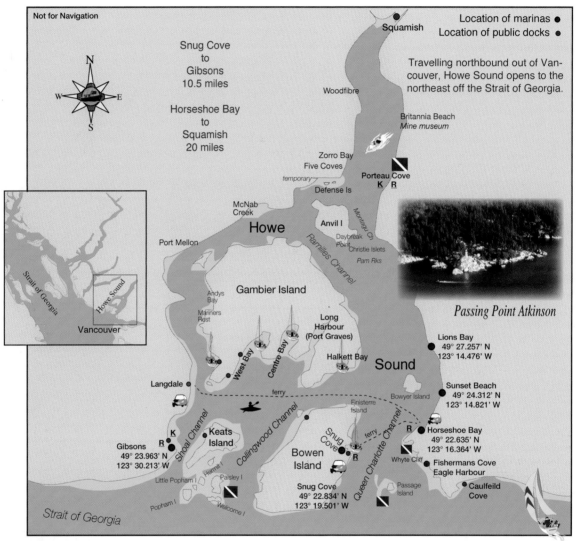

Not for Navigation

Location of marinas ●
Location of public docks ●

Snug Cove
to
Gibsons
10.5 miles

Horseshoe Bay
to
Squamish
20 miles

Travelling northbound out of Vancouver, Howe Sound opens to the
northeast off the Strait of Georgia.

Squamish

Woodfibre

Britannia Beach
Mine museum

Zorro Bay
Five Coves
temporary
Defense Is

Porteau Cove
K R

McNab
Creek

Howe

Anvil I

Daybreak
Point
Christie Islets
Pam Rks

Port Mellon

Gambier Island

Andys
Bay

Mariners
Rest

West Bay

Centre Bay

Long
Harbour
(Port Graves)

Halkett Bay

Sound

Lions Bay
49° 27.257' N
123° 14.476' W

Langdale

ferry

Bowyer Island

Sunset Beach
49° 24.312' N
123° 14.821' W

Passing Point Atkinson

Finisterre
Island

Shoal Channel

Keats
Island

Collingwood Channel

Gibsons
49° 23.963' N
123° 30.213' W

R K

Snug
Cove

Bowen
Island

Queen Charlotte Channel

ferry

R

Whyte Cliff

Horseshoe Bay
49° 22.635' N
123° 16.364' W

Fishermans Cove
Eagle Harbour

Caulfeild
Cove

Passage
Island

Little Popham I

Hermit I

Paisley I

Snug Cove
49° 22.834' N
123° 19.501' W

Popham I

Welcome I

Strait of Georgia

Strait of Georgia

Howe Sound

Vancouver

When time or means do not permit a trip to Desolation Sound, Howe Sound is a very good alternative.

Howe Sound

This large inlet off the Strait of Georgia, lying within 16 kilometres of Vancouver, has been a popular playground for local mariners and ferry travellers since the early days of settlement. Captain George Vancouver was the first European known to enter the Sound, in 1792. He named it for the Royal Navy's Admiral Howe.

Departing Vancouver by way of English Bay, the trip into

Howe Sound begins with a passage around Point Atkinson into Queen Charlotte Channel. On the east side of the channel the Grebe Islets and surrounding rocks protect the entrance to **Eagle Harbour** and **Fishermans Cove**, home of the large Thunderbird Marina and the West Vancouver Yacht Club. Nearby, Whyte Cliff Park is a popular scuba diving training site. The underwater life is a good representation of what lo-

Top, left: Approaching Point Atkinson from English Bay. Centre, left: Sailing at Point Atkinson. Bottom, left: Passage Island and the West Vancouver shoreline. Above: The big Fishermans Cove and Eagle Harbour marinas in West Vancouver.

cal waters have to offer. Anchoring is possible, but only for smaller boats, in the shallows near the floats. Access (also small boats only) is along the north side of Whyte Islet but watch for bubbles indicating scuba divers in the water, and beware of possible ascents of divers.

This eastern entrance to Howe Sound sees a constant coming and going of BC Ferries vessels between Horseshoe Bay and Vancouver Island. In the middle of Queen Charlotte Channel is Passage Island. The ferries pass to the west and north of it. The island was named by Captain Vancouver for its location in the waterway. There are those who believe rather, that it was for its prominence in aiding navigators find the passage from the southern Strait of Georgia to avoid the shallows at Roberts Bank off the Fraser River. When Passage Island is lined up with Anvil Island, mariners are able to navigate safely past the river mouth.

Thunderbird Marina

5776 Marine Drive, West Vancouver BC V7W 2S2.
Phone 604-921-7434

The marina offers limited guest moorage. There is 15 and 30 amp power and water at the docks. The marina's work yard has a 25 ton travel lift. On the property, there is a restaurant and a large marine chndlery that sells boat hardware, clothing, accessories, books and charts. Fuel is available in Howe Sound at the Horseshoe Bay fuel dock, selling gas and diesel.

Above: The entrance to Howe Sound, showing Erwin Point, Eagle Harbour, Fishermans Cove, Eagle Island, and Whyte Cliff Point with the Grebe Islets in the foreground. Left: Caulfeild Cove. Opposite page: The Bowen Island ferry crossing Queen Charlotte Channel to Horseshoe Bay. In the bottom photo Bowyer Island is seen at the top and Horseshoe Bay in the foreground. The bay's waterfront is seen in the inset.

Queen Charlotte Channel is used extensively by mariners who keep their boats moored in Vancouver, as well as visitors from farther afield, to access Snug Cove and Mannion Bay on Bowen Island. Bear in mind the winds that blow down Howe Sound. The northerly winds are known as Squamish winds and they can cause a large build-up of seas in the southern section of the sound and affect conditions beyond into the Strait of Georgia.

Horseshoe Bay

This BC Ferries terminal village is a short haul across Queen Charlotte Channel from Snug Cove to West Vancouver on the Lower Mainland. There is fuel, a launch ramp and numerous restaurants and stores.

Some mooring is available at Sewell's Marina and the public dock. It is a busy cove with the constant movement of ferry traffic.

Mannion Bay is a fair weather anchorage. The lagoon at lower left, is part of a very scenic waterfront. Inset: The launch ramp at Snug Cove.

Sewell's Marina

6409 Bay St., Horseshoe Bay, West Vancouver
BC V7W 3H5. Phone 604-921-3474
info@sewellsmarina.com   www.sewellsmarina.com
Marina services include a limited amount of mooring space. Reservations are suggested. Gas, diesel, engine and outboard oils are available. The Boat Centre and marine store offers marine repairs, sales and service. Horseshoe Bay village has a variety of stores and restaurants adjacent to the ferry terminal. A public launch ramp is located nearby.

A short way north of Horseshoe Bay the shallows extending off the south end of **Bowyer Island** provide some temporary day anchorage in calm conditions, but prolonged stays require careful monitoring of wind forecasts. The cove at the south end has private docks and mooring buoys.

Farther along the eastern shore of Howe Sound lie the home marinas of **Sunset Beach** and **Lion's Bay**. They cater to some visiting boats, but call ahead to check on available space. Check details in ***Docks and Destinations***.

Beyond these is Porteau Cove, a popular park and recreational area for campers and scuba divers. It has a launch ramp and inactive ferry landing (see page 41).

Bowen Island

For decades the Union Steamships carried passengers to resorts on Bowen Island and elsewhere in Howe Sound where dancing and outdoor games were the weekend entertainment. As recently as the latter part of the 20th century remnants of the large Union Steamship Company resort at Mannion Bay (also known as Deep Bay) included riding stables, a large dance pavilion, tennis courts, weekend cottages and other outbuildings of the former resort, which were eventually removed to make way for new development. Other historic buildings at Snug Cove include the Cottage Museum and former Union Steamship Company store which now houses the library. The tourism office and post office are nearby.

Snug Cove

The big Union Steamship Company Marina at the head of Snug Cove is one of the busiest on the coast. It was developed from a small enterprise, by Rondy and Dorothy Dike, into the large, beautifully designed facility that it is, and now has many slips available, with many services visitors need, including a store, laundry, washrooms and showers. A wooden sidewalk connects the store and marina access to restaurants,

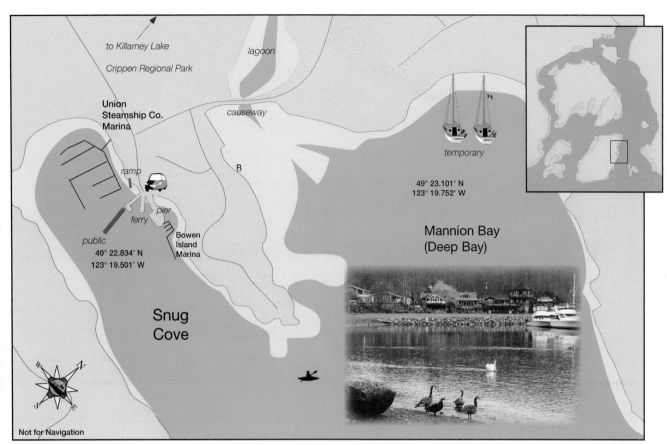

to Killarney Lake

Crippen Regional Park

lagoon

causeway

Union
Steamship Co.
Marina

ramp

R

Mannion Bay
(Deep Bay)

temporary

49° 23.101' N
123° 19.752' W

pier

ferry

Bowen
Island
Marina

public

49° 22.834' N
123° 19.501' W

Snug
Cove

Not for Navigation

Temporary anchorages may be found at Apodaca Cove and Seymour Bay on the east side of Bowen Island and at Tunstall Bay and Bowen Bay on the west side. Galbraith Bay and Grafton Bay lie in the lee of Hutt Island and offer some fair weather shelter. Collingwood Channel off Hood Point is a busy waterway with some temporary, daytime shelter in the coves either side of Finisterre Island.

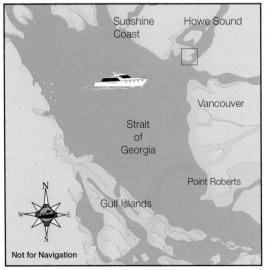

Sunshine
Coast

Howe Sound

Vancouver

Strait
of
Georgia

Point Roberts

Gulf Islands

Not for Navigation

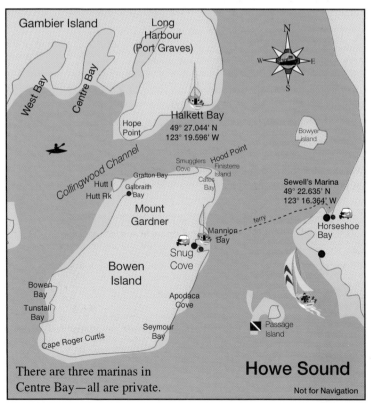

Gambier Island

Long
Harbour
(Port Graves)

West Bay

Centre Bay

Hope
Point

Halkett Bay
49° 27.044' N
123° 19.596' W

Bowyer
island

Collingwood Channel

Smugglers
Cove

Hood Point

Finisterre
Island

Grafton Bay

Cates
Bay

Sewell's Marina
49° 22.635' N
123° 16.364' W

Hutt I.
Hutt Rk

Galbraith
Bay

Mount
Gardner

Mannion
Bay

ferry

Horseshoe
Bay

Snug
Cove

Bowen
Island

Bowen
Bay

Apodaca
Cove

Passage
Island

Tunstall
Bay

Seymour
Bay

Cape Roger Curtis

There are three marinas in
Centre Bay—all are private.

Howe Sound

Not for Navigation

Above: The buildings at Union Steamship Company Marina house the marina office and store. Below: Farmers' Market kiosks on the waterfront at Snug Cove. Opposite: Snug Cove docks and marinas. Sailboat Up and Down *at the marina. Mannion Bay anchorage from the causeway.*

restored historic cottages and a variety of shops. Walk up the hill beyond the marina, where there are more shops including bakeries, bistro, gift shops, restaurants and pubs which feature Bowen Island Brew. The general store is a short walk from the marina. Other island stores include a pharmacy, liquor store, art shops, health food and specialty stores. ATM, post office, and medical services can be found near the marina. Enjoy the outdoor market on the foreshore in summer.

The large Crippen Regional Park entrance is just across the road from the marina. Check in at the Union Steamship Company store, then enjoy a tranquil walk along the trails around Killarney Lake (take the official walking tour) or just stroll along the Lady Alexandra promenade at the marina. The road alongside the post office and park reception building leads across a small bridge over a causeway where water gently pours out of a lagoon as the tide recedes in Mannion Bay. The road beyond leads into the residential area on what was once part of the grounds of the resort. A more strenuous hike entails following the pathways that lead to the summit of 760 metre Mount Gardner. From its peak, the views over the Sunshine Coast, Howe Sound, and south across the border are stunning.

Mannion Bay, the large basin immediately north of Snug Cove, is an exposed anchorage subject to the wash of passing vessels but protected from most summer breezes. Winter easterlies sweep into both Snug Cove and Mannion Bay.

Union Steamship Co. Marina

431 Trunk Rd. PO Box 250
Bowen Island BC V0N 1G0
Phone 604-947-0707
marina@ussc.ca www.ussc.ca

The marina has many slips with accommodations for vessels up to 64 metres. Reservations are suggested. Power at the docks is 30 and 50 amps. Facilities include internet access, laundry,

showers, washrooms, and garbage disposal. On shore there is a busy chandlery offering boating supplies, gifts, novelties, books, charts and snacks. At the marina or nearby you will find tackle, bait, hardware, ice, grocery store, fresh produce, frozen foods, and most necessary supplies.

Snug Cove public dock

There is a 105 metre public dock that serves as a breakwater, alongside the ferry landing. The public dock has a garbage disposal unit and washrooms ashore. Water taxis and other small vessels frequent the breakwater dock.

Alongside the landing in Snug Cove, there is a pier adjacent to the private **Bowen Island Marina** on the outside of the ferry dock, that includes a café, an ice cream stand and a craft store. There is a shuttle bus service at the ferry terminal.

The water taxi *Apodaca*, was named after the former name of Bowen Island. Apodaca was a Spanish naval officer who was honoured by Narvaez while exploring the Sound in 1791.

Events and activities

Annual summer events include live entertainment in the pub on Saturday nights, the Bowen Island Parade and Festival on the Saturday prior to Labour Day, and the Dog Days of Summer on the second Sunday in August.

In mid July the local Historians and Memorial Garden Society host a People, Plants and Places Tour. Roads and trails give access to much of the island. Other activities on the island include golf.

Left: The public dock at Snug Cove. This forms an effective breakwater for the marina that lies beyond.
Bottom left: Doc Morgan's Pub overlooking the Union Steamship marina in Snug Cove. Below: There is a small private marina on the approaches to Snug Cove ferry landing, pier and public dock. The aerial photographs at the bottom of the page show Snug Cove and Mannion Bay.
Inset: The library building was once the general store.

At the time of European settlement, Snug Cove was the summer camp of the Squamish First Nations, who used it as their fishing and hunting camp. The Spanish explorer Narvaez charted the entrance to Howe Sound in 1791. The area he covered included Passage Island, Bowen Island and the Pasley group. The first white settlers to claim Bowen Island, landed there in 1874. In the 1990s a small store on the main street was named the Sannie Shop. It memorialized the old Sannie Transportation Company which ran steam launches across Queen Charlotte Channel in the 1920s. The Union Steamship Company operated the Terminal Resort which catered to tourists off their ships.

Bowen Island was named for Rear-Admiral James Bowen master of Lord Howe's flagship HMS *Queen Charlotte*. Less than 15 years after the naming, land was pre-empted by the first settler, William Eaton.

A circumnavigation of Bowen Island would reveal few suitable overnight anchorages. Hood Point is a prominent feature at the northeast end of Bowen Island. It protrudes into Queen Charlotte Channel with **Cates Bay**, **Enchanta Bay** and Finisterre Island at its tip. These, and adjacent **Columbine Bay** and **Smugglers Cove** on the northwest side, are sometimes used as temporary anchorages. This is a very busy point with commercial traffic, recreational vessels travelling to and from Gambier Island destinations, and the ferries that ply between Horseshoe Bay and Langdale, passing it constantly. **Mount Gardner Park** has a public dock with a 17 metre float.

In Collingwood Channel at the northwest side of Bowen, pass **Galbraith Bay** and **Hutt Rock** south of Hutt Island. The latter and another rock in the passage between Bowen and Hutt Islands are well marked. The small public dock at Galbraith Bay, with its immediate access to Mount Gardner Park, does not offer secure overnight moorage.

Mount Gardner looms over Collingwood Channel. It was named for a rear-admiral who had served as lieutenant under

Above: Looking northwest from Hope Point, Long Bay opens into the southeast section of Gambier Island, with Centre Bay lying alongside to the west. Port Graves is at the head of Long Bay.

Captain George Vancouver before the famous captain's arrival in British Columbia.

Cape Roger Curtis, at the southwest corner of Bowen is a major navigation landmark. Nearby **Tunstall Bay** and **Bowen Bay** are used by some vessels for day anchoring in good weather. Close to the Strait of Georgia, Tunstall Bay gives good views of the conditions to those waiting to continue to destinations on the Sunshine Coast or Vancouver Island.

Gambier Island

Gambier Island was named for British Admiral of the Fleet, Lord James Gambier, by Captain George Henry Richards who conducted the first hydrographic survey of the sound aboard HMS *Plumper* in 1889.

Port Graves public dock

The dock has a 10 metre float used mostly for the disembarking of visitors to Camp Artaban.

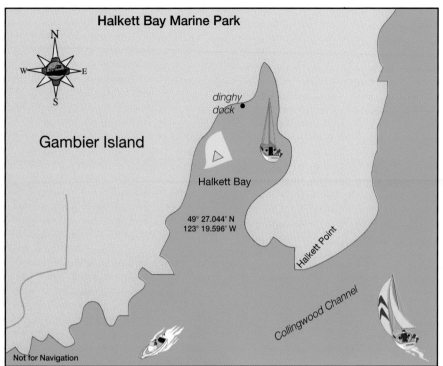

Halkett Bay Marine Park

N
W E
S

Gambier Island

dinghy
dock

Halkett Bay

49° 27.044' N
123° 19.596' W

Halkett Point

Collingwood Channel

Not for Navigation

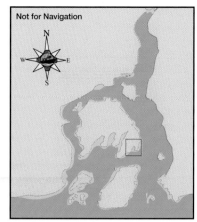

Not for Navigation

N
W E
S

*Below: A ferry passes Halkett Bay in
Collingwood Channel.*
*Bottom: Halkett Bay has a dinghy dock
and park access to shady meadows and
wide pathways. Anchorage is considered
temporary.*

Above: Halkett Bay opens into the southeast end of Gambier Island. Ramilles Channel continues between Gambier and Anvil Island, seen beyond Halkett Point, to the left. Montagu Channel leads to Squamish Harbour in the direction of the tall, snow-capped mountains.

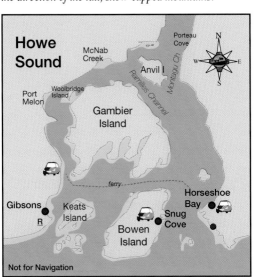

Howe Sound

Porteau Cove
McNab Creek
Anvil I
Woolbridge Island
Port Melon
Ramilles Channel
Montagu Ch
Gambier Island
ferry
Gibsons
Keats Island
Horseshoe Bay
Snug Cove
Bowen Island
R

Not for Navigation

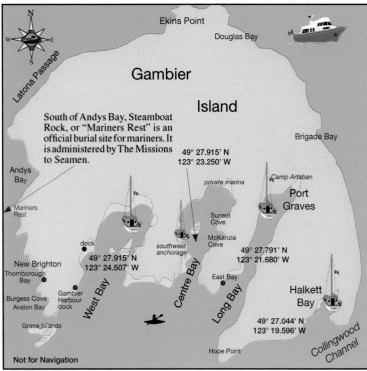

N
W E
S

Ekins Point
Latona Passage
Douglas Bay
Gambier
Island
Brigade Bay

South of Andys Bay, Steamboat Rock, or "Mariners Rest" is an official burial site for mariners. It is administered by The Missions to Seamen.

49° 27.915' N
123° 23.250' W

private marina
Camp Artaban
Port Graves

Andys Bay
Mariners Rest
Sunset Cove
McKenzie Cove
49° 27.791' N
123° 21.680' W

dock
49° 27.915' N
123° 24.507' W
southwest anchorage

New Brighton
Thornborough Bay
East Bay
West Bay
Centre Bay
Long Bay
Halkett Bay

Burgess Cove
Avalon Bay
Gambier Harbour dock

Grace Islands

Hope Point

49° 27.044' N
123° 19.596' W

Collingwood Channel

Not for Navigation

Gambier Island has some attractive landings and anchorages. At the southeast corner of the island, **Halkett Bay** opens to a marine park that has forested slopes with trails leading to Mount Artaban. The park is undeveloped, with a dinghy dock, pit toilet and campsites. Enter well to the east of the islets and a shallow area near the entrance, and anchor in 5 to 15 metres off the centre of the bay. The bay gives a broad sweeping view of passing ferries and other boat traffic. Halkett Bay is a fair weather anchorage, protected from most wind conditions.

Like stubby fingers protruding from a tight fist, peninsulas extend from the island to form a series of deep bays that affords varying amounts of protected anchorage. West of Hope Point is **Long Bay** with **Port Graves** at its head. At the entrance

Above: Centre Bay on Gambier Island. Left: This view shows Alexandra Island clearly, to the left. It is the property of the Royal Vancouver Yacht Club. Another private property is the Centre Bay Yacht Station at the head of the bay. The West Vancouver Yacht Club outstation is on the east side. Long Harbour opens to the right.

Below: Yachts tied up at the Royal Vancouver Yacht Club outstation at Alexandra Island in Centre Bay. Opposite page: West Bay is another popular anchorage. Beware of a reef in the middle of the bay. There is a dock on the west side that provides walking access across the lower end of the island to New Brighton.

to the bay a small dock is located at a nook called **East Bay**. This is suitable only for short stops.

Anchorage in Port Graves is fairly sheltered but not too popular due to the remnants on the seabed of former logging operations. The main feature in the port is an Anglican summer children's camp, Camp Artaban, which is located at its head. Floats serving the camp are private and the small public dock is limited to brief stops. Visitors are welcome to go ashore by dinghy and walk the unrestricted trails at the camp. Established in 1923, the camp is one of the oldest of its type in British Columbia.

Centre Bay is a popular destination, with facilities along its shores belonging to West Vancouver Yacht Club and the Royal Vancouver Yachts Club (on Alexandra Island), as well as the Centre Bay Yacht Station at its head. All of these are private, but it is possible to anchor in 5 metres in the small cove at the southwestern corner of the bay. Private docks lie along this shoreline, restricting stern tying and scope. Other anchorages can be found on the east shore of the bay at locally named **Sunset Cove** and **Mackenzie Cove**. An islet separates the two coves and anchorage can be taken in its lee along a steep wall between the coves.

West Bay is the westernmost of the inlets offering anchorage on Gambier Island. Enter by keeping well to the west side, avoiding rocks in the middle of the entrance. This has been a popular anchorage for many years, with preference given to tying up alongside log booms in the early days.

The Sir Thomas Lipton Park abuts a gravel beach at the head of the bay. The park is named for the wreck of the former log booming vessel *Sir Thomas Lipton*, which lies at the southwest end of the beach. The park is separated from private property by a small stream with the delightful name of Whispering Creek. We walked up the lower reaches of this creek one winter when it, and its low, cascading waterfall were totally iced over. Anchor in 10 metres off the beach or on the opposite side, stern tying to the steep shore. Some old cables lie on the seabed. Two small public docks extend from the beach on the east shore beyond the confines of the bay. One is at the entrance to West Bay and the other, called **Gambier Harbour**, lies closer to the south tip of the island. It has 30 metres of moorage space and is equipped with power for lighting, but is not recommended for overnight stays.

At this juncture you may want to head for Squamish. Cross Ramilles and Montagu Channels on the east side of Gambier Island, passing Porteau Cove and Britannia Beach. Or from Horseshoe Bay, travel up the eastern shoreline of Howe Sound, where you can see numerous waterfront homes or small settlements, including Sunset Beach and Lions Bay.

Porteau Cove and Britannia Beach

Porteau Cove lies in the upper reaches of Howe Sound, on the east shore of Montagu Channel. There is a boat launching ramp which is exposed to open water conditions. An extensive beach is an attraction for campers and day visitors who arrive by vehicle. It has walk-in campsites with toilets and potable water. There are mooring buoys off the beach and anchoring is possible off the campsite area for short periods provided the wind is not blowing. Temporary anchorage is possible also at **Glen Eden**. For scuba divers there are change rooms and an interpretive presentation display with access from the beach to several artificial reefs, comprising a number of sunken vessels. These are a scuba diving attraction and are marked by buoys, to the north of the ramp.

One of the major landmarks on the steep-sloped eastern

Above: Looking down Montagu Channel from Porteau Cove on Howe Sound's east shore. Mount Arteban rises above Halkett Point (to its left). Below: The ferry from Snug Cove on the east side of Bowen Island. Bowyer Island is to the right, Gambier to the left, beyond Bowen Island. Anvil Island is at centre in the distance, and Porteau beyond the point to the right. Opposite: Divers explore the cove's waters and wrecks, and the launch ramp at Porteau Cove. Inset above: The museum at Britannia Mine; below: The picturesque waterfall at Shannon Falls near Squamish.

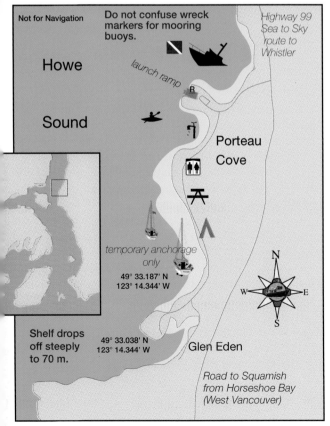

Not for Navigation

Do not confuse wreck markers for mooring buoys.

Howe

Sound

Highway 99 Sea to Sky route to Whistler

launch ramp

B

Porteau Cove

temporary anchorage only
49° 33.187' N
123° 14.344' W

N
W — E
S

Shelf drops off steeply to 70 m.

49° 33.038' N
123° 14.344' W

Glen Eden

Road to Squamish from Horseshoe Bay (West Vancouver)

shore of Howe Sound is **Britannia Beach**, site of a former copper mine, with its scarred hillside from early mining operations. This mine, which is now a museum and popular tourist attraction, was founded by a prospector Dr. A.A. Forbes, in 1888.

The next year a mining engineer, George Robinson helped establish the mine and by 1904 ore was being shipped to a smelter on Vancouver Island. By 1916 the mine was producing 2,000 tons of ore a day, despite a catastrophic event in 1915, when a landslide destroyed one of the labourer camps, killing 60 people–men, women and children. Later that same year, another 37 were killed when a flood struck the small town at the base of the mine. The mine was shut down in 1974, turned into a museum the following year, and named a national historic site in 1988. The mine is conspicuous by its cascading structure down the side of a steep cliff. The waterfront is exposed and poor for stopping, moorage or anchoring. The dock is suitable for dinghies only.

Top: The mill at Port Mellon is an imposing sight on the west shore of Howe Sound. It lies to the west of Gambier Island. Passage is between Mariners Rest (point) and Whitherby Point.

Left and below: The Squamish Yacht Club, at the entrance to the river, welcomes visitors.

Squamish

Howe Sound tapers northward into an inlet. This becomes Squamish Harbour, where at its entrance lies Porteau Cove and Britannia Beach. At the head of the sound lies the town of Squamish. Passing Britannia en route, proceed along the eastern shore into the well-marked entrance of the Squamish River and look for temporary moorage at the Squamish Yacht Club. Keep an eye on depths, as parts of the waterway are reported to be silting up. The club is private but members generally invite guests to tie up and visit the clubhouse. The adjacent public docks include an outer section for transient boats to about 16 metres, and the old public dock which is often occupied by tugs. There is power and water as well as garbage disposal and pumpout. Some mariners may choose to tie up to nearby log booms, but be ready to move if tugs arrive to tow the logs. The town is a short walk away from the marina. Range markers assist in navigation farther up the river through Mamquam Blind Channel to a private marina.

Squamish Yacht Club

Contact through *www.squamishyachtclub.com*

Above: The public marina adjacent to the yacht club on the Squamish River. In summer there is a farmers' market on Saturdays in the town of Squamish.

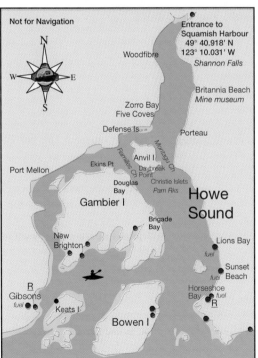

Not for Navigation

Entrance to
Squamish Harbour
49° 40.918' N
123° 10.031' W
Shannon Falls

Woodfibre

Britannia Beach
Mine museum

Zorro Bay
Five Coves

Defense Is

Porteau

Anvil I

Daybreak
Point

Christie Islets
Pam Rks

Port Mellon

Ekins Pt

Douglas
Bay

Gambier I

**Howe
Sound**

Brigade
Bay

New
Brighton

Lions Bay
fuel

Sunset
Beach
fuel

Horseshoe
Bay *fuel*
R

R
Gibsons
fuel

Keats I

Bowen I

The passage to Squamish up the western shore of Howe Sound passes from Gibsons via New Brighton on Gambier Island, Port Mellon, the privately owned facilities of two yacht clubs at Ekins Point, McNab Creek on the opposite shore, and the Defence Islands.

Above: Taking a slow run up Mamquam Blind Channel in the Squamish River towards a private marina. Spectacular views of the precipitous Stawamus Chief and adjacent mountain ridges reward the mariner venturing all the way up Howe Sound to Squamish.

New Brighton

Passage around the southwestern corner of Gambier can be taken around Grace Islands or through the passage created by them. It is a shallow passage with rocks at either side so careful use of a chart and GPS is recommended. Pass Avalon Bay and Burgess Cove and drop the hook in the northwest part of **Thornborough Bay** just beyond the large but usually full public dock, which serves the settlement at **New Brighton**. Or tie up if space is available. The outer dock is used for the ferry commuter vessel to and from Langdale, where the Horseshoe Bay/Gibsons ferry lands. A short walk up the road at New Brighton leads to a corner where a small grocery store and café is located between the forks of the road. Continuing along the road will take you to West Bay. New Brighton public dock has a float length of 120 metres.

Circumnavigating Gambier Island clockwise, pass either side of Woolridge Island, through Latona Passage or on the Port Mellon side of the island. Port Mellon is a long established pulp mill and its stacks and vapours can be seen from a long distance off.

Ekins Point

At the north end of Gambier, Ekins Point shelters Burrard Yacht Club and Thunderbird Yacht Club outstations. McNab Creek, to the north, on the mainland shore, can be accessed by way of a small private dock. A substantial unpaved road at **McNab Creek** provides the opportunity to walk through open, light shrub where logging has long since left the land sparsely covered. Be cautious, as we have encountered bears on this stretch of road. It is possible to take temporary anchorage along the beach adjacent to McNab Creek, but be advised, the shallows drop off quickly and steeply.

Ekins Point was named for Sir Charles Ekins, an early captain of HMS *Defence*, later under the command of Captain James Gambier. It was this latter commander for whom Captain Richards later named Gambier Island.

To the north of Anvil Island, the **Defence Islands** are not ideal for anchoring, but temporary stops may be made in the shallower areas in the lee of the larger of the islands. Beware of currents along the shore. The isthmus protruding from the shore just north of the Defence Islands offers temporary anchorage off the beach on either side. These anchorages are known locally as **Five Coves** and **Zorro Bay**.

Opposite: The New Brighton wharf and docks in Thornborough Bay. Top: A ferry heading west in Collingwood Channel off the south end of Gambier Island. Above left: There is a popular grocery store and cafe near the landing at New Brighton. Right: Most dock space is taken up with local boats. Inset opposite page: Passengers at New Brighton awaiting the ferry to Langdale.

Anvil Island lies between Ramilles Channel and Montagu Channel at the entrance to Squamish. It is a steep-sided 760 metres high island with limited opportunity for anchoring. A temporary stop is possible either side of **Daybreak Point** on the southwest shore of Anvil Island. Nearby Christie Islets and Pam Rocks are home to sea lions and an underwater habitat for a variety of interesting fish and invertebrates. Scuba divers will find ratfish, dogfish and giant jellyfish. It is also home to a large colony of seabirds.

The eastern shore of Gambier Island has a few indents, the most notable of which is **Brigade Bay** where there is limited shelter from northerly outflow "Squamish" winds that blow down the sound, all too often in summer, and even more frequently in winter. The best place to anchor, in calm conditions, is in the north end of the bay, or in the lee of a small islet at the other end. The bay is the site of a one-time summer camp for boys. An early homesteader developed the property where he raised horses and birds and left trails that lead to various parts of the island including Port Graves. The east shore coves are deep except for **Douglas Bay** which has extensive shallows at the Gambier Creek mouth and is suitable only for temporary anchorage.

Hopkins Landing has a small public dock attached to a long wharf. It is worthy of note. This, like several other landings, was an early stop for the steamships that carried passengers to and from their coastal homesteads. Typically such landings would have small grocery stores and a post office to serve local residents. The dock can accommodate a few small boats, but is recommended for brief stops only.

Gibsons Landing

Lower Gibsons has a variety of stores near two major marinas. An uphill hike leads to upper Gibsons where there are strip malls with more restaurants and stores.

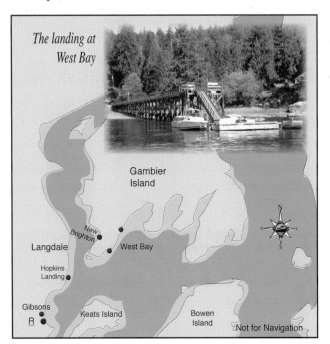

The landing at West Bay

Gambier Island

New Brighton

West Bay

Langdale

Hopkins Landing

Gibsons
R

Keats Island

Bowen Island

Not for Navigation

Gibsons Landing public docks. These are behind a breakwater that also protects Gibsons Marina. It was the site of the filming of a long running television series, The Beachcombers.

The two marinas are behind a substantial breakwater. One is the large Gibsons Marina with a vast number of slips, many of which are available for transient vessels, and the other is the public dock, which has room for commercial and several recreational craft. Rafting is allowed at the public dock.

Some mariners drop the hook outside the breakwater when wind forecasts allow. Others looking to anchor, venture across Shoal Channel to Keats Island and Plumper Cove.

Gibsons is a busy community of residents, transient ferry travellers, business people and boat operators docking their craft at the community dock or at Gibsons Marina. This large facility is one of the biggest and best of its kind in local coastal waters. It provides all services required by mariners, from the chandlery store at the head of the dock to nearby repair facilities.

In the waterfront village of Gibsons Landing there are stores, restaurants, a pub, post office, pharmacy, museum, bank machines, a book store and convenience stores. Craft and art stores have become a major attraction. Or hike, take a cab or the bus up to the main shopping centre.

The Beachcombers, Molly's Reach, Nick Adonidas and Relic are names that became synonymous with Gibsons in the 1970s and 80s. The long-running television series that was filmed at Gibsons until 1991 told lively tales of beachcombing, and characterized the small communities along this stretch of coast. Each week, viewers gathered at their TV sets to watch the antics of Nick the Greek (Bruno Gerussi) and Relic (Robert Clothier) as they faced off in a

Above: A small dock serves Grandma's Pub outside the breakwater at Gibsons. Moorage or anchorage is temporary, as afternoon outflow winds often disturb the tranquility of the waters in Shoal Channel.
Right: There is a well-stocked store for mariners at Gibsons Marina.

competitive but amusing clash of wills and objectives, with the local policeman (Jackson Davies) and First Nations' Jessie and others of the cast gathering at their favourite restaurant, Molly's Reach. For the duration of the show, this was just part of the movie set and not open to the public. But in recent years it has been turned into a real restaurant, and along with popular places like nearby Grandma's Pub, is open to local and visiting customers.

Gibsons was also long known as a base for outstanding sports fishing in the area. The shallows in The Gap at Shoal Channel drew hundreds of boats at a time. Although the activity is not what it was, there is still a fair amount of action during fishing seasons, openings and good salmon runs. The shallow water requires a cautious approach in rough seas.

Gibsons Marina

67 Prowse St, PO Box 1520, Gibsons BC V0N 1V0
Phone 604-886-8686
There are 400 permanent and transient berths. Reservations are suggested for visiting boats. Dock A is the main visitor dock. The marina is equipped with portable pumpout, garbage disposal, laundry, showers, washrooms, power at the docks and a launch ramp. Marine supplies are available at the chandlery alongside the marina office. Walk along the waterfront to the village. There is an hourly bus service between the Langdale ferry, Gibsons and Sechelt.

Also available in Gibsons are gas, diesel, oils, marine service, haul-outs and repairs, boat equipment sales and vehicle rentals.

Above: Gibsons Landing and Home Island at the southern tip of Keats Island. Left: Gibsons from the north east and, bottom left, a closer view of Lower Gibsons. Below: Marinas at Gibsons protected by Steep Bluff. The islands beyond include Keats Island, Home Island and the Pophams at top centre and right. Hermit Island and Pasley Island are at top left. Opposite, top: Layout of the harbour. Bottom: Molly's Reach at Gibsons is located up the ramp from Gibsons Landing public marina.

Gibsons Landing Harbour Authority

PO Box 527, Gibsons BC V0N 1V0

Phone 604-886-8017

glha@telus.net

Transient moorage is available. Rafting is allowed at this busy commercial facility. It has water at the dock, a pumpout station, washrooms, showers and laundry. There is a launch ramp nearby. Power is 15 and 30 amps. The marina is immediately inside the breakwater and has close access to the nearby restaurants and shops.

Pasley Island and its surrounding archipelago of smaller islands, Worlcombe, Popham, Hermit and Ragged Islands, provide sheltered passage between Cape Roger Curtis and Keats Island. Formerly a centre for whaling and sealing, these islands attract people who love to explore in small boats. Select a nook and drop anchor if you want a temporary place that is tranquil and quiet, disturbed only occasionally by some vessels that pass through the islands between Barfleur Passage and Collingwood Channel. This is part of the northwestern entrance to Howe Sound. Worlcombe Island has a clearly marked shallow ledge on its north side. Scuba diving attracts divers who know the area. The north side of Worlcombe Island is a popular site with lots to see underwater at shallow to moderate depths. Anchor at the north end of Pasley Island in the protection of the small **New Islet**, but beware of rocks

and drying ridges, similar to those at nearby Hermit Island. Temporary anchorages can be found also at other coves indenting the shores of these islands. **Popham Island** offers shelter at its south end where, like **Tunstall Bay**, a weather watch can be maintained on the Strait of Georgia before venturing out. Respect private property on these islands.

Plumper Cove

The most popular anchorage in Howe Sound is at Plumper Cove on **Keats Island**. This marine park, opened in 1960, has a set of floats extending from a pebble beach and there are many features on land for mariners and campers. These

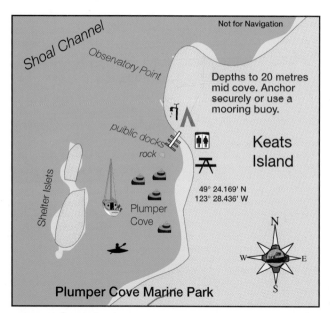

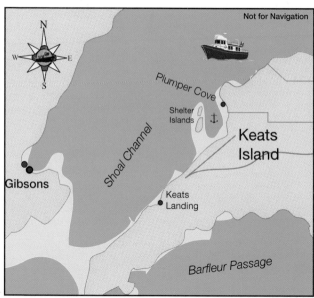

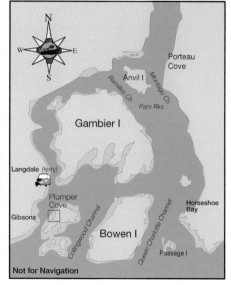

include potable water, pit toilets, picnic tables and campsites with fire pits. Its location on a beautiful promontory of land around Observatory Point overlooks Gibsons Landing across Shoal Channel. Plumper Cove is protected by the Shelter Islets and has numerous mooring buoys and space to drop the hook. Beware of the rock a short way off the dock, marked by a yellow buoy. Also be mindful of the deep water to 20 metres in the centre of the cove. An easy trail courses through the park and leads to Keats Landing farther down island. Here a small dock gives access for foot passengers arriving from the BC Ferries terminal at Langdale. It has little room for lengthy stops, but does have power and water available.

Howe Sound is subject to strong Squamish (or outflowing) winds and these can cause discomfort at some anchorages, including Plumper Cove, at times.

Passage Island and Anvil Island were named by Captain Vancouver during his two day exploration of Howe Sound. Later, Captain Richards named many of the islands, coves and other features of the Sound. Most were named for battles, ships, prominent lords, admirals and high ranking officers of the Royal Navy. In his book *British Columbia Coast Names*, Captain John Walbran provides a comprehensive list of place names and their origin.

June 1st, 1794 was a prominent date for producing place names. This was the date on which Lord Howe gained a massive victory in the first major fleet battle of the French Revolutionary war. From this war, its ships, battles and men, Captain Richards gave names to places in Howe Sound, including Queen Charlotte Channel, Ramillies Channel, Cape Roger Curtis, Bowen Island and many others.

Plumper Cove lies behind the Shelter Islands in the lee of Observatory Point on Keats Island.

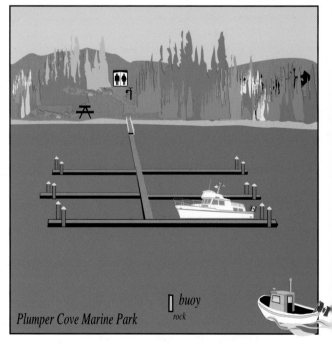

Plumper Cove Marine Park

buoy
rock

Top: Boats tied up at Plumper Cove Marine Park on Keats Island.
Left: Relaxing aboard while anchored in the cove.
Above: The docks layout at Plumper Cove.

Above: Gibsons Landing, on the left, and the ferry to Horseshoe Bay from Langdale passing to the north of Keats Island. Below, and inset: Plumper Cove and the Shelter Islets in Shoal Channel. Plumper Cove is opposite Gibsons Landing. Note the mooring buoys. The bottom photograph was taken in 2008.

Sechelt Peninsula
The Sunshine Coast and Adjacent Inlets

Charts 3311, 3512, 3535, 3536, 3312, 3513, 3514, 3538

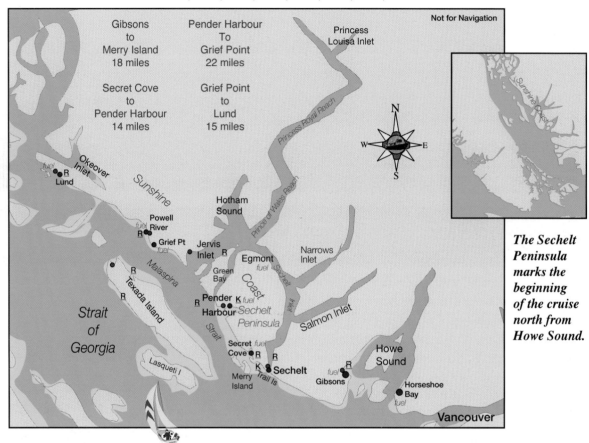

The Sechelt Peninsula marks the beginning of the cruise north from Howe Sound.

The Sunshine Coast

The Sunshine Coast is a popular destination for mariners. It also appeals to vacationers by land and people looking to settle in an area with a mild climate. Temperatures on the Sunshine Coast are idyllic, ranging on average between three and 21 degrees Celsius.

While winters can be wet, and usually are, they are milder on the Sunshine Coast than surrounding coastal areas. Equally, the summers are drier. The average number of hours of sunshine recorded at Pender Harbour is 1,906 annually and the rainfall 300 mm. Snowfall averages a mere 93 cm per year.

Leaving Howe Sound for the Sunshine Coast destinations of Secret Cove and Pender Harbour, pass Gower Point and follow the coastline past Roberts Creek and Wilson Creek to the Trail Islands off Sechelt.

If the wind is coming from the west, you are likely to encounter an uncomfortable quartering or beam sea. Strong northwesterlies can build up a large head sea, diminishing as you approach Welcome Passage and Merry Island. The shallow waters off the initial stretch may cause more discomfort than those deeper and farther into the Strait. Take a bearing on White Islets and pass either side of them on approaches to Sechelt and beyond to Merry Island. Although it is safe to pass fairly close, keep your distance off these islets. The reason they are white is largely because of the bird colonies that make them home.

There is nowhere to stop on the southern approaches to Sechelt other than possibly at Port Stalashen, and then preferably in calm conditions. However, it would be only rough weather that would call for an urgent stop as this harbour is private with no overnight facilities for transient vessels.

The **Trail Islands** provide some protection from rough conditions, and anchorage in Trail Bay may be taken in the lee of the islands, notably on the west side of the island marked 58 on the chart.

Sechelt–Selma Park

The town of Sechelt sits on a narrow isthmus dividing the Strait of Georgia from Sechelt Inlet. Save a visit to the town for a trip down the Inlet from Egmont (see page 97). On the strait there is nowhere to stop at Sechelt. However, at Selma Park, as you approach Sechelt, there is a breakwater and launch ramp and a small set of floats on First Nations land. It is possible to anchor behind the breakwater, near the floats, to wait out unsettled weather. Beyond Sechelt, **Sargeant Bay**, lying in a bight north of the Trail Islands, offers fair weather temporary anchorage. Mind the exposed and drying rocks off Kenyon Creek.

Merry Island

This major coastal feature marks the passage to Secret Cove. Its prominent lighthouse is a beacon to those approaching Welcome Passage, Halfmoon Bay and the Thormanby Islands.

Merry Island was named for the owner of a racehorse named Thormanby, that won the Derby in England at the time the coast was being surveyed by Captain Richards. The lighthouse was established in 1902 and rebuilt in 1966. The trees on the island are home to eagles, cormorants and gulls.

Top: Sechelt, with Selma Park in the foreground and Sechelt Inlet on the other side of the isthmus. The Selma Park breakwater is to the right of the larger deep water terminal.
Above: Just northwest of Sechelt is Sargeant Bay. The Trail Islands are in the left foreground and Merry Island, the Thormanby Islands and Texada Island beyond.

Part of the island is private but small boats may be beached on public land for visits to the lighthouse. Temporary anchorage may be taken between Merry Island and Franklin Island on its west side. Mind the rocks to the south.

Above: The public dock (left of centre) and nearby private docks at Halfmoon Bay. Anchorage is taken near the private docks in Priestland Cove behind the islets off Redroofs.

Left: Aerial view of Merry Island.

Below: The marina at Wilson Creek, known as Stalashen, is private. Access in emergency requires a passage through an entrance which is shallow, especially at low tide.

Bottom, left: The First Nations landing at Selma Park is one of a few sheltered spots on the Sunshine Coast. The breakwater provides an escape from rough seas, but dock space is reserved for private use. Mariners forced to take shelter here should drop anchor, out of the way of the launch ramp and dock activity.

Above: The lighthouse at Merry Island. It is a coastal sentinel, used as a beacon for navigation up and down the Sunshine Coast. Right: The historic general store not far from the public wharf and dock at Halfmoon Bay. The dock is somewhat exposed and overnight moorage is not recommended unless the weather forecast is very favourable.

Halfmoon Bay

Halfmoon Bay has a public dock with limited access, and space nearby for temporary anchorage near **Redroofs**, in **Priestland Cove**. From the dock a road curves through the small settlement and leads to the historic grocery store and post office.

Opening off Halfmoon Bay are **Brooks Cove**, a popular dive site but not a recommended anchorage, and sheltered **Frenchman's Cove.** This latter cove is narrow and best entered in calm conditions. Stay mid channel and watch for rocks. The cove opens in the lee of Jedediah Point and its adjacent land extends into Smuggler Cove Marine Park on the opposite side of the peninsula. Pass through Welcome Passage and round Wilbraham Point and Grant Island to reach the entrance of Smuggler Cove.

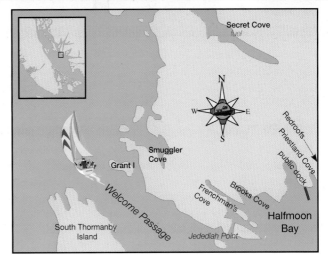

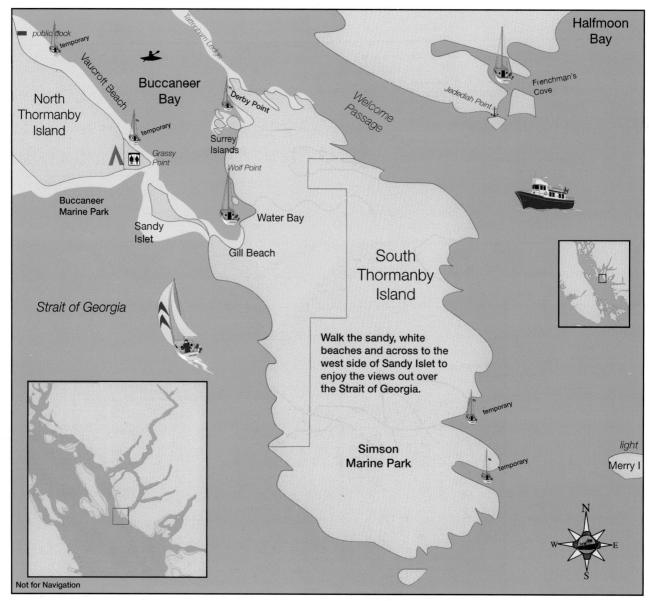

Not for Navigation

Halfmoon Bay public dock

There is a store nearby. The float length is 26 metres with lights, but no amenities.

Buccaneer Bay

Beautiful Buccaneer Bay, with its white sandy beach, is entered from Thormanby Channel at the south end of Malaspina Strait. When approaching from Welcome Passage or Secret Cove, take care to avoid the shallows of Tattenham Ledge, stretching northward from Derby Point. Rather than chance a grounding, round the Tattenham Ledge light to avoid the reefs it marks. The bay lies between North and South Thormanby Islands which are almost one. They are separated only by a shallow shoal adjacent to a low lying stretch of white sandy

beach on the south island, that extends along Sandy Islet from the bottom of the bay at Gill Beach. The beach continues north along the east shore of North Thormanby Island. Local wildlife includes colonies of sea lions and seals, which may be found in the water and on the beaches at times.

Anchor in **Water Bay**, taking extra caution in wind conditions, or off the beach between Grassy Point and Gill Beach. Also anchor in the lee of the **Surrey Islands** at the entrance to the bay. Temporary anchorage may be taken also in the small coves on the south eastern side of South Thormanby Island.

There is a small community dock at **Vaucroft Beach** in Buccaneer Bay, with access ashore for beachcombing and sunbathing. Anchor out temporarily for excursions to the beach by dinghy. Or anchor lower down in the bay off the beach with overnight stays dependant on weather forecasts.

Above: Looking south across Buccaneer Bay. North Thormanby Island, seen at right, is separated from South Thormanby by Sandy Islet. Vaucroft Beach extends beyond Grassy Point on the North Thormanby shore and includes the small public dock.
Right: Gill Beach at Buccaneer Bay extends from the lower left to Sandy Islet and beyond to Grassy Point.
Below, left: Anchored off the beach.
Below Right: Frenchman's Cove is tucked in behind the rocks and islets at Jedediah Point on the west side of Halfmoon Bay.

Top and left: Sandy Vaucroft Beach at Buccaneer Bay extends along the lee shore of North Thormanby Island. The small public dock gives limited access ashore, and is used mostly by residents of the island. Holiday homes and cottages line the beach. Opposite page: The convoluted nooks in Smuggler Cove and a boat arriving to anchor there. Note the dog in the dinghy.

In summer, wind conditions generally allow for comfortable overnight anchoring. The park is known for wilderness camping. There are pit toilets but no amenities and no potable water.

Smuggler Cove

This is one of the best and most sheltered anchorages on the coast. A marine park since the early 1970s, Smuggler Cove comprises a number of cozy nooks off its maze of coves. Swimming is popular in the warm, shallow water.

Easy walking trails run through the adjacent parkland, extending to the island road and visitor parking lot nearby, and to the lane that leads to Frenchman's Cove. Along the trail following the south shore, there are viewpoints with good vistas of the anchorages. The entrance is protected by Isle Capri from the effects of northwesterly winds.

Keep to the north side of the passage when entering, as rocks and shallows extend from the south shore. Anchor in the first nook beyond the narrow entrance and all the way around the convoluted shoreline as well as in the middle of the coves. Stern tie wherever possible. Stern lines can be tied to eyebolts at places on shore.

Note: A reef in the main cove extends well out from the islet marked 9 on the chart and could leave a boat touching bottom at low tide, so be careful to anchor in suitable depths. Pass between Kathleen Islet and France Islet carefully to reach the inner basin. Entry at low tide will provide an exposed view of the reefs.

If you imagine the name of Smuggler Cove has anything to do with sunken or buried treasure, don't go searching for it. The name comes, yes, from a smuggler of sorts. A former seaman of the Royal Navy, by name of Larry Kelly, was said to have smuggled labourers into the USA from Canada. He used the cove as a hideout and also, during the prohibition era in the 1920s, it was reportedly used to store illegal liquor from stills on Texada Island.

Walk in the park but do not disturb the nesting birds or beaver dams. This is a wetland habitat for them. Visitors are reminded to keep pets on a leash. The park offers camping, swimming and hiking.

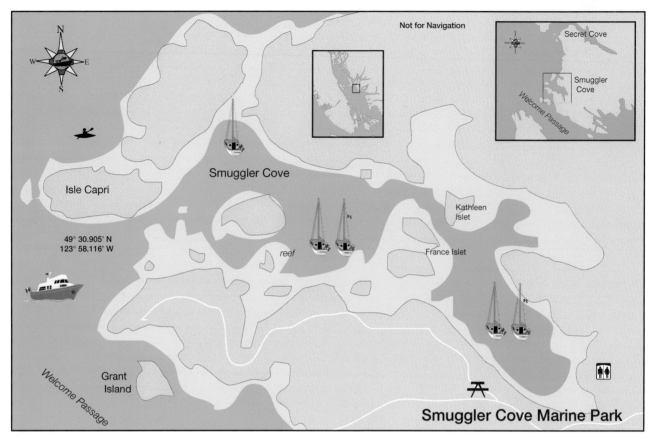

Not for Navigation

Secret Cove

Smuggler Cove

Welcome Passage

N
W E
S

Smuggler Cove

Isle Capri

49° 30.905' N
123° 58.116' W

reef

Kathleen
Islet

France Islet

Grant
Island

Welcome Passage

Smuggler Cove Marine Park

Below left: Poking about in Smuggler Cove. The view is north towards a distant Pender Harbour. Between the bow of the boat and the facing island is an extended reef that is very shallow. Below right: Park Rangers at the entrance to the popular marine park at Smuggler Cove.

Secret Cove

Enter from Malaspina Strait north of Welcome Passage. Pass the entrance to Smuggler Cove Marine Park when approaching from the south. Go around the south end of Turnagain Island when approaching from the north. The water in the cove is shallow but adequate for pleasure craft. A large marina occupies the largest basin in the cove, while yacht club facilities, small marinas and private docks abound along the remaining shorelines. The southeast arm, occupied by the

Royal Vancouver Yacht Club outstation, becomes shallow. Its entrance is narrow. Avoid the rock that protrudes from the north side after entering. Watch also the shoals at the main entrance to the cove adjacent to Jack Tolmie Island and off the island in the centre of the cove.

Anchor in the lee of Turnagain Island opposite the fuel dock and marina. Approach with caution, minding the reefs east of the fuel dock. Anchor also in the lee of **Jack Tolmie**

Above: The entrance to Secret Cove. It is located a short distance from Smuggler Cove, making this area an ideal destination with anchorage and moorage in close proximity. Jack Tolmie Island lies just inside the entrance. Note the reef to starboard of the sailboat.

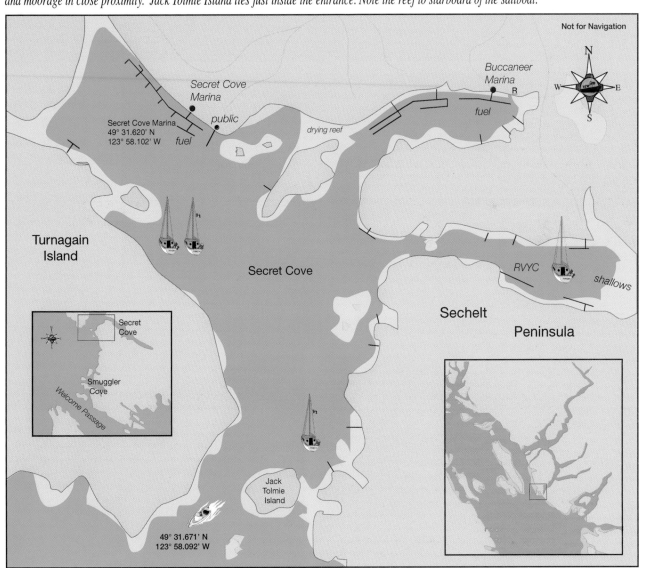

Not for Navigation

Secret Cove Marina

Buccaneer Marina

R

fuel

Secret Cove Marina
49° 31.620' N
123° 58.102' W
fuel

public

drying reef

N
W   E
S

Turnagain
Island

Secret Cove

RVYC

shallows

Sechelt

Peninsula

Secret
Cove

Smuggler
Cove

Welcome Passage

Jack
Tolmie
Island

49° 31.671' N
123° 58.092' W

The photographs above and on the opposite page combine to show the extent of Secret Cove's main arm and the northeast arm. Left and below: The docks at Secret Cove Marina. The restaurant is upstairs in the building on the dock.

Above: Note the entrance to the southeast arm (lower right). The Royal Vancouver Yacht Club outstation is located farther inside.
Right: The store at Secret Cove Marina.

Island or near the Royal Vancouver Yacht Club facility.

Provisions, fuel, moorage, restaurants and hotel facilities are available in Secret Cove. There is a public dock, which is small and usually very busy. Good service, fuel and plentiful moorage is available from the large marina in the north arm. Repairs, fuel and yard work are available at the marina in the northeast arm.

Secret Cove is a popular home for recreational fishing enthusiasts, many of whom keep their boats dry stored at Buccaneer Marina or in the water, and commute to access the adjacent fishing grounds off Thormanby and Merry Island or the Bjerre Shoals up the coast towards Pender Harbour.

Secret Cove Marina

The two photographs above show the continuous waterway to Buccaneer Marina, past the private docks at the entrance.

Bottom: The Mercer family has operated Buccaneer Marina for decades. It is a popular facility for sports fishermen who keep their boats at the marina. Fuel is available at the dock.

Secret Cove public dock
Float length is 44 metres with power.

Secret Cove Marina
5411 Secret Cove Rd, PO Box 1118
Sechelt BC V0N 3A0
Phone 604-885-3533
Toll free 1-866-885-3533
info@secretcovemarina.com www.secretcovemarina.com
Marina services are seasonal between Easter and Thanksgiving. There are 35 transient slips. Gas, diesel and oil are available at the fuel dock. Power at the docks is 15 and 30 amps. Customer services include showers, washrooms, fish cleaning tables, picnic tables, and garbage disposal for moorage customers. A large general store and liquor agency carries marine supplies, fishing gear, licences, charts, bait, ice, electronics, accessories, books and gifts. Wireless internet access is available. A restaurant with a patio is located above the store on the fuel dock. A water taxi service is available. There is good fishing a short run from the marina.

Above: The northeast arm of Secret Cove ends at Buccaneer Marina. This facility provides boat servicing, repairs and storage. It is a busy place in summer when tenants and visitors stop at the dock, below, for fuel and supplies. Holiday cottage owners on the Thormanby Islands also use this as a base to reach their properties.

Buccaneer Marina &Resort

5535 San Souci Rd
Halfmoon Bay BC V0N 1Y2
Phone 604-885-7888
Toll free: 1-877-885-7888
buccaneermarina@telus.net
www.buccaneermarina.com

Marina services include haulouts, gas, diesel, oil sales, and a small store. Occasional overnight slips are available. A repair dock offers a 12 metre marine ways, and service, parts and repairs.

The marina offers garbage disposal, boat rentals, charts, fishing gear and licences, live and frozen bait. Ice and propane are also available at the marina.

A water taxi service to Thormanby Island and Sechelt operates from the dock.

Pender Harbour
Francis Peninsula, Green Bay, Agamemnon Channel

Charts 3535, 3311, 3312, 3512, 3514

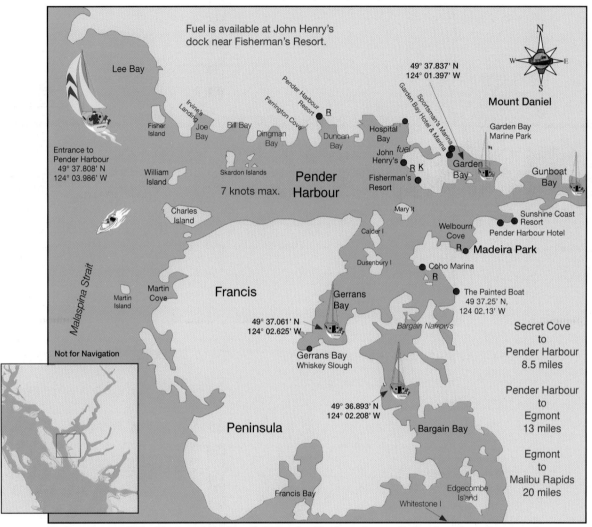

Fuel is available at John Henry's dock near Fisherman's Resort.

Lee Bay

Mount Daniel

49° 37.837' N
124° 01.397' W

Entrance to Pender Harbour
49° 37.808' N
124° 03.986' W

Irvine's Landing

Fisher Island
Joe Bay
Bill Bay
Dingman Bay
Duncan Bay
Pender Harbour Resort
Farrington Cove

Hospital Bay
John Henry's *fuel*
Fisherman's Resort

Garden Bay Hotel & Marina
Sportsman's Marina

Garden Bay Marine Park

Garden Bay

Gunboat Bay

William Island
Skardon Islands

Pender Harbour

7 knots max.

Charles Island

Mary It

Calder I

Welbourn Cove

Sunshine Coast Resort
Pender Harbour Hotel

Madeira Park

Dusenbury I

Martin Island
Martin Cove

Francis

49° 37.061' N
124° 02.625' W

Gerrans Bay

Coho Marina

The Painted Boat
49 37.25' N,
124 02.13' W

Gerrans Bay
Whiskey Slough

Bargain Narrows

Secret Cove to Pender Harbour
8.5 miles

49° 36.893' N
124° 02.208' W

Peninsula

Bargain Bay

Pender Harbour to Egmont
13 miles

Egmont to Malibu Rapids
20 miles

Francis Bay

Edgecombe Island

Whitestone I

Malaspina Strait

Not for Navigation

Referred to as "The Venice of the North," Pender Harbour is a well-developed marine vacation area with every option as a cruising destination–with anchorages, marinas and public docks.

Bargain Bay

From Buccaneer Bay and Welcome Passage, chart a course to Whitestone Islands. Passing to the northeast of them will lead to the entrance of Bargain Bay just west of Edgecombe Island off the Francis Peninsula. While this is not an entrance to Pender Harbour, its shallow Bargain Narrows will allow the passage of a very small boat, at higher tides.

There is a rock in the centre of the entrance to Bargain Bay, but the chart shows it as deeper than six feet at low tide.

This bay is a pleasant, sheltered anchorage, in 7 metres, from which one can explore Pender Harbour in a shore boat.

Pender Harbour

Continuing around Francis Peninsula, pass Francis Point and Francis Bay, proceeding north between Martin Island and Charles Island to enter Pender Harbour either side of Williams Island. The reef to the southeast of Williams Island is marked.

Above: View from the south of Pender Harbour showing its entrance and numerous private and public docks. Bargain Bay and Gerrans Bay are on the left, Madeira Park on the far right. Right: Bargain Bay from above Coho Marina in the lower right foreground.

Another marker stands on the reef off the Skardon Islands. The most used passage is north of the Skardon Islands along the Pender Harbour north shore.

Pender Harbour's 32 miles of shoreline has anchorages and facilities to meet most needs of cruising mariners. The neighbouring waters are renowned for excellent fishing. Fuel, however is available only at one place, John Henry's Marina, in Hospital Bay. Available services and facilities for mariners, include moorage at a number of marinas. There are restaurants, stores, post office, pubs and launching ramps.

Many mariners use dock facilities in Pender Harbour and many anchor out. The available docks include private marinas and the public docks at Hospital Bay, Madeira Park and Gerrans Bay. Refer to marinas in ***Docks and Destinations.***

Joe Bay

Immediately north, inside Pender Harbour, Joe Bay is the site of Irvine's Landing. For decades this landing was the major settlement of Pender Harbour, with Union Steamships Com-

Above: Gerrans Bay is protected by Calder and Dusenbury Islands. Below left and right: The entrance to Pender Harbour. Opposite top: Pender Harbour Resort. Opposite lower: Pender Harbour Resort and Fisherman's Resort and Marina.

pany vessels calling regularly at its substantial landing.

In more recent years it was the location of a popular marina with fuel, overnight moorage and a pub and restaurant to serve visitors and locals. Charlie Irvine was the namesake and possibly the first settler at the Landing, arriving there in 1865. Prior to his arrival, however, it is believed a fish saltery was founded at the landing by a Chinese family. Later, Joe Gonsalves, known as Portuguese Joe, became the owner and he and his family built the marina, pub and hotel that became the focus of the Union Steamships recognition of Pender Harbour. In the early years of the 21st century Irvine's Landing was closed, fuel supplies discontinued, and the docks removed. Future development may provide facilities once again for mariners. It was Joe Gonsalves of Irvine's Landing who brought the Portuguese influence to Pender Harbour and gave Madeira Park its name.

Following the north shore of Pender Harbour you will pass two notable coves before reaching Hospital Bay. The first, **Farrington Cove**, is the site of a new development that has replaced a once homey settlement owned by the Whittaker family. They ran it as a fishing and scuba diving resort in the 1980s. The second, **Duncan Cove**, has a marina and store, **Pender Harbour Resort**, with some lodging in rustic cabins. The marina accommodates regulars and visiting

Pender Harbour Resort

boats. The cove was named for a Scots settler who founded a blacksmith shop there in the early 1900s. Other prominent settlers at Pender Harbour included industrious Japanese and German immigrants.

Pender Harbour Resort and Marina

4686 Sinclair Bay Rd
Garden Bay BC V0N 1S0
Phone 604-883-2424 Toll free 1-877-883-2424
info@penderharbourresort.com
www.penderharbourresort.com

Marina services include showers, laundry, washrooms, ice, water, 15 and 30 amp power and garbage disposal. The resort offers some snacks, fishing licences, rental boats, access to a heated pool. It is also a busy RV resort, with campsites, chalets, yurts and cabins.

Pender Harbour Resort

There are many places in Pender Harbour for small craft to moor. Vessels can be anchored in Garden Bay in an open area, which is generally protected from wind, although the occasional southerly blow may cause some discomfort. Drop anchor in 6 metres near the shore at the marine park.

Anchor also in Gerrans Bay with attention to wind forecasts. Drop anchor in 4 metres at the head of the bay or off Calder and Dusenbury Islands. Sheltered anchorage can be found inside **Gunboat Bay**. This bay lies at the east end of Pender Harbour. It has a narrow entrance and dries at the far end.

Dusenbury Island was named for an enterprising settler who set up a sealing operation and boat repair facility there

Fisherman's Resort and Marina

Above: Fisherman's Resort and Marina in the foreground with the Hospital Bay public dock to its left. Garden Bay is on the other side of the isthmus. Left: A favourite with locals and visitors is Laverne's Grill at Hospital Bay, known for its great fish and chips.

in 1905. Pender Harbour was once the centre of a large population of the Coast Salish people. It was part of their home base on the Sunshine Coast and a venue for winter potlatches. They thrived on fishing, berry gathering and hunting. At one time huge longhouses occupied some landings, such as at Garden Bay.

Note: Caution should be exercised in parts of Pender Harbour due to rocks and reefs, shallows and other obstacles. Use a large scale chart such as the close up section in the Sunshine Coast strip chart 3311.

Hospital Bay

Hospital Bay anchorage is exposed to more wind than some other parts of Pender Harbour, but there is sheltered overnight moorage available at Fisherman's Resort or try for space at the Hospital Bay public float.

The former hospital, overlooking this bay, functioned in more recent years as a lodge and restaurant, but has since been sitting almost derelict. The hospital, interestingly, was built in 1930 by one of the coast's more notable missionaries, John Antle, who travelled by boat up and down the BC coast

Hospital Bay

Events and activities

The Pender Harbour Blues Festival is held in June. A Music Festival is held in August and a Jazz Festival is held in September. Like the Blues Festival, the Jazz Festival is held at venues and restaurants throughout the area. Phone 604-883-2130 for details. A Wooden Boat Festival is held in August. The annual May Day festival at Pender Harbour is notable. Visit the Gallery at the former Forestry Station at Madeira Park. Stroll the reed marsh boardwalk near the shopping centre in Madeira Park.

with the Columbia Coast Mission.

For light meals, try Laverne's, a small eatery located on the isthmus between Hospital Bay and Garden Bay. For patio and lounge dining visit Garden Bay Hotel and Pub.

Top: The fuel dock at John Henry's and busy summer moorage at Fisherman's Resort and Marina in Pender Harbour's Hospital Bay. The old hospital (seen in the photo opposite, top) still overlooks the bay for which it is named. Below: The small launch ramp adjacent to the fuel dock. Bottom: John Henry's Marina, store and fuel dock.

Fisherman's Resort & Marina and John Henry's fuel.

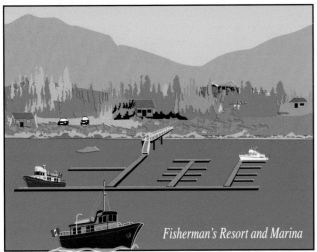

Fisherman's Resort and Marina

Top: Fisherman's Resort and Marina docks in Hospital Bay, with John Henry's fuel dock and small boat marina in the foreground.

Opposite page, clockwise from top: The store, office, garden and docks at Fisherman's Resort and Marina in Hospital Bay. Owners, David Pritchard and Jennifer Love at Fisherman's Resort. A group from the Schooner Cove Yacht Club meet Pacific Yachting magazine editor Peter Robson (at left) during happy hour at Fisherman's Resort marina. The resort's garden overlooking Hospital Bay.

Fisherman's Resort & Marina

4890 Pool Lane PO Box 68, Garden Bay BC V0N 1S0
Phone 604-883-2336
fishermans@dccnet.com
www.fishermansresortmarina.com
Marina services include moorage at over 700 metres of dock space. Reservations are suggested. Power at docks is 20 and 30 amps. There is water at the docks. Facilities include laundry, showers and washrooms. Ice, tackle, marine charts, books, clothing, fishing gear and licences are available. The resort has several waterfront cabins for rent. There is internet access at the marina.

Fishing is good in the general area as is scuba diving. There are four lakes nearby, and swimming, golfing, mountain biking, animal and marine life viewing are popular pastimes.

John Henry's Marina

4907 Pool Lane, PO Box 4907, Garden Bay BC V0N 1S0
Phone: 604-883-2253
This is the only fuel dock in Pender Harbour. It has gas, diesel, oil and propane. On the property, there is a substantial store, which sells ice, groceries, pharmacy items, liquor, marine and fishing supplies. There is also a post office and ATM. There is a small launch ramp on the road between John Henry's and Fisherman's Resort Marina..

Right: West side of the public docks at Pender Harbour, with the east side continuation and adjacent Madeira Marina on the opposite page. Below, top to bottom: Madeira Park marina offices; Hospital Bay and Garden Bay either side of the Garden Peninsula. Note the anchorage in Garden Bay; The docks and pub/restaurant on the waterfront with boats at the Garden Bay Hotel and Marina docks.

Madeira Park Marina

Garden Bay Hotel & Marina

Hospital Bay public dock
Pender Harbour Authority
The float length totals 158 metres. Available facilities include garbage disposal, portable type toilets, water, and 15 and 20 amp power. It is located close to John Henry's grocery store and marina.

Garden Bay
Of the many nooks and crannies in which to anchor in Pender Harbour, Garden Bay is one of the most popular. The bay is located on the north shore of the harbour fronting a majestic designated marine park which has a shoreline of about 200 metres. A dinghy float in Garden Bay provides access to the park. Four marinas are located in Garden Bay. Two are yacht club facilities and the others are the Sportsmans Marina Resort and the Garden Bay Hotel and Marina, both providing overnight moorage.

The upper reaches of **Garden Bay Marine Provincial Park** include Mount Daniel. The local Sechelt people refer to the mountain as Kwiss Chiam, which is of great ceremonial and ritual significance. The summit of the mountain and a cemetery on the waterfront are protected archaeological sites.

Gunboat Bay
In Gunboat Bay the recommended spot to anchor is near **Goat Islet**. Mind the depths in this shallow bay. Beware of the rock to port in the narrow entrance. Leaving Gunboat Bay and following the east and south shores of Pender Harbour, Sunshine Coast Resort and Pender Harbour Hotel, have moorage and facilities. Just beyond, Madeira Park is approached through Welbourne Cove. Here Madeira Marina has been a long established service and repair centre and marina, accommodating local tenants. Alongside is the public dock.

*Above: The public docks at Madeira Park. Below, right: The pub
and restaurant at Garden Bay overlooking the marina and adjacent
Royal Vancouver Yacht Club facility. Below: Approaching the docks in
Garden Bay, some mariners use this bay as an anchorage while others
tie up at a marina or the nearby Royal Vancouver Yacht Club floats.*

Garden Bay

Garden Bay Hotel & Marina

4985 Lyons Rd, PO Box 90
Garden Bay BC V0N 1S0 Phone 604-883-2674
gbhm@dccnet.com   www.gardenbaypub.com
Guest moorage: 1,200', reservations are suggested. Water and
15 and 30 amp power at the dock. Garbage disposal. Dining
at the pub and waterfront restaurant with live entertainment.
Kayak and canoe rentals and fishing charters are available.
Laundry and showers are located nearby and washrooms can
be found at the pub overlooking the docks.

Pender Harbour Hotel and Marina

Sportsman's Resort and Marina

Top: The walk to the Madeira Park shopping centre.
Above, centre: Boats at Pender Harbour Hotel and Marina docks.
Above: Sportsman's Resort and Marina in Garden Bay.

Madeira Park public wharf

PO Box 118, Madeira Park V0N 2H0
Phone: 604-883-2234 *penderauthority@telus.net*
A large set of floats and an aircraft float are adjacent to the launch ramp. The marina has garbage disposal, pumpout, washrooms, showers, water, lights, and 15, 30 and 50 amp power. Nearby there are restaurants, supermarket and shops. Madeira Marina is adjacent to the public dock.

Madeira Marina

12930 Madeira Park Rd
Madeira Park BC V0N 2H0
Phone 604-883-2266
This is a full service marine centre with mechanics and a marine store. It has haulout and repair facilities, but no transient moorage.

Sportsman's Resort & Marina

PO Box 6 Garden Bay, BC V0S 1N0
Phone 604-883-2479
info@sportsmansmarina.com www.sportsman_marina.com
Visitor moorage. Services include laundry, showers and washrooms. Water and 20 and 30 amp power available.

Sunshine Coast Resort & Marina

12695 Sunshine Coast Hwy. PO Box 213
Madeira Park BC V0N 2H0
Phone 604-883-9177
vacation@sunshinecoast-resort.com
www.sunshinecoastresort.com
Limited guest moorage is available seasonally from Easter to Thanksgiving. Much of the dock space is allocated as the

Top: Boats anchored and docked in Garden Bay.
Right: the Sunshine Coast Resort and Marina docks.

Sunshine Coast Resort and Marina

Nanaimo Yacht Club outstation. Power at the dock is 15 and 30 amps. Visitors have access to laundry, washrooms, showers and garbage disposal, plus boat rentals, live bait and internet access. Quality accommodations with sundeck and hot tub are available to resort and marina guests. There is free transportation to and from the local golf course.

Pender Harbour Hotel & Marina

12671 Sunshine Coast Hwy BC V0N 2H0
Phone 604-883-9013
bal@penderharbourhotel.com
www.penderharbourhotel.com
Guest moorage offers 20, 30 and 50 amp power, pub/restaurant, liquor, beer and wine store. Banquet room and hotel. Hotel and pub shuttle pick up at the marina.

Madeira Park

This is the site in Welbourn Cove of the public dock and launch ramp, with access to the large shopping centre nearby, for banking, liquor and grocery shopping. The fingers on the public dock provide overnight moorage. Sometimes the dock is busy with commercial and visiting pleasure craft and rafting up is necessary. An art gallery at the adjacent former forestry station overlooks the docks.

Gerrans Bay

Enter Gerrans Bay from Welbourn Cove and follow the shoreline into the rugged basin that opens eastward. If you are heading directly to Coho Marina (it has a launch ramp), from the entrance of the harbour, pass into Gerrans Bay between

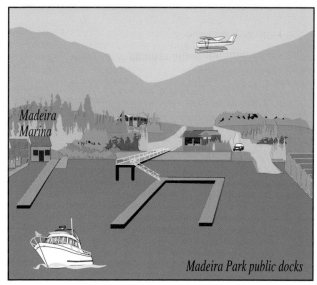

Madeira Marina

Madeira Park public docks

The Painted Boat Resort

Above: A view over the sheltered waters of Pender Harbour from the Sunshine Coast Resort. Its marina lies at the foot of the slope with Garden Bay beyond. Left: The docks at The Painted Boat Resort. The fingers on the south side of the marina are for transient boats. Coho Marina is at far left. Inset, left: Overlooking the docks from The Restaurant and the lodge at The Painted Boat Resort.
Opposite page: Madeira park. The public marina with the adjacent launch ramp, is in the middle. The road running to the nearby shopping centre passes the school. The Painted Boat Lodge is seen in the upper right hand corner.

Madeira Park.

Calder Island and Mary Islet, or go east of Mary Islet, and use the reef markers on approach to Coho Marina as a reference. Follow these channel markers to Coho Marina. There is little space for visitors at this marina so call ahead if you hope to tie up there. Its launch ramp is used by visitors hauling boats by trailer. Beyond Coho Marina is the Painted Boat Resort. The Restaurant at the resort is open for lunch and dinner and for refreshments. Mariners moored at nearby marinas can access the resort's restaurant docks by dinghy or runabout. Or visit by boat and dine and stay overnight, by arrangement with the restaurant.

Keep south of the islands marked 9 on the chart and follow the channel to the dock. The waters north of the two small islands are shallow and subject to drying. Explore these areas by kayak or small runabout (dinghy) at high tide. The shallows in the south end of the cove lead to Bargain Narrows and Bargain Bay. Gerrans Bay has many private floats, and Whiskey Slough, a larger, public dock, lies at the head of the bay.

Coho Marina Resort

12907 Shark Lane,
PO Box 160, Madeira Park BC V0N 2H0
Phone 604-883-2248 *cohomarina@dccnet.com*
Hazard: Rocks in the bay–marked by beacons. Consult charts.
This marina has limited visitor moorage.
There is a launch ramp on site.

The Painted Boat Resort
Spa and Marina

Lagoon Rd, Madeira Park BC. PO Box 153, V0N 2H0
Phone 604-883-2456 Toll free 1-866-902-3955
therestaurant@paintedboat.com www.paintedboat.com
Moorage is available for overnight and for The Restaurant customers. The marina accommodates visitors' boats to about 20 metres. Check with the restaurant management. Water and 30 and 50 amp power are available at the docks. No showers, washrooms or garbage removal. Lodge guests have facilities and amenities including spa and pool. Accommodation in luxury time-share units. Shops nearby at Madeira Park.

Whiskey Slough public dock

Phone 604-883-2234
Moorage 100 metres in summer. 15 amp power, water.

Leaving Pender Harbour, there are two ways to proceed north. One is by way of Agamemnon Channel and the other along the coast past Cape Cockburn. Agamemnon Channel is the passage to Hotham Sound, Egmont, Sechelt Inlet and Princess Louisa Inlet.

If you are not continuing to Princess Louisa or Sechelt, turn west in Jervis Inlet and make for Malaspina Strait. You will pass Hardy Island to port and Saltery Bay and Scotch Fir Point to starboard. In rough conditions in Malaspina Strait, you can avoid Cape Cockburn by using this latter route.

Above: Agamemnon Channel from Lee Bay and Daniel Point to Green Bay. From Daniel Point, Lee Bay sweeps to the right and abuts the entrance of Pender Harbour. In the adjoining photograph, Lee Bay is seen to the left. Fisher Island is at the east end of the bay in both photographs.

Green Bay, Agamemnon Channel

If you find Pender Harbour a bit on the busy side for your liking and wish for more tranquility, try the anchorage at Green Bay a short distance up Agamemnon Channel. Out of Pender Harbour turn north along Agamemnon Channel. Green Bay opens to port a short way up the passage. The bay is a quiet, sheltered anchorage but has a large reef in the middle of the arm that opens northwards. It is possible to anchor south of the reef but the most protected place (mostly from passing traffic) to drop the hook, is north of the reef. Anchor in 8 to 10 metres. Watch for rocks near the surface in the centre and the head of the bay. This is a good place to wait out the daytime southerly breezes or overnight northerlies.

The north end of Agamemnon Channel opens into Hotham Sound. Just to starboard as you leave the channel is the Earl's Cove to Saltery Bay ferry terminal. Beyond that, at the entrance to Sechelt Inlet is the turbulent Sechelt Rapids at Skookumchuck Narrows and the settlement of Egmont. To port, Captain Island can be passed either side. However, if you are heading for Princess Louisa or Egmont you will pass well to the east of it. Between **Nile Point** and **Captain Island** there is a tiny nook created by a small island with a reef attached to shore that dries at low tide. Temporary anchorage in this nook is possible. It is a good place for a swim (page 116).

Agamemnon Channel is named for Admiral Nelson's gunship and Nelson Island for the famous man himself. Many name places were taken from ships and captains exploring the coast as well as famous or respected naval characters they

honoured in this way. Such names include Fearney Point, Captain Island (HMS *Captain*), Malaspina Strait, Hardy Island, Vanguard Bay (Nelson's flagship HMS *Vanguard*) and the list goes on. Check Walbran–*BC Coast Names*.

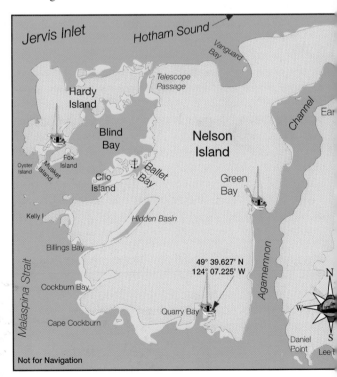

Nelson Island

anchorage
49° 42.705' N
124° 04.874' W

Keep far over to the east side passing the reef. Note: Some GPS maps show the reef farther north than its actual location. Use the large scale chart 3589, especially at high tide when the extent of the reef is not visible.

reef

private dock

Green Bay

waterfall

N
W   E
S

Green Bay entrance
49° 42.580' N
124° 04.863' W

Agamemnon Channel

Hotham Sound

Foley Head

Miller Rk

N
W   E
S

Jervis Inlet

Captain Island

Egmont Point

Nelson Island

Agnew Passage

Nile Point

Agamemnon Channel

Sechelt Inlet

Sutton Its

Top: Pender Harbour. The entrance is protected by Williams Island with the Skardon Islands beyond. The boat leaving the harbour is passing Henry Point on the north shore. This is the main entranceway to the harbour. Hospital Bay lies beyond the Skardon Islands and Madeira Park is off to the far right. The body of water at left of Pender Harbour's north shore is Hotel Lake. Above and inset: The reef inside Green Bay and Agamemnon Channel continuing north.

A sunny day at Garden Bay public dock, Pender Harbour. John Henry's Marina and Fisherman's Resort and Marina are also located in Hospital Bay.

It is hard to believe that just a short distance away from the tranquility at Egmont, bottom photo, the currents can be running up to 16 knots in Sechelt Narrows. The bottom photo was taken at Secret Bay in Egmont, the top, courtesy of Justin Taylor, looking down on the rapids.

Sechelt Inlet
Egmont, Skookumchuck Narrows, Sechelt Rapids, Porpoise Bay

Charts 3312, 3512

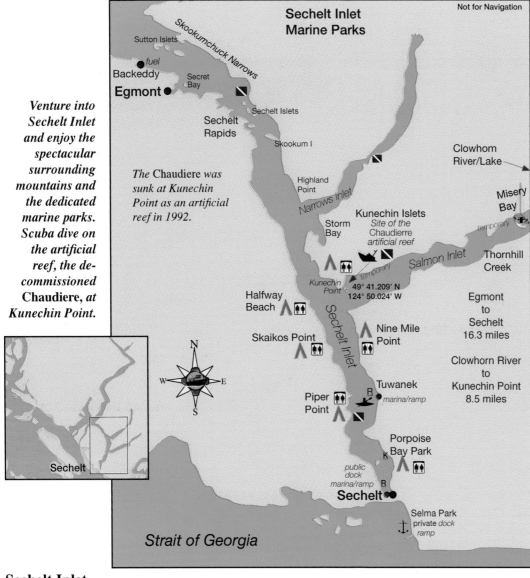

Sechelt Inlet
Marine Parks

Not for Navigation

Sutton Islets

Skookumchuck Narrows

fuel
Backeddy
Egmont ●

Secret Bay

Sechelt Islets

Sechelt Rapids

Skookum I

Clowhom River/Lake

The Chaudiere *was sunk at Kunechin Point as an artificial reef in 1992.*

Highland Point

Misery Bay

Narrows Inlet

Kunechin Islets
Site of the Chaudierre artificial reef

temporary

Storm Bay

Salmon Inlet

Thornhill Creek

Kunechin Point
temporary
49° 41.209' N
124° 50.024' W

Egmont to Sechelt
16.3 miles

Halfway Beach

Nine Mile Point

Skaikos Point

Clowhorn River to Kunechin Point
8.5 miles

Sechelt Inlet

Tuwanek
marina/ramp

Piper Point

N
W — E
S

Porpoise Bay Park

public dock marina/ramp

Sechelt ●●

Selma Park
private dock ramp

Strait of Georgia

Sechelt

Venture into Sechelt Inlet and enjoy the spectacular surrounding mountains and the dedicated marine parks. Scuba dive on the artificial reef, the de-commissioned Chaudiere, at Kunechin Point.

Sechelt Inlet

This large sheltered inlet opens to the east of the Sechelt Peninsula and features eight marine park areas. It is accessed from Jervis Inlet via the tidal Skookumchuck Narrows with its famous Sechelt Rapids, which are known to reach speeds up to 16 knots. This occurs usually during spring tides when overfalls can reach a stunning five metres. This is one of the most dangerous waterways on the coast and should not be used without tide and current tables and good charts. Passage should be made only during slack tides, preferably at high tide. There are several launching ramps inside Sechelt Inlet which can be reached by road from the Sunshine Coast.

Egmont

The town of Egmont, at the entrance to the inlet, is a short distance to the south of Jervis Inlet. It has marinas and facilities with supplies and amenities for mariners.

Tied up at the public dock at Egmont. Here one waits for either the slack tide at Sechelt Rapids ("The Skookumchuck") to enter Sechelt Inlet, or for the appropriate time to set off for Princess Louisa Inlet.

While at Egmont it is possible to hike in and watch the powerful Sechelt Rapids at Skookumchuck Narrows. Walk to the Skookumchuck Narrows Provincial Park Heritage Centre and take the trail to the rapids viewpoint. There is a bakery at the head of the trail.

Kayakers enjoy riding the waves when the currents are strong. The "ride" through the rapids by scuba divers is a regular underwater event, but at slack tide. I had the pleasure of doing it in company of several other divers, and even at slack tide we were swept along the bottom at a good speed.

The public dock is next door to Bathgate Marina. Egmont is the nearest base before a trip to Princess Louisa Inlet. The ferry to Princess Louisa Inlet and Malibu Club leaves from a nearby dock. Contact them at *www.malibuyachts.com*.

Bathgate General Store Resort & Marina

6781 Bathgate Rd,
Egmont BC V0N 1N0
Phone 604-883-2222
bathgate@lincsat.com
www.bathgate.com

Gas, diesel, propane and oils are available at this facility. Visitors may reserve moorage. It has a marine ways to 40 tons, a marine mechanic on duty and water at the dock. Power at the docks is 15, 20 and 30 amps.

A deluxe waterfront motel with wheelchair access overlooks the marina. The adjacent grocery store has fresh meat and vegetables, fishing tackle, licences, a liquor agency and a bank machine (ATM).

There are RV and tent sites nearby. The washrooms, showers and laundry are available for marina customers. Other services include video rentals, ice and internet access.

Hazard: There is a marked drying reef in the middle of Secret Bay stretching from the approaches to the Bathgate Marina fuel dock to near the government dock, noted on your chart.

Backeddy Resort and Marina

16660 Backeddy Rd., Egmont BC V0N 1N0
Phone 604-883-2298 Toll free: 1-800-626-0599
info@backeddy.com www.backeddy.com

This is a fuel stop for gas, diesel, oils, two stroke oil, frozen bait and supplies. Guest moorage is available, with laundry, showers, washrooms, 15 and 30 amp power, water, ice, tackle, fishing licences, books, some groceries and supplies.

The Backeddy Marine Pub is a long established restaurant and pub, overlooking the marina. Guests enjoy long-weekend live entertainment in summer. Tours to Princess Louisa Inlet can be arranged. This is a Boat US participating marina. In 2008 youthful new owners took over ownership and improvements and changes were in the works.

Above and right, top: The public dock and Bathgate Marina at Secret Bay in Egmont. Note the Sutton Islets, Egmont Point and the beginning of Prince of Wales Reach–the route to Princess Louisa Inlet.
Above, right: The docks at Backeddy Marina.

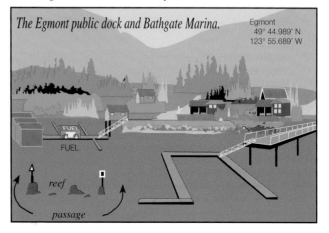

The Egmont public dock and Bathgate Marina.

Egmont
49° 44.989' N
123° 55.689' W

FUEL

reef

passage

91

Top: The Sutton Islets off the west side of Backeddy Marina.

Above: Bathgate Marina from the ramp to the adjacent public docks at Egmont.

Right: Unbelievable calm at Sechelt Rapids. As the tide turns the currents increase to make this one of the fastest flowing tidal waterways on the coast. By contrast, note the flow during ebb, inset.

Left: Carla with Suzanne Allan, co-owner of the Backeddy Marina.

Skookum Whitewater Challenge–September
Professional kayak rodeo at the extreme whitewater of Skookumchuck Rapids
For information call the Backeddy Pub, 604-883-2298.

Automobile fuel is available at Bathgate Marina and marine fuel is obtainable nearby at Backeddy Marina (formerly Egmont Marina).

Egmont Public Dock

Egmont Harbour Authority. Phone 1-877-988-3838.

The float length of 145 metres includes an aircraft float, and marina services provide garbage disposal and safe overnight moorage. There is a reef between the two passage markers nearby. Within easy reach of the marinas, the **West Coast Wilderness Lodge**, offers fine dining and accommodation.

Sechelt Inlet has been described as an incredible inland sea. It is a kayaker's paradise, with many calm hours and lee shores to explore. It is home to a variety of animals and birds, sea lions, dolphins, otters, herons, eagles and kingfishers. The inlet is lined with marine parks but there are not many sheltered anchorages.

The cove in **Storm Bay** between Sockeye Point and Cawley Point at the entrance to Narrows Inlet, is a suitable overnight anchorage. Anchor in the lee of the small islet in 4 to 6 metres. Or try **Misery Bay**, up Salmon Inlet. Anchor in about 14 metres. Fellow yachtsman Dave Short says he and

friends have anchored at the head of the inlet many times over the years. They enjoy the reported mild conditions and often go ashore to stroll along the logging road for a swim in the warm summer water of Clowhom Lake.

Sechelt Inlet parks are most popular among small boat operators, canoeists and kayakers. They are **Tzoonie Narrows**, on the northern shore of Narrows Inlet, **Kunechin Point** on the north side of Salmon Inlet, **Thornhill Creek** at the mouth of the creek of the same name on the south shore of Salmon Inlet, **Nine Mile Point** just south of the entrance of Salmon Inlet, **Tuwanek** on the east side of Sechelt Inlet, **Piper Point**,

Skaiakos Point and **Halfway Beach** on the west side.

There is camping, but limited development at the marine parks and little protected overnight anchorage. Exceptions are the tiny coves at either side of Kunechin Point.

There is a reef in the small basin on the Salmon Inlet side of the point, so take care when anchoring. Although this cove is generally protected from most winds, some effects of a blow down Salmon Inlet can be felt at times.

Many place names come from the First Nations settlers of the area. Notably the Qenetcin, the Tuwanekq and the Skaiakos people are recognized in name places of the inlet.

Above: Sechelt Inlet showing Four Mile Point and the view north. Left: A view of Sechelt Rapids from the shore at the end of the hiking trail at Skookumchuck Narrows. Sechelt Rapids is commonly known as "The Skookumchuck". It lies at the entrance to Sechelt Inlet from near Jervis Inlet and two miles from the marina in Skookumchuck Narrows. Bottom: Backeddy Marina. The Sutton Islets are in the background.

Above: Narrows Inlet opens off Sechelt Inlet at Cawley Point, seen in the lower foreground with Sockeye Point opposite. Storm Bay is in the lower centre and angled off to the right. Below: Take a close look. The Sechelt Rapids is a waterway to be respected.

Left: Kunechin Point and the Kunechin Islets. Temporary anchorage may be taken in the lee of the islands or the point.
Below: The interpretive centre and museum at Egmont with a mural inside by local artist Emily Gray. The centre and museum features logging and fishing artifacts from the Egmont historic community. It is a pleasant walk to the museum from either marina in Skookumchuck Narrows. There is a bakery nearby, on the trail from the centre to the viewpoint overlooking the Sechelt Rapids.

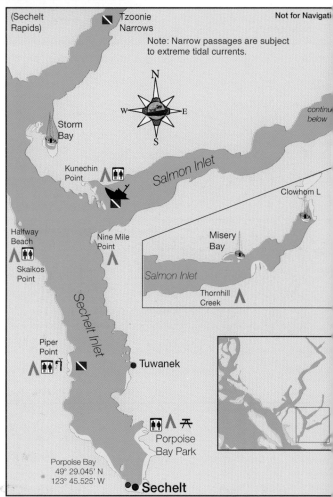

(Sechelt Rapids)

Tzoonie Narrows

Not for Navigati

Note: Narrow passages are subject to extreme tidal currents.

Storm Bay

Kunechin Point

Salmon Inlet

Clowhom L

continu below

Halfway Beach

Skaikos Point

Nine Mile Point

Misery Bay

Salmon Inlet

Thornhill Creek

Sechelt Inlet

Piper Point

Tuwanek

Porpoise Bay Park

Porpoise Bay
49° 29.045' N
123° 45.525' W

Sechelt

Above: Looking north up Sechelt Inlet. Kunechin Point can be seen at the north side of the entrance to Salmon Inlet, on the east side of Sechelt Inlet. This is the site of the sinking of the former HMCS Chaudiere *as an artificial reef, in December 1992, for the enjoyment of scuba divers.*
Right: A large crowd gathered to watch the event of the sinking of the ship. It has become a popular attraction for the diving community.

Sechelt Inlet was a major feature in the book *The Curve of Time* by M. Wylie Blanchet. The author and her children wrote a novel account of a killer whale named Henry who swam into the inlet and could not find his way out. It was based on numerous versions of just such an actual incident.

Sechelt

The town of Sechelt has marinas and launching facilities as well as services and stores for all needs at Porpoise Bay, which lies at the head of Sechelt Inlet. Scuba diving is popu- lar at several places in the inlet, particularly the site of the *Chaudiere*, a sunken artificial reef off Kunechin Point, and at the Skookumchuck, Tzoonie Narrows and Tuwanek.

See the dive guide book *151 Dives* by Betty Pratt-Johnson. It's highly recommended that you use a local dive charter boat for diving the inlet.

Several small marinas and a launch ramp are located behind a breakwater on the east shore of the south end of Sechelt Inlet. These include Poise Cove Marina (private moorage) and Choquer and Sons Marina located inside the breakwater.

*Opposite page:
Looking up Narrows Inlet
from Sechelt Inlet. Tzoonie
Narrows can be seen
at centre. This is a fast
running tidal passage that
should be negotiated at
slack water.
Above: Porpoise Bay and
Poise Island from above
Sechelt. Sechelt Inlet can
be reached from Egmont
via Skookumchuck Narrows
and Sechelt Rapids.
Right: The docks at
Porpoise Bay. The public
docks are clustered alongside the launch ramp.*

Choquer and Sons

This marina offers 100 metres of dock space, launch ramp, and haulouts to 12 metres. Phone 604-885-9244.

Porpoise Bay, Sechelt public dock

District of Sechelt

This fairly substantial dock, with a length of 132 metres, faces into the inlet and provides secure moorage for a good number of boats. It includes an aircraft float and has a launch ramp and grid alongside. Garbage disposal, power and water are also available. Nearby are restaurant, hotels and shops. Scuba diving is popular in the vicinity.

Lighthouse Marina and Pub

5764 Wharf Rd PO Box 137, Sechelt BC V0N 3A0
Phone 604-885-9494

info@lighthousepub.ca   www.lighthousepub.ca

The marina docks were being upgraded in 2008. Its facilities provide guest moorage with power available, and the convenience of access to ice, laundry, showers, washrooms, pumpout, garbage disposal, restaurant and pub. Internet access and ATM are available. There is a beer and wine store nearby. The marina is adjacent to the launch ramp and public docks. Porpoise Bay is located on the Sechelt Inlet side of the isthmus, not far from downtown Sechelt.

Above: Poise Cove at Tilicum Bay in Sechelt Inlet. The Lamb Islets can be seen in the upper left corner. Inset: Poise Cove Marina and adjacent Choquer and Sons marine facility that includes a marina and marine services, inside the breakwater. Right: Marina docks in Porpoise Bay.

Above: Porpoise Bay at the head of Sechelt Inlet. The docks at upper left in the photograph are adjacent to the public launch ramp.
Right: Porpoise Bay showing Poise Island and Snake Bay directly behind it.

Above: The public dock at Sechelt.
Right: On the sundeck of the Lighthouse Marina and Pub at Sechelt.
Opposite page: Looking up Sechelt Inlet from above Porpoise Bay Provincial Park. In the foreground is a First Nations reserve. Beyond is Four Mile Point then the Lamb Islets tucked in to the right at Tuwanek ahead of Nine Mile Point and Kunechin Point at Salmon Inlet. In the far distance the inlet tapers to Skookumchuck Narrows.

Princess Louisa Inlet. The dock at the park.

Princess Louisa Inlet
Chatterbox Falls, Malibu Rapids, Hotham Sound

Charts 3312, 3514, 3512, 3311

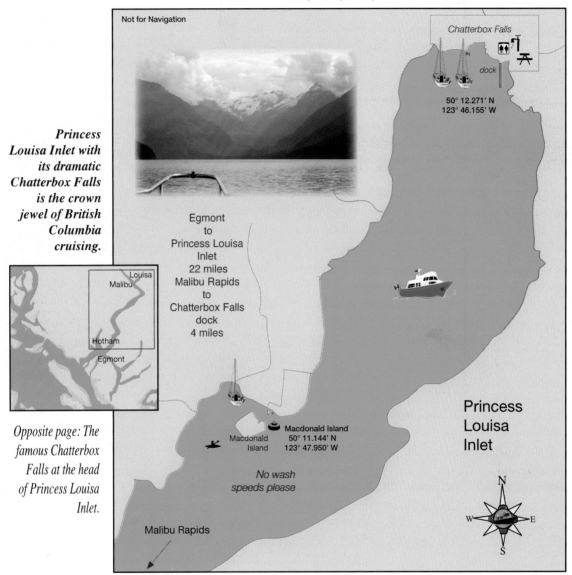

Not for Navigation

Princess Louisa Inlet with its dramatic Chatterbox Falls is the crown jewel of British Columbia cruising.

Opposite page: The famous Chatterbox Falls at the head of Princess Louisa Inlet.

Chatterbox Falls

dock

50° 12.271' N
123° 46.155' W

Egmont to Princess Louisa Inlet 22 miles Malibu Rapids to Chatterbox Falls dock 4 miles

Louisa
Malibu
Hotham
Egmont

Macdonald Island
Macdonald Island   50° 11.144' N
                    123° 47.950' W

Princess Louisa Inlet

No wash speeds please

Malibu Rapids

N
W   E
S

Princess Louisa Inlet

Princess Louisa Inlet and its beautiful Chatterbox Falls are among the most famous coastal attractions in British Columbia.

Take the time to travel up Jervis Inlet to Princess Louisa Inlet. Waterfalls and tall craggy mountains are the features of this deep inlet that cuts into the Coast Range. The passage begins at Jervis Inlet and Hotham Sound. From Egmont Point pass Miller Islet and Goliath Bay as you enter Prince of Wales Reach. Pass Vancouver Bay as you approach the tall Marlborough Heights reaching over 1,500 metres above the

106

waterway. The tall peak in the background is Mount Churchill at nearly 2,000 metres. From these heights streams run to the inlet with some cascading into waterfalls that tumble into the ocean, such as the one at Glacier Creek in Princess Royal Reach. There is possible temporary shelter from outflowing winds, at **McMurray Bay** on the west shore of the Reach. Take shelter from opposing winds, in the north side of the bight beyond McMurray Bay.

Deserted Bay is a wide, open bight, so named because of its having been found abandoned except for the bodies of a number of First Nations people who had succumbed to smallpox. It is not a suitable place to stop, so continue up Queens Reach to Malibu Rapids at the entrance to Princess Louisa Inlet.

Due to strong tidal flow between tides, passage through Malibu Rapids should be undertaken with caution, using a large scale chart and the tide and current tables. Note: The reference port is Point Atkinson and the secondary port is Malibu Rapids. Monitor wind forecasts.

Aerial photo courtesy of the Princess Louisa International Society.

Above and right: The dock at Princess Louisa Marine Park. Note the shallows and check tidal depths when dropping anchor. Opposite page: Visitors by boat congregate at their vessels and on the dock. The park ranger, the shelter and a view of Chatterbox Falls with boats at the dock The inlet is flanked by towering mountains.

Princess Louisa Inlet was named for Queen Victoria's mother, the Duchess of Kent, Victoria Maria Louisa. It was missed by Captain Vancouver who initially thought it was a river. The original name for Princess Louisa Inlet, given by the early First Nations of the area was Suiuoolot or Suivoolot (sway-we-lat), which means a place of warmth and sunshine. This was appropriate for the summer months when winds are minimal and sea temperatures reach a balmy 17 to 20° C.

Above: A tranquil anchorage with mooring buoys, in the lee of Macdonald Island, part way up Princess Louisa Inlet.
Opposite page: Anchored off Chatterbox Falls at the head of the inlet. Low tide exposes a sandy beach below the falls, but when anchoring near the outflowing river, remember the shallow ledge drops off quite quickly.

The astounding scenery, with steep mountains reaching some 2,500 metres above the deep fjord, is legendary. From these snow-capped and glacial mountains, streams tumble into the sea along the shore, with the most spectacular of them all reaching its end in the gushing Chatterbox Falls.

Pass through Malibu Rapids during slack tide. Once inside the inlet, proceed at no-wake speeds. If it is mid summer, or even shoulder season, expect to find the 200 metre dock filled with boats. No rafting is allowed and boat size is restricted to 18 metres in length. Time limit is 72 hours.

In the park there are walk-in campsites, a rain shelter, pit toilets, picnic tables, drinking water and panoramic views from several viewpoints. Hike up the mountainside to the remnants of a trapper's cabin. An easy trail leads to the base of Chatterbox Falls.

Note: A strong word of caution: the area at the top of the falls is extremely dangerous, even though it appears to be safe. Slippery rocks have led to the death of a number of people over the years and visitors are urged to not proceed any higher.

There are mooring buoys on the north side of **Macdonald Island.** This was formerly Hamilton Island and was renamed to honour James F. (Mac) Macdonald who settled on the land at Chatterbox Falls in 1927 making it his home for the remainder of his life. Despite several generous purchase offers, in 1953 Mac deeded it to the Princess Louisa International Society and in 1964 it became a BC provincial marine park under the guardianship of the society. Mac continued to live there aboard a houseboat, as caretaker and custodian of his former property. He died in 1978. The park has since been expanded with the provincial acquisition of surrounding land. The society continues to play a significant role in managing and conserving the park.

In 1974 I had the pleasure of meeting Bruce Calhoun, author of *Mac and the Princess.* He had traveled to the inlet many times and knew Mac in his latter days. My first trip to Princess Louisa Inlet was with a well-known aviator, Blackie Apsouris, aboard his Tyee Airways Beaver floatplane out of Sechelt. The view of the inlet, Chatterbox Falls and the surrounding mountains from the air is spectacular. We landed

Above and top: The current-swept passage at Malibu Rapids.
Right: Shops serving the youth that attend the camp at Malibu, and the
author's boat tied up at the their dock. Short visits
to the facility by passing mariners are invited.
Opposite: Malibu Club with a view from Princess Louisa Inlet towards
Queens Reach. A group of young people from the nearby Malibu camp
are dropped off to pay a short visit to the marine park at Princess
Louisa Inlet. Arriving at the Princess Louisa
dock near Chatterbox Falls.

Opposite page: Vessels leaving Princess Louisa Inlet through Malibu Rapids. Above: Hotham Sound. The Harmony Islands are at far right.

at the head of the inlet and tied up at the float that was once Macdonald's landing. There was not much park development back then and Mac was still alive, but no longer residing at his beloved Princess Louisa.

At the entrance to Princess Louisa Inlet, the Malibu Club Young Life summer camp at Malibu Rapids is an imposing property. It was originally a resort, built by aviation industrialist Thomas F. Hamilton, to cater to his yachting friends and visitors. The original Malibu Club was closed in 1950 and later sold to the present owners.

If you think of going to Princess Louisa Inlet in winter, remember it can partially freeze over near the waterfall, where the surface water is freshest. In addition, strong winds are known to howl down from the north.

Harmony Islands, Hotham Sound

The Harmony Islands are located on the east side of Hotham Sound to the north of Granville Bay and near the 430 metre high cascading Freil Lake waterfall. The sound is reached from Jervis Inlet past St Vincent Bay and around Elephant Point. It is a good stopover near Princess Wales Reach, the passage to Princess Louisa Inlet.

This is a quiet and tranquil park area with no facilities or development. The most sheltered anchorage is in the tiny basin created by the natural formation of three islets north of the main island (park). Watch for rocks and reefs in the entrance and anchorage areas. It is possible to anchor between the park

and the mainland but use a large scale chart, being mindful of the shallows in the passage. There is no stern tying or access on private islands. It is best to keep off these, and any other private islands on the coast.

There are other small coves in the vicinity to be discovered, such as **Dark Cove** in **Goliath Bay**. Cruise around Hotham Sound and stop in the lee of **Junction Island** in St Vincent Bay for a magnificent view of the mountains and waterfall on the opposite shore.

Princess Louisa Inlet access

For calculating tides and currents, use Point Atkinson high tide plus 24 minutes. Or low tide plus 36 minutes, allowing extra time for extreme tides. There is a short "S" shaped, fast running passage into the Inlet around the Malibu Young Life Camp which allows only single-lane traffic. Mariners entering or leaving should announce their intentions, at low power, on VHF channel 16: "Securite securite securite, this is (*boat name*), (*size of vessel*) power/sailing vessel entering Malibu, opposing traffic please advise, over."

This assures safe passage and advises oncoming traffic of your intentions. Inside the Inlet, limit your speed to 5 knots, and no wash from Malibu to Chatterbox Falls.

—*Bill Herringshaw (Princess Louisa International Society).*

Above: The Harmony Islands in Hotham Sound.
Left: Looking across Hotham Sound towards Freil Falls with the Harmony Islands in the distance at left. Junction Island and Elephant Point are in the foreground.
Bottom: Quarry Bay, looking towards Texada Island, and Cockburn Bay, on the south and west sides of Nelson Island.

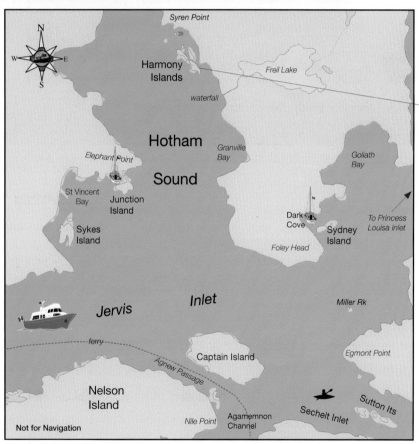

Syren Point

N
W E
S

Harmony
Islands

Freil Lake

waterfall

Hotham

Granville
Bay

Sound

Elephant Point

Junction
Island

St Vincent
Bay

Sykes
Island

Goliath
Bay

Dark
Cove

Sydney
Island

To Princess
Louisa Inlet

Foley Head

Inlet

Miller Rk

Jervis

ferry

Captain Island

Egmont Point

Agnew Passage

**Nelson
Island**

Nile Point

Agamemnon
Channel

Sechelt Inlet

Sutton Its

Not for Navigation

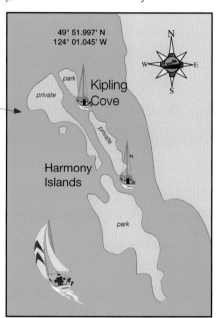

49° 51.997' N
124° 01.045' W

N
W E
S

park

private

Kipling
Cove

private

Harmony
Islands

park

Not for Navigation

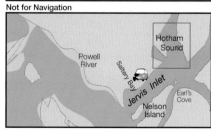

Powell
River

Saltery Bay

Hotham
Sound

Jervis Inlet

Earl's
Cove

Nelson
Island

Quarry Bay

Cockburn Bay

Nelson Island
Blind Bay, Ballet Bay, Hardy Island, Saltery Bay, Jervis Inlet

Charts 3312, 3311, 3512, 3514

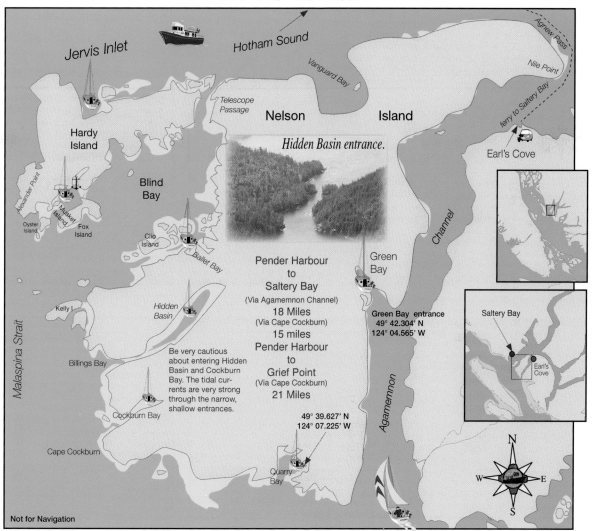

Jervis Inlet

Hotham Sound

Vanguard Bay

Nelson Island

Telescope Passage

Hardy Island

Hidden Basin entrance.

Blind Bay

Alexander Point

Musket Island

Oyster Island

Fox Island

Clio Island

Ballet Bay

Kelly I.

Malaspina Strait

Hidden Basin

Billings Bay

Be very cautious about entering Hidden Basin and Cockburn Bay. The tidal currents are very strong through the narrow, shallow entrances.

Cockburn Bay

Cape Cockburn

Pender Harbour
to
Saltery Bay
(Via Agamemnon Channel)
18 Miles
(Via Cape Cockburn)
15 miles
Pender Harbour
to
Grief Point
(Via Cape Cockburn)
21 Miles

49° 39.627' N
124° 07.225' W

Quarry Bay

Green Bay

Green Bay entrance
49° 42.304' N
124° 04.565' W

Channel

Agamemnon

Agnew Pass

Nile Point

ferry to Saltery Bay

Earl's Cove

Saltery Bay

Earl's Cove

N W E S

Not for Navigation

Many mariners reach the tranquil and sheltered coves in Blind Bay and make that their final destination.

Nelson Island

Quarry Bay, a short way out of Pender Harbour, lies at Nelson Island's southern shore. Anchorage here is good in about 10 to 12 metres. Caution–there is a rock near the shore. Anchor in the bight to starboard after entering the bay.

Cockburn Bay and **Hidden Basin** are both sheltered anchorages but have limited and very difficult access. The entrances are narrow and subject to drying, rocks and tides. If

you do get inside you will find these are sheltered anchorages. Be on the lookout for the drying rock in Billings Bay.

Blind Bay

If you round Cape Cockburn and are looking for shelter, or a place to spend some quality time at anchor, cruise into the southern portion of Blind Bay and make your way between

Blind Bay with Ballet Bay in the foreground, a clear view of Telescope Passage at the top. Below: Billings Bay, at the entrance to Hidden Basin, is in the foreground. Kelly Island and Fox Island straddle the main entrance to Blind Bay. Hardy Island and Jervis Inlet lie beyond.

Justin Tayl

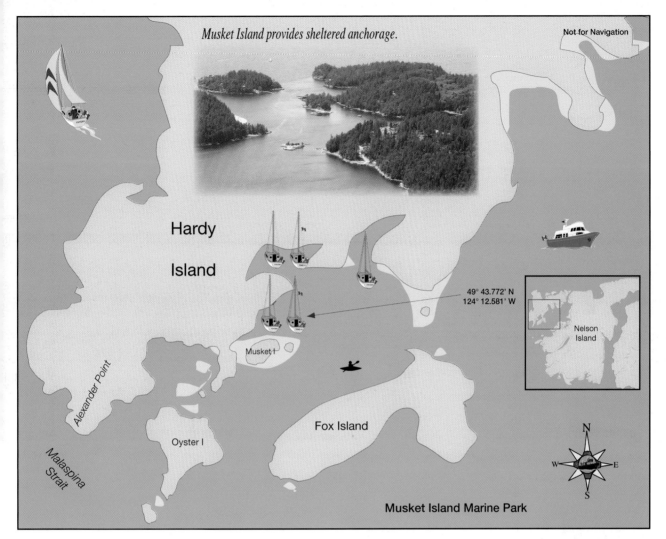

Musket Island provides sheltered anchorage.

Not for Navigation

Hardy

Island

49° 43.772' N
124° 12.581' W

Nelson
Island

Musket I

Alexander Point

Fox Island

Oyster I

Malaspina Strait

N
W E
S

Musket Island Marine Park

the northwest shore of Nelson Island and Clio Island. Passage into Blind Bay is possible for small boats going east of Kelly Island. Be careful of shallows and rocks lining the passage. Blind Bay is located off Jervis Inlet and is often a destination as a layover gateway to Princess Louisa Inlet.

On the northwest side of Nelson Island after entering Blind Bay, **Ballet Bay** is a very popular anchorage, while on the opposite shore of the bay, Musket Island is the primary anchorage and an official marine park.

Great care should be taken navigating into Ballet Bay due to rocks and reefs, some of which dry at low tide. Anchor in the inner or outer coves. The best protection against wind is deep inside the anchorage. This bay has been one of the anchorages of choice for mariners seeking shelter en route up and down the Sunshine Coast, or as a destination where warm water swimming and a cosy setting are their priority.

There are several indentations and coves on the Blind Bay side of Hardy Island, which offer temporary shelter. But it is best to use the **Musket Island Marine Park** anchorage.

Hidden Basin on the west side of Nelson Island is a sheltered anchorage. However, as the tide drops, the tidal entranceway is swift, shallow and narrow. Enter or leave at high tide slack, favouring the passage south of the island at the mouth. Use Point Atkinson tide tables.

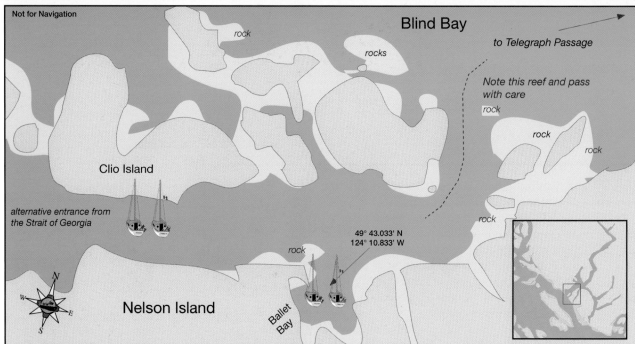

Blind Bay

rock

rocks

to Telegraph Passage

Note this reef and pass
with care

rock

rock

rock

Clio Island

*alternative entrance from
the Strait of Georgia*

49° 43.033' N
124° 10.833' W

rock

rock

Nelson Island

Ballet
Bay

W N E S

Musket Island is a small island that lies just off the south shore of Hardy Island, tucked in behind **Fox Island** in Blind Bay. It is undeveloped and the anchorage nearby and in the shadow of Hardy Island makes it a remote and tranquil place to stop. Best anchorage is in the lee of Musket Island. Anchor directly behind it or in the adjoining coves to its north. Access Musket Island Marine Park either west or east of Fox Island, but mind the reef on the east side. Entering Blind Bay from Jervis Inlet through Telescope Passage, pass either side of the small island marked 26 on the chart. Keep well over to the Nelson Island side to avoid rocks in the centre of the narrow part of the passage. Then move away from Nelson Island to avoid a reef where the passage widens.

Vanguard Bay, located beyond Telescope Passage in Jervis Inlet, is a large open bay with log booms at times, and has a rather exposed anchorage.

Opposite page: Blind Bay from the Jervis Inlet side of Hardy Island. A log boom is stretched out along the northwest side of Blind Bay.
Above: Musket Island Marine Park and its busy but spacious anchorage. Anchor in 2 to 10 metres near the shore.

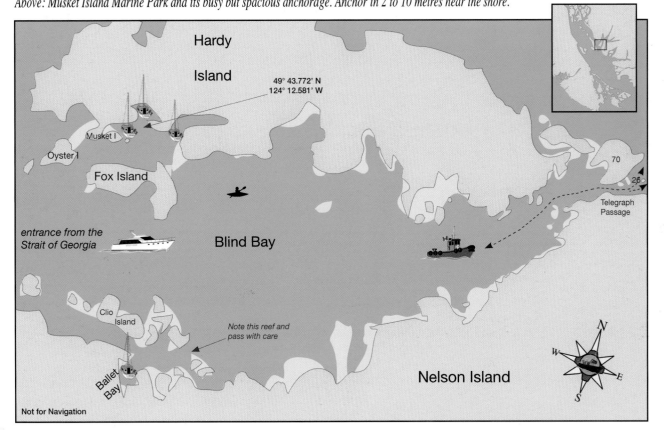

Hardy

Island

49° 43.772' N
124° 12.581' W

Musket I

Oyster I

Fox Island

70

26

Telegraph
Passage

entrance from the
Strait of Georgia

Blind Bay

Clio
Island

Note this reef and
pass with care

Ballet
Bay

Nelson Island

N
W E
S

Not for Navigation

121

Above: The sheltered anchorage at Musket Island Marine Park. Beyond the anchored vessels is Musket Island with Fox Island off to the left. The small island in the distance lies at the entrance to Blind Bay.

Left: Vanguard Bay (foreground) on the north side of Nelson Island. The adjacent body of water is West Lake. Beyond that is Agamemnon Channel and Green Bay.

Below: Boats at anchor in Ballet Bay, one of the most popular anchorages on the coast.

Photograph above courtesy of Justin Taylor.

Right: Looking down the north side of Hardy Island towards the entrance to Jervis Inlet. Temporary anchorage may be taken in the nook behind the islands. Off to the right is Scotch Fir Point on the Sunshine Coast. Texada Island can be seen across Malaspina Strait.

Below: Looking up Malaspina Strait over Scotch Fir Point. The north end of Texada Island lies beyond, with the mountains of Vancouveer Island in the distance. Off to the far right in the photo, McRae Cove entrance opens immediately beyond the point.

Anchored in the western approaches to Ballet Bay between Nelson Island and Clio Island.

Left: A busy Hummingbird Marina near Saltery Bay.

Saltery Bay Sunshine Coast public dock

The float length is 133 metres, with garbage disposal. There are no other amenities at this marina. It is adjacent to the Earl's Cove Saltery Bay ferry terminal and is often busy with local commercial divers coming and going.

Hummingbird Cove Marina

Saltery Bay, BC. Phone 604-487-1499

Nearby, beyond a small peninsula is Hummingbird Marina. Located in Hummingbird Cove west of the Saltery Bay ferry landing, this marina is small and space is limited. There are cottages for rent by reservation and an oceanside barbecue available. It is known for its walking trails and beach, as well as wildlife, birds and sea life.

Off Saltery Bay Provincial Park, a sunken bronze casting of a mermaid, known as the ***Emerald Princess***, stands nearly 3 metres tall underwater in about 20 metres in Mermaid Cove. It was sculpted by BC sculptor Simon Morris and placed there by the British Columbia scuba diving community.

Saltery Bay

There is a cosy public dock at Saltery Bay. It is not large nor is it the most sheltered, but it does offer protection from the winds that sometimes blow through Jervis Inlet.

We once spent several days there in a small boat waiting for winds to drop in Malaspina Strait, to continue a trip up the Sunshine Coast. This is where the ferry from Egmont lands, so there is a large ferry landing alongside the dock. A small food concession is located outside the ferry terminal, and pleasant walks can be taken along the adjoining roadway. A small logging operation alongside the dock has the cove partially closed off for log storage.

The bay had its beginnings as a landing in the early 1900s as a Japanese-owned salmon saltery and fish packing plant, hence the name, Saltery Bay.

Doug Pemberton photo.

Above: The docks at Saltery Bay, alongside the ferry landing. In the background, Telescope Passage opens into Blind Bay between Nelson Island and Hardy Island. Right, top to bottom: Saltery Bay and nearby Hummingbird Cove. The food stand near the ferry terminal entrance at Saltery Bay. Inset: The Emerald Princess.

Jervis Inlet

Saltery Bay
Hummingbird Cove

Texada Island

Malaspina Strait

Lasqueti Island

Strait of Georgia

Not for Navigation

Saltery Bay
This is the trailhead for the 180 km Sunshine Coast Trail.

Hummingbird Cove

Powell River
Grief Point, Texada Island, Lund, Copeland Islands

Charts 3311, 3536, 3538, 3513

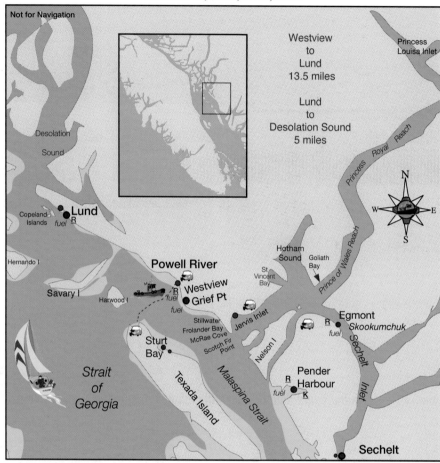

After navigating Malaspina Strait, the safe havens at Grief Point, Westview and Lund allow the mariner to stop for refreshments and supplies before continuing up the coast to the Copeland Islands and Desolation Sound.

North to Desolation Sound

Cruising north from Jervis Inlet, round Scotch Fir Point and enter Malaspina Strait. Several small coves offer possible shelter just beyond the point. **McRae Cove** provides some protection in the lee of the islands at its entrance. **Frolander Bay**, **Stillwater Bay** and several bights along the coast to Westview, are suitable for temporary daytime stops.

At the north end of Malaspina Strait is **Grief Point** on the approaches to Westview and Powell River. The prominent breakwater at **Beach Gardens Resort** can be seen from a distance. In all weather, this sheltered marina offers overnight moorage and fuel. If you choose to linger at the marina, transportation is available to visit nearby shops. Accommodations are available at the resort.

Beach Gardens Resort and Marina

7074 Westminster Ave, Powell River BC V8A 1C5
Phone toll free 1-800-663-7070
beachgardens@shaw.ca www.beachgardens.com

The marina entrance is at the breakwater just south of Grief Point. Stop here for fuel: Gas, diesel, oil and ice are available in season. This is a permanent marina with overnight moorage slips, laundry, showers, washrooms, and 15 and 30 amp power at the docks.

The hotel has waterfront accommodations and an adjacent restaurant, the *Savoury Bight*. There is a liquor store nearby, selling cold beer, wine and spirits. Walking trails, road access, and some beachfront walks start at the marina. Ask about fish-

Above: View north from Grief Point. Left: At Grief Point just south of Westview and Powell River, Beach Gardens Resort and Marina offers overnight moorage and fuel. Below: The harbour is protected by a substantial rock breakwater. It's a short jaunt across Malaspina Strait to Sturt Bay on Texada Island.

Above: A view of the public docks at Westview, Powell River. Many vessels tie up here, mostly commercial, but there is usually space for transient recreational boats. A wharf outside the breakwater is the landing for the Comox and Texada Island ferries. Mind their operations when leaving the harbour. Below: A friendly reception from Carmen at the fuel dock at Westview, Powell River.

Clockwise from above: An aerial view shows the large marina complex at Powell River's Westview. Transient docks are in the south marina, to the left; the Powell River-Comox ferry lands outside the breakwater of the south marina; looking north over Westview towards the mill; the launching ramp on Powell Lake.

ing charters, sail charters, sea kayaking and wilderness canoe routes. Scuba diving arrangements and sightseeing charters are available–ask at the hotel for details.

There is a grocery store and post office nearby and, in season, a shuttle service to town, for restaurants and stores. Golf and hiking are popular in the area.

Powell River

A few miles beyond Grief Point is the entrance to the large Powell River harbour at **Westview**. There is a fuel dock in the south harbour, and moorage for visitors in the marina. Enter past the fuel dock, located immediately inside the breakwater.

Less than a block up the road there is the well-stocked *Marine Traders* store and nearby hotel and restaurants.

City restaurants, shops and hotels are near the waterfront. Try *The Little Teapot* tearoom for an extraordinary "High Tea" experience.

Powell River is the location of the old paper mill on which the town was founded. There is no moorage here as the harbour at Westview serves Powell River. Fronting Powell River and its tall chimneys of the pulp mill, is a string of derelict vessels. These are Liberty ships that served in World War II. Known

as *The Hulks*, they have been a popular site for scuba diving for decades. The vividly coloured growth on the cement hulls is magnificent and represents a vast number of marine species typically found in the Emerald Sea (a scuba diving community term used for the Strait of Georgia).

Westview South Harbour

Wharf St, Powell River
Phone 604-485-5244
www.powellriver.ca

With over 625 metres of floats, this is one of the larger harbours on the coast. Rafting is permitted at the docks. No reservations are taken.

The marina has garbage and waste oil disposal, 15 and 20 amp power, and washrooms with showers and laundry. Internet access is available at the docks. A free shopping shuttle bus to the city mall operates in July and August. Adjacent is a major ferry terminal for vessels to Comox, Vancouver Island and Texada Island. Gas, diesel and ice are available at the Westview fuel dock, phone 604-485-2867.

Powell River events and activities
Blackberry Festival, Sea Fair, International Choral *Kathaumixw* in July, August and September. Sunshine Coast Music Festival on Labour Day. Phone 604-485-4701 for details and dates.

Westview North Harbour

This is a Transport Canada dock and boat harbour.
Phone 604-485-5244. No transient moorage.
This harbour is reserved for permanent mooring tenants.
There is a launch ramp located at the north end.

Texada Island

If you are travelling along the south of Texada Island you will find anchorage in Anderson Bay just as you head north up the east side of the island. The late Corporal Bob Teather of

Top: Anderson Bay on the southeast side of Texada Island makes a comfortable temporary anchorage when northerly winds come down Malaspina Strait. Above: An eagle keeps watch over the entrance.

If you travel up the Sunshine Coast by road and have a trailer and boat in tow, visit Powell Lake. There is a fine launching ramp and lots of water to explore. This good fishing lake is extensive, reaching 51 kilometres in length.

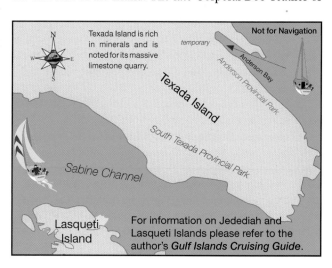

Texada Island is rich in minerals and is noted for its massive limestone quarry.

Not for Navigation

temporary

Anderson Bay

Anderson Provincial Park

Texada Island

South Texada Provincial Park

Sabine Channel

Lasqueti Island

For information on Jedediah and Lasqueti Islands please refer to the author's *Gulf Islands Cruising Guide.*

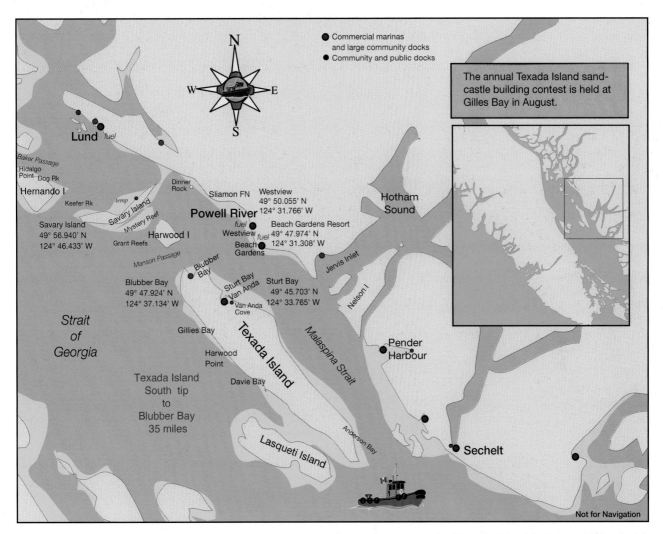

The annual Texada Island sand-castle building contest is held at Gilles Bay in August.

Commercial marinas and large community docks
Community and public docks

Lund *fuel*

Baker Passage
Hidalgo Point
Dog Rk
Hernando I
Keefer Rk
temp
Savary Island
Mystery Reef
Dinner Rock
Sliamon FN
Powell River
Savary Island
49° 56.940' N
124° 46.433' W
Grant Reefs
Harwood I
Manson Passage
Blubber Bay
Blubber Bay
49° 47.924' N
124° 37.134' W

Strait of Georgia

Gillies Bay
Harwood Point
Texada Island South tip to Blubber Bay 35 miles
Davie Bay

Lasqueti Island

Westview
49° 50.055' N
124° 31.766' W
fuel
Westview *fuel*
Beach Gardens
Beach Gardens Resort
49° 47.974' N
124° 31.308' W
Van Anda
Sturt Bay
Van Anda Cove
Sturt Bay
49° 45.703' N
124° 33.765' W
Texada Island
Malaspina Strait
Anderson Bay

Hotham Sound
Jervis Inlet
Nelson I

Pender Harbour

Sechelt

Not for Navigation

the RCMP introduced me to this bay. He once told me it was his preferred place of shelter in the area, and going ashore he had encountered good walking trails with breathtaking views. Some reports advise mariners to watch for wind from the southeast. Farther north on Texada Island is Van Anda.

From Grief Point, cross Malaspina Strait to Van Anda and **Sturt Bay** on Texada Island. This cove offers good mooring at the Texada Boating Club. Anchorage opposite the club docks, near the mouth of Sturt Creek, is good in all but unsettled weather, when winds blow from the east.

Continuing around Texada Island, Blubber Bay at the north end provides temporary anchorage and limited moorage at a company dock, if space is available. On the west side of Texada Island there is mostly temporary sheltered anchorage at **Gillies Bay**, **Harwood Point** on Texada Island, and **Davie Bay**. Gillies Bay has a rock in the middle of it and is exposed to the south. Harwood Point is the site of a large, popular campsite and park, and has a launch ramp that is suitable for use in calm conditions. Davie Bay offers temporary anchorage in the lee of several islands and rocks. Across Sabine Channel

from the south end of Texada Island is Lasqueti Island with its many cosy nooks and anchorages.

See *Gulf Islands Cruising Guide* by this author for information on Lasqueti Island.

Texada Boating Club

PO Box 196, Van Anda BC V0N 3K0
Phone 604-486-7574
Located on the northeast side of Texada Island, almost opposite Grief Point. Guest moorage includes 15 amp power, garbage disposal and a launch ramp. A hotel nearby offers showers, restaurant, ATM, ice, liquor store, grocery store, laundry at the garage, walking club on Saturdays, and an interesting old mine on the opposite beach. Rough conditions occur in strong southeasterly winds. This makes the marina not suitable for larger boats in very windy weather.

Blubber Bay public dock

Texada Island. BC Ferries landing nearby.
Limited facilities and moorage at a 13 metre float. Shore

Above: The launching ramp and docks at the Texada Boating Club at Van Anda, also seen at bottom.

Centre, left: The wharf at Van Anda Cove does not offer protected moorage. It faces onto Malaspina Strait with a view across towards Grief Point. Centre, right: One of two launch ramps at Gillies Bay on Texada Island's west side. This one, as can be seen, dries at low tide.

Opposite page: Savary Island from the west shows its shallows and sandy beaches as well as its temporary anchorage. Some of the reefs on the south side of the island are visible, extending far out towards Harwood Island.

access is possible by dinghy. Try the Texada Boating Club docks at Sturt Bay to the south. Recommended docks are also at Westview in Powell River and good moorage is available at Beach Gardens Resort and Marina at Grief Point.

Continuing to Lund beyond Westview and Powell River, set a course past Sliammon First Nations village for the east end of Savary Island. Pass to the east of Harwood Island and west of Atevida Reef and Dinner Rock. Mystery Reef lies to the west of the passage on the north side of Shearwater Passage. This is a dangerous mess of rocks and shallows, that extends all the way to the south and south west side of Savary Island. If Shearwater Passage is to be used to cross the Strait of Georgia for Mitlenatch Island and possibly Campbell River, it is advisable to pass south of the red bell buoy marking Grant Reefs. Vivian Island and Rebecca Rock, off the west side of Harwood Island, are popular scuba diving sites.

Savary Island
In calm conditions vessels anchor off the beach at Savary Island. The preferred spot is at the far west side facing north. The extensive shoals keep boats away from the south side of the island. To the north of Savary Island, explore Manson Passage only in a small boat. Avoid Keefer Rock when continuing from Savary Island to Hernando Island. On this latter island there is anchorage also only in fair conditions. Drop the hook

in Dog Bay on the east side of **Hidalgo Point** taking care to avoid Dog Rock. A water taxi service links Lund with Savary Island. Its lovely sandy beaches are popular for swimming. There are many easy launching sites for kayaking.

Savary Island was settled by Jack Green. He built a home and established a store on the island. Green, who was murdered on the island, was honoured when his name was given to Green Point near the site of the government wharf. The one-time bustling Royal Savary Hotel at Indian Point was built by another group of settlers, the Ashworth family.

Savary Island public dock
Transport Canada public dock. Float length 11 metres. No moorage–the dock is for loading only.

Lund
Lund is the northernmost town on the Sunshine Coast road, and an interesting place to visit. It lies just south of the entrance to Thulin Passage and the Ragged or Copeland Islands. It has an historic hotel, restaurants and numerous facilities including a well-stocked grocery store. There is a waterfront marine service centre and chandlery, catering year-round to the local community. Under relatively new ownership, the buildings and installations go back to the earliest days of settlement on the coast. Today, as in the past, Lund is a prominent fuel stop before entering Desolation Sound.

MV Gulf Stream Sinks at Dinner Rock

It was October 11, 1947 and the passenger ferry MV Gulf Stream *had been filled to capacity with nearly 200 people making their way home for the Thanksgiving Day weekend. Most of the passengers disembarked in Westview, while the remaining 19, with a crew of 22 continued on to Lund. Once the ship was safely through the passage between Mystery Reef and the Atevida Reef markers, Captain Jack Craddock turned the wheel over to the second mate, Roy Ketchum.*

Dinner Rock rises above the surface like a small island off the mainland near Savary Island, eight miles north of Powell River. Ketchum peered through the windows trying to see through the darkness and rain, having lost track of the coastal signs. Suddenly, the Gulf Stream *plowed into Dinner Rock. The force of the 174 ton vessel hitting the rock at 15 knots drove the stern underwater and most of the bow up on the rock.*

"About a 15 knot wind was blowing. It was low overcast, a very dark night, with a light rain," according to Henry Pavid, a passenger on the Gulf Stream. *Pavid and his wife Josephine had been sitting in the aft lounge. Their eighteen month old daughter, Jean was asleep on the seat in front of them. On impact, the lights died and the stern rapidly filled with freezing water. Pavid made a lunge for his sleeping daughter, but he missed her by about an inch, as the water swept him upwards. Fortunately for him, he came up under a window—and a bubble of air. Henry managed to smash the safety glass and escape with his wife and another passenger. Henry and Josephine frantically searched for their daughter but to no avail. Four other passengers –two women and two children–also died. Their bodies were later recovered by divers. Little Jean was never found.*

After the accident, Henry placed a cross on Dinner Rock. In 1991 a new, eight foot, 1000 pound cross was lifted into place on Dinner Rock by a helicopter and a memorial plaque was unveiled at the Dinner Rock Forest Service campsite. The original cross went to the Powell River Historical Museum.

—From an article in **Diver Magazine**, *by Catherine Adler.*

Left, top: The west end of Savary Island offers temporary anchorage off its white sandy beach at Indian Point, or in the shallows near the wharf that extends off the island's north side. Note: Be careful if you venture to the south side of the island, as it is full of rocks and shallows that make navigation difficult. Left: Dinner Rock, south of Savary Island near the mainland, is the site of a famous shipwreck, the 45 metre MV Gulf Stream that went down in 1947. Opposite: Lund, its harbour, hotel and marina, including an historic photo of the hotel.

A boardwalk follows the shore around Lund to a restaurant overlooking the marina. The coming and going of fishing charter and water taxi vessels add to the activity in the harbour.

On the slopes above the marina are more stores, a restaurant, a scuba diving store, arts, souvenirs and gifts, pizza and ice cream vendors, an information kiosk and a clothing store.

Swedish settlers, the Thulin brothers, Fred and Charles, founded Lund, and it was for them that the main passage north to Desolation Sound was named. Charles had rowed from Vancouver in a small boat with a makeshift sail in search of a place to settle. In her book *Coastal Villages*, Liv Kennedy details his travels, and the establishment of Lund. Some of the settlers in Lund were Finnish, hence the name Finn Cove in the adjacent nook in the lee of Sevilla Island.

Lund Small Craft Harbour

Public dock with visitor moorage. Phone 604-483-4711
There is over 150 metres of moorage with water and 20 and 30 amp power for transient use. There are washrooms and showers available to visitors. A substantial launch ramp is a feature of the marina. The Lund Hotel, restaurants, shops, ATM, and laundry are nearby. Rafting is permitted at the docks. A 30-ton travel lift is available at an adjacent service dock.

Lund water taxi dock.

Lund fuel dock and the historic Lund Hotel

Phone 604-483-4711

Gas and diesel are available at the fuel dock. Some moorage is available on fairly exposed fingers. Garbage may be dropped for a fee. The hotel offers accommodation, a restaurant and a pub that is open seven days a week. Showers, washrooms, laundry and ice are available at the hotel or the store adjacent to it. There is an art store in the hotel building that carries a wide range of local work, painting, sculpture (done on site) kayak rentals and more. The complex includes a post office and general store that carries groceries, tackle, marine supplies, some hardware, meats and fresh produce, books and charts. There is a liquor agency, a deli and a bakery.

Finn Cove

Appropriately named for the early Finnish settlers in the area, this cove opens immediately north of Lund and although it has limited space to anchor or to tie up at the small public float, it is a more sheltered spot than Lund, particularly in a northwesterly blow. The public float is not attached to shore. It is usually busy with commercial or local vessels.

Note: Mind the rock on the approach to Lund from the south and another after leaving Finn Cove to proceed north.

Finn Cove public float, Lund

This is a public float that has no ramp to the shore. The float length is 49 metres.

Below: Businesses and buildings at Lund have given the town growth and prosperity. Top: The fuel dock, breakwater, water taxi dock and hotel on the Lund waterfront.

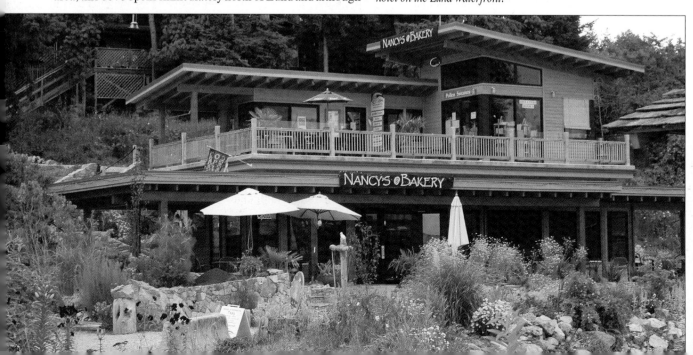

Above: A restful garden setting overlooking the Lund Harbour and the north end of the Strait of Georgia.
Right: The Lund Hotel is a familiar landmark to mariners who have navigated local waters for many years.
Bottom: The fuel dock at Lund, Julia at the information kiosk, and Jamie, an assistant harbourmaster at Lund.

Top: Finn Cove entrance with its unattached public float. It can be seen also in the photograph at the top of the opposite page. Above: Commercial operations in Finn Cove. Right: Artist and sculptor Debra Bevaart at her Salish-named Tug-Gumh Gallery at Lund. Below: A restaurant on the boardwalk overlooks the marina. Opposite, bottom: The harbour and docks at Lund.

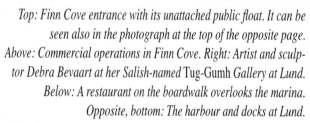

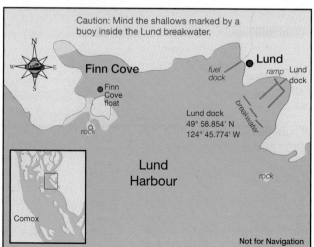

Caution: Mind the shallows marked by a buoy inside the Lund breakwater.

Finn Cove

Finn Cove float

rock

Lund

fuel dock

ramp

Lund dock

breakwater

Lund dock
49° 58.854' N
124° 45.774' W

Lund Harbour

rock

Comox

Not for Navigation

Copeland Islands Marine Park

Thulin Passage, which separates the Copeland Islands from the mainland, is the passage of choice for continuing into Desolation Sound. The islands are a designated marine park. There are several temporary, protected or semi protected spots to anchor in 5 to 10 metres. The most popular and sheltered of these is behind the islands that form a cove opposite the steep cliffs on the opposite shore half way through the passage.

Sharpes Bay is open and subject to the wash of passing vessels. It was one time the site of Ragged Islands Marine, a fuel stop that was popular among the locals and regular visitors. The shore is up for development and there may be a landing in the cove again. But for now, most vessels pass by and continue on to Desolation Sound.

Bliss Landing is located in Turner Bay at the north end of Thulin Passage. It has a private marina belonging to shareholders at the settlement. Overnight moorage is available to visitors when resident boats are away. Check with them at 604-483-8098.

After entering Desolation Sound via the Copeland Islands, there is the choice of continuing past Sarah Point and heading for Grace Harbour and Okeover Inlet, or rounding Zephine Head and voyaging on to Prideaux Haven.

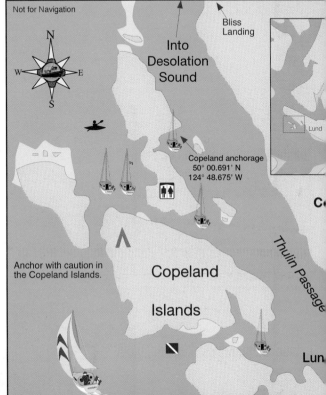

Not for Navigation

Bliss Landing

Into Desolation Sound

Lund

N
W   E
S

Copeland anchorage
50° 00.691' N
124° 48.675' W

Anchor with caution in the Copeland Islands.

Copeland

Islands

Thulin Passage

Lun

Above: Bliss Landing lies in semi-exposed Turner Bay on the mainland, at the north end of Thulin Passage. Below: The dock at Bliss Landing. Opposite page: Immediately north of Lund Thulin Passage divides the Copeland Islands from the mainland. This is the preferred route into Desolation Sound from the Sunshine Coast. The islands are a designated Marine Park, and offer several sheltered anchorages.

Looking southeast down Malaspina Inlet towards Okeover Inlet. In the distance is Coode Island, Coode Peninsula and Trevenen Bay. The boat is approaching Beulah Island to its port, off the Josephine Islands.

Okeover Inlet
Grace Harbour, Lancelet Inlet, Theodosia Inlet

Charts 3559, 3538, 3312, 3513

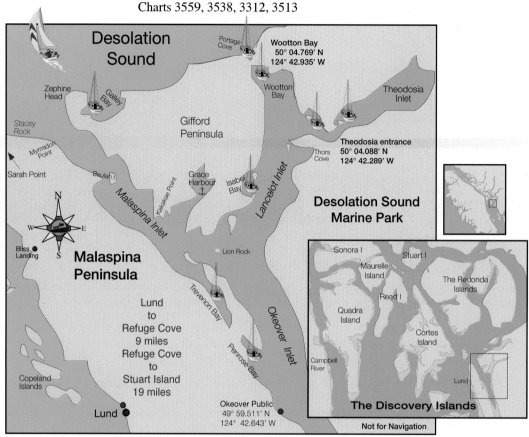

Captain George Vancouver, exploring Desolation Sound in 1792, found it to be a depressing place. But it has turned out to have more appeal to cruising vacationers today than he ever would have imagined. It is at Kinghorn Island in the sound where the tides meet, flooding north and south from that point or ebbing away from it.

Grace Harbour

Many visitors to Desolation Sound travel to this destination for its several large but sheltered coves, and in doing so miss out on the virtues of Grace Harbour.

Grace Harbour lies in the nape of a wishbone-shaped configuration of waterways. Its entrance is almost at the point where Malaspina Inlet on the west side and Lancelot Inlet join the north end of Okeover Inlet.

When cruising north past Sarah Point you are reminded to beware of Stacey Rock on the approach to Myrmidon Point, as it is unmarked and dries at low tide. Many vessels have come to grief on this massive reef. It cannot be overemphasized that it is best to continue towards Zephine Head after rounding Sarah Point before turning into Malaspina Inlet. The most direct route into the inlet is between Beulah Island and Josephine Islands, passing to the south of Rosetta Rock off Cross Islet. Keep a watchful eye on the chart, for Malaspina Inlet is dotted with reefs. Follow the mid channel between the above-mentioned islands.

There are a few spots to anchor temporarily in the lee of the Gifford Peninsula. These are along the shore opposite the **Josephine Islands** and **Neville Islet**. Be aware of the tidal currents that flow quite strongly down the centre of the passage.

Just beyond Kakaekae Point temporary anchorage may be taken in the small cove that I have called **Myrita Cove** for our long-time good friends and boating companions Walter and Rita Lee, who often anchored there in their 54' Monk McQueen, *Myrita*, occupying the tiny anchorage overnight in calm conditions. Pass Kakaekae Point and enter Grace Harbour around Scott Point.

If you go farther into Desolation Sound than Grace Harbour, you will not find much better. It is part of Desolation Sound Marine Park and is made up of a shallow rocky basin north of **Jean Island** at the entrance, just off the passage to the main basin. A large open bay lies farther inside where, in mid summer, it is possible to find boats tied up to one another,

Above: Looking out of Malaspina Inlet to Desolation Sound with Kinghorn Island and smaller Station Island to its right. The boat in the foreground is coming from the direction of Scott Point and Grace Harbour. Isbister Islands and the tip of Coode Island are to its starboard in the foreground. Below: Grace Harbour. Anchor behind Jean Island or deep inside the bay. There is a low waterfall at the head of the inner bay in Grace Harbour that can be reached by trail or small dinghy. This is a popular anchorage in the marine park and becomes crowded in mid summer. Lancelot Inlet can be seen to the right. Inset: Behind Jean Island in Grace Harbour.

Above: The photograph shows a continuation of the top one on the previous page. It includes a section of Grace Harbour and the coast past Selina Point, Salubrious Bay and Edith Island into Lancelot Inlet. Below: Madge Island at the north end of Isabel Bay in Lancelot Inlet.

anchored in the centre, or stern tied to shore. At the far side of the anchorage is a small stream with a waterfall that has a good flow of cool water, popular among those searching for a cooling down, for bathing and showering, or refreshing themselves after several days aboard their boats. There is a place to land in a small boat at the base of the park sign. The area has developed trails for hiking, swimming in the nearby lake, or just sitting and enjoying the views.

Lancelot Inlet

While exploring this area consider Lancelot and Theodosia Inlets. Pass Salubrious Bay and Edith Island and put into **Isabel Bay**, a quiet but popular anchorage just inside Lancelot Inlet. Be careful of the rock off **Polly Island** as you enter. Anchor in 4 metres in the lee of **Madge Island** in a shallow nook with a small beach, being considerate of other vessels by stern tying wherever possible. The opposite side of the bay, in the lee of Polly Island, also offers protected anchorage. A small, shallow bay at the northeast side of Madge Island, formed by the island and a drying reef, is sometimes used by the more adventurous, with a small boat. Farther into Lancelot Inlet lies **Thors Cove**, **Wootton Bay** and **Theodosia Inlet**.

Aquaculture has taken over some cosy coves, but sometimes mariners will find them moved from their noted positions. Their locations can usually be verified on the latest charts.

A small nook in the south side of Thors Cove is protected from the winds that blow from the south up Lancelot Inlet. A better anchorage is in 8 metres in the lee of the **Susan Islets** at the entrance to Theodosia Inlet, or in a sheltered corner

Above: Theodosia Inlet showing Susan Islets and the reefs in the entrance. Beyond the island on the right is Gallahad Point. Anchor in the lee of Susan Islets or in the lee of the island just inside the inlet.

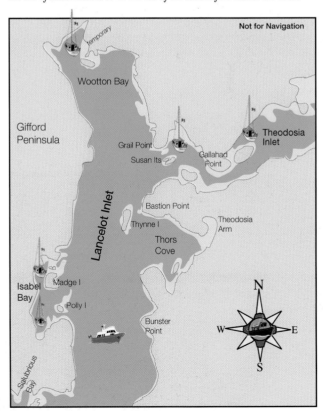

Top: The dock at Okeover Inlet. It is quite busy at times and suitable mostly for smaller craft.
Left: A view over the lower part of Okeover Inlet from the nearby restaurant property.
Below: Restaurants such as this, overlooking coastal waterways, attract a regular clientele of mariners in summer. They usually offer fine dining to go with a magnificent setting.

Dining at Okeover.

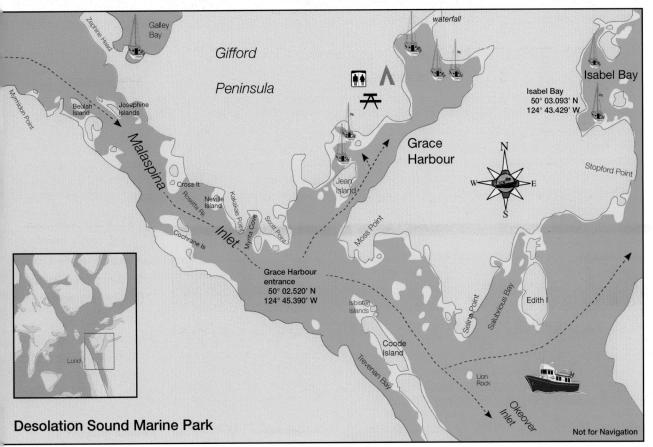

Desolation Sound Marine Park

Not for Navigation

inside Theodosia. Wootton Bay is suitable as an anchorage although it is exposed to southerly winds. Anchor to the west of the little promontory at the head of the bay, avoiding the reef at its southern tip as you approach.

Okeover Inlet

Some mariners anchored at Grace Harbour, and possibly in the less sheltered **Trevenon Bay** or **Penrose Bay**, take a late afternoon cruise in their shore boats to visit a well-known restaurant that overlooks Okeover Inlet. It is a distance of about four miles from Grace Harbour to the dock. There is a landing comprising several floats behind a floating log breakwater, with enough room inside for small boats to tie up temporarily. An early dinner allows an easy return to the anchorage before dark in summer. Use your chart to determine your course as there are charted rocks a short way out of Grace Harbour. Pass to the south of Lion Rock at the confluence of Malaspina Inlet, Lancelot Inlet and Okeover Inlet.

The route into Lancelot Inlet and thence to Theodosia Inlet passes Lion Rock on either side, but be aware of the extended shallows on its north side if favouring that approach.

Okeover public dock

This small landing, with a total float length of 35 metres, has

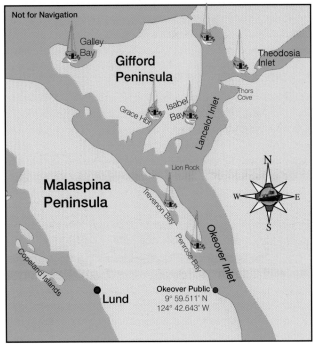

20 amp power at the dock, but no other amenities. Temporary anchorage is possible in the shallows nearby. The Laughing Oyster Restaurant overlooks the landing.

Desolation Sound and the Discovery Islands

When mariners refer to Desolation Sound they generally include the overall area that encompasses nearby and adjacent waterways, islands, mainland inlets and shorelines. The Discovery Islands archipelago includes Cortes and Marina Islands, the Redonda Islands, Quadra, Thurlow and Hardwicke Islands, Maurelle and Read Islands and Sonora Island. While Cortes Island and Quadra Island are the main islands of the Discovery Group, Maurelle, Read, the Redondas, Sonora, Stuart, Raza, East and West Thurlow and the Rendezvous Islands are considered the Outer Islands. Other islands peripheral to the group are the Copeland Islands, Hernando and Savary Islands to the south, the Octopus Islands, the Penn Islands, Mink Island in Desolation Sound and Twin Islands off Cortes.

Desolation Sound lies in the southeast corner of the Discovery Islands archipelago. Anchorages in the proximity of the Desolation Sound Marine Park attract the vast majority of cruising vessels visiting the archipelago each summer. The more popular and sheltered anchorages and cosy nooks in the park become quite crowded compared to other parts of the Discovery Islands. There are many alternative anchorages where it is possible to remain for days on end in the summertime, or set up home aboard for an entire vacation. The choices include the coves and bays of Grace Harbour, Prideaux Haven, Pendrell Sound, Walsh Cove, Roscoe Bay, Theodosia Inlet, Van Donop Inlet and Squirrel Cove to name a few. Some mariners play musical moorages and move from one to the next as they spend their summer vacation in this warm water oasis in BC. To avoid difficulty in finding a place to drop anchor in some of the busier bays, move early in the day.

To the west is Campbell River or Heriot Bay for moorage and fuel, and Drew Harbour with its anchorage behind Rebecca Spit. Go to Surge Narrows from Heriot Bay, or cross over and spend the rest of your vacation at Gorge Harbour, one of the most sheltered large bays in the area, with a fine marina and restaurant to keep you in comfort for your stay. Kayaking is also drawing increasing numbers to this area each year.

One of the best-known events of coastal history was the naming of Desolation Sound. When Captain Vancouver was charting the coast in 1792 he sailed into the waters north of Sarah Point and found himself in what he considered a very desolate place and promptly gave the sound its controversial name. Mariners visiting Desolation Sound ever since have wondered at the captain's dubious choice of names. For anyone gazing across the waters of the sound on a tranquil summer day will be awed by the beauty of the waterway and surrounding islands with the backdrop of the tall Unwin Mountains rising to the north.

The early settlers took up homesteads and became involved in the land's major industries, comprising fishing, logging, trapping and mining. They built homes made of logs, some of which can be seen dotting shorelines to this day, sometimes standing side by side with new, modern homes. Anchor in a cove and enjoy the varied surroundings.

Any on-shore man-made structures could well represent a significant part of the coastal history. In most communities immigrants brought with them their handicraft and trades, built saw mills, homes and boats. Some even established businesses to serve the other settlers. Rummaging through forest undergrowth, one may well come across remnants of homesteads and settlements that were tried and abandoned. Remember to keep off private land.

The people who settled in Desolation Sound and influenced place names, included Joe Copeland, the Palmer brothers, the Owen family, the Thulin brothers, the Andersons and the Hansons. An early property owner at Galley Bay was Axel Hanson who set up a prosperous logging operation in 1907. One of the Palmer daughters was Sarah. However, Sarah Point, at the entrance to Desolation Sound, is said to have been named for Captain Vancouver's sister.

The population of the Discovery Islands, like other, more remote parts of the coast, increased notably during the latter part of the 1800s and the early 1900s. The Union Steamship Company was flourishing at the time and their vessels carried hundreds of settlers into the islands. There were steamship stops at all major islands and settlements and many of those who stepped off the ships had arrived from Europe and the United States. In addition to Lund, Finns settled also at Granite Bay on Quadra Island, where they established a fair sized community complete with school, hotel, post office and store. Americans, mostly from North Dakota, settled on Read Island and established a school at Evans Bay in 1894, and another, later, at Surge Narrows.

Quadra Island, originally named Valdes Island, was initially thought to be larger than it is. Before it was properly explored, it was thought that Maurelle and Sonora islands were part of its land mass.

Today, small public docks, sometimes considered too exposed for functional use, remain in place at bays such as Granite Bay, Evans Bay and Owen Bay. Remnants of the steamships landings have gone, along with many families of the early settlers. In their stead are weekend and holiday homes scattered throughout the islands, some having private moorage, others sharing available docks left behind by logging, fishing, whaling and early communities.

Prideaux Haven
Galley Bay, Tenedos Bay, Mink Island, Eveleigh Anchorage, Melanie Cove, Laura Cove

Charts 3555, 3312, 3538, 3559, 3513

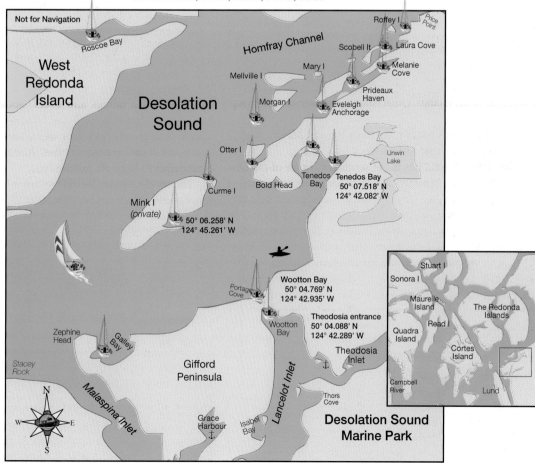

This is one of the most spectacular and popular anchorages on the BC coast. Its many nooks and coves are filled with boats at the height of summer.

Desolation Sound Marine Park's best known anchorages are at Prideaux Haven, Laura Cove, Melanie Cove, Tenedos Bay and Grace Harbour. Popular access to these harbours is north through the Strait of Georgia and Malaspina Strait, via the Copeland Islands and east, northeast around Sarah Point.

Once in Desolation Sound you will not be stuck for fuel because there is a long established fuel stop at Refuge Cove. This facility is the local centre for all supplies and provisions to serve the cruising mariner.

Galley Bay

Although this is quite an open bay, on the north side of the Gifford Peninsula, Galley Bay affords shelter from south and southeasterly winds, and many mariners favour anchoring here for extended periods. Anchor in the lee of the island

on the east side or off the small nook on the west side of the bay. Avoid the rocks in the centre. They dry at low tide, one as much as three metres.

Where once there was a family homestead and later a busy commune at Galley Bay, today there remains only a small piece of private property, which lies within the bounds of the large marine park area. A short distance east of Galley Bay is **Portage Cove** which is passed en route to Tenedos Bay. Anchorage at this narrow indent in the coastline is temporary, but possible only at high tide. A stern line to shore is recommended.

Mink Island

Almost opposite Galley Bay and Portage Cove, at the entrance to Homfray Channel, lies Mink Island, about midway

Two views of Galley Bay. The one above shows the south end of the bay and Malaspina Inlet in the background. Okeover Inlet tapers away in the distance. The bottom one shows the anchorage in the opposite corner of the bay with the waters of Desolation Sound beyond the point.

This painting by marine artist John M. Horton depicts Desolation Sound in recent years, little changed from the time of its exploration by Captain Vancouver in 1792. Visit www.johnhorton.ca

between the Gifford Peninsula and Prideaux Haven. Mink Island is not included in the Desolation Sound Marine Park designated area and is privately owned. However, anchorage may be taken in the outer part of the bay on its south side. This is somewhat exposed, but weather seems to miss the anchorage, making it mostly secure for overnight stays. The docks on the inner part of the cove are private. Nearby, on its east shore, the **Curme Islands** offer anchorage in fair weather. Temporary anchorage may be taken in the narrow, shallow channel between the two larger islands at the north end of the group.

Desolation Sound Marine Park

This is the largest marine park in British Columbia. Its 14,000 acres of land with over 6,000 of that being shoreline, encompasses many bays, inlets and coves. The park area includes anchorages, shore access with toilets, trails, beaches, hiking, fresh water from lakes, bayhing areas, waterfalls and scenic viewpoints.

Prideaux Haven is the popular, centrally located anchorage preferred by most yachtsmen heading for Desolation Sound. The park was established in 1973, protecting what is without a doubt, one of the best boating destinations in the world.

In one of artist John M. Horton's famous paintings, Cap-

tain George Vancouver's ships, HMS *Discovery* and HMS *Chatham* (see page 6), are accurately depicted approaching the entrance to Prideaux Haven. Naming the place for his feelings of desolation may seem inappropriate to those who know and love the area, but it certainly conjures up the right mood for a tranquil place to lie at anchor in peaceful surroundings.

The mild climate and abundance of marine life in Desolation Sound are the result of warm summer temperatures. Conditions are good for swimming as well as aquaculture. Hence the presence of oyster farms in numerous coves that were once considered good anchorages.

Tenedos Bay

This cosy nook is another of the most popular anchorages in the park. It lies in the shadow of Bold Head. There are rocks near the entrance to Tenedos Bay. Ray Rock is a serious navigational hazard, so be cautious approaching or leaving the anchorage. The spacious anchorage is good for a quite a number of boats.

While the water is deep, over 100 metres in the middle

Desolation Sound from above Mary Point on Cortes Island. Kinghorn Island is beyond with Mink Island to the right. The Unwin Mountains rise in the distance. Mount Addenbroke is tall on East Redonda Island. Refuge Cove is to the left.

Calm Tenedos Bay, Desolation Sound.

Top: *This view of the anchorage at Mink Island shows the private docks and the preferred place to drop the hook, along the adjacent shoreline.*
Above: *Anchored at Mink Island. This is a privately owned island, located in the centre of Desolation Sound.*

Looking across Desolation Sound towards Prideaux Haven, from Mink Island, at the south end of Homfray Channel. Ray Rock can be seen off Bold Head, centre, marking the entrance to Tenedos Bay.

of the bay, there are several suitable spots to drop the hook in the coves around its perimeter. Note that the narrow point between the island in Tenedos Bay and the nearby shore dries or is extremely shallow at low tides.

Warm water bathing in Unwin Lake attracts many people anchored in Tenedos Bay. The shortest hike to the lake is from the anchorage on the east side of Tenedos Bay.

Nearby **Otter Island** has a very secluded cove opening to the north. The adjoining passage is suitable only for small boats. Stern tie and keep an anchor light on at night. Watch for Sky Pilot Rock on the north approaches to the cove.

Other anchorages and parks in the vicinity include Roscoe Bay on West Redonda Island and at Pendrell Sound on the other side of Waddington Channel. Homfray Channel is a spectacular body of water. This is so partly because of the magnificent Unwin Range, rising to more than 1,300 metres, looming over it and forming a backdrop to the many anchorages in the park.

Above: Slipping into Prideaux Haven through its narrow entrance. There is lots of room to anchor. In summer, arrive early in the day, as the anchorage fills up quickly.

Prideaux Haven

Entrance to Prideaux Haven is from Homfray Channel to the east of Eveleigh Island. Keep the reef in the centre of the channel to port as you enter.

The anchorage at Prideaux Haven is busy in summer, with boats dropping the hook in every available cove, including **Eveleigh Anchorage**, **Melanie Cove** and **Laura Cove**. Eveleigh Anchorage is almost part of Prideaux Haven. The two anchorages are divided by a reef which extends part way across the passage. If mariners decide to enter Prideaux Haven through the anchorage they should keep well over to the island side to stay clear of the reef, and only at high tide. Anchor in Eveleigh Anchorage close to Eveleigh Island.

Another place to anchor is in the small cove on the east

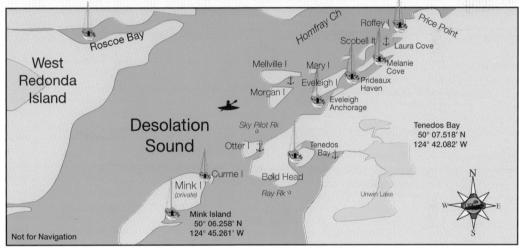

Roscoe Bay

Homfray Ch

Roffey I

Price Point

Scobell It

Laura Cove

West
Redonda
Island

Mellville I

Mary I

Melanie
Cove

Eveleigh I

Prideaux
Haven

Morgan I

Desolation
Sound

Sky Pilot Rk

Eveleigh
Anchorage

Tenedos Bay
50° 07.518' N
124° 42.082' W

Otter I

Tenedos
Bay

Curme I

Bold Head

N

Mink I
(private)

Ray Rk

Unwin Lake

W   E

Mink Island
50° 06.258' N
124° 45.261' W

S

Not for Navigation

Top: From above Bold Head and Tenedos Bay (not seen) looking towards Mink Island. The Curme Islands lie off Mink Island. To the right is Otter Island. Note Ray Rock in the foreground.
Right: Early season at Prideaux Haven. An opening behind the boats leads into Melanie Cove.

Above: From above the Gifford Peninsula, Mink Island lies in the foreground with Prideaux Haven and Homfray Channel beyond. The tall mountains are part of the Unwin Range. Below: A busy Prideaux Haven and Melanie Cove.

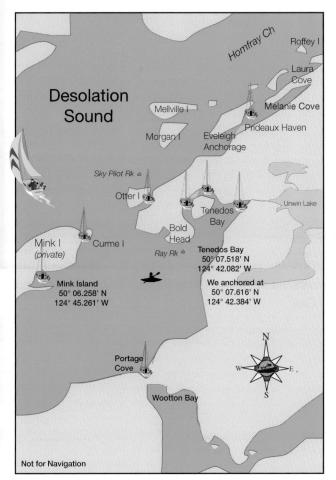

Desolation
Sound

Homfray Ch

Roffey I

Laura
Cove

Mellville I   Melanie Cove

Prideaux Haven

Morgan I   Eveleigh
Anchorage

Sky Pilot Rk

Otter I   Unwin Lake

Tenedos
Bay

Bold
Head

Mink I
(private)   Curme I

Ray Rk

Tenedos Bay
50° 07.518' N
124° 42.082' W

Mink Island
50° 06.258' N
124° 45.261' W

We anchored at
50° 07.616' N
124° 42.384' W

N
W   E
S

Portage
Cove

Wootton Bay

Not for Navigation

Top, right: Roffey Island anchorage. Bottom: Prideaux Haven with Laura Cove in the foreground. The Curve of Time refers to early settlers' cabins on the shores of these coves. They have all but gone with time and weather. Make your way ashore to explore the remnants of early settlement, but respect posted private land.

side of **Roffey Island**. There are rocks in this cove and careful navigation is required to use it as a passage or entrance to the anchorage. It is suitable anchorage only for a few boats.

There are trails in some park areas and these are marked by signboards ashore at the trail heads. The largest fresh water body in the park is Unwin Lake, located south of Prideaux Haven and east of Tenedos Bay.

A garbage scow at Refuge Cove will accept garbage from vessels for a fee. Other than that, there is no garbage disposal at Desolation Sound Marine Park anchorages, so pack it out.

Sewage discharge is also an issue. BC Parks has requested, in keeping with provincial legislation, "that due to poor tidal circulation in Desolation Sound, Prideaux Haven and Grace Harbour are closed to sewage discharge."

The park includes several properties that are private and mariners are asked to respect the privacy of the owners.

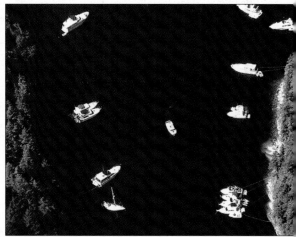

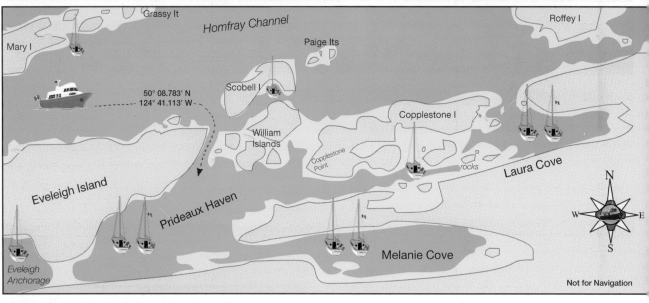

Grassy It

Homfray Channel

Roffey I

Mary I

Paige Its

Scobell I

50° 08.783' N
124° 41.113' W

William
Islands

Copplestone I

Copplestone
Point

rocks

Laura Cove

Eveleigh Island

Prideaux Haven

N

W   E

S

Eveleigh
Anchorage

Melanie Cove

Not for Navigation

Prideaux Haven

Above: Stern tied in the eastern nook of Tenedos Bay in Desolation Sound Marine Park. A trail leads from here to Unwin Lake. Below: Prideaux Haven. The entrance is marked by a rock on the east side. Opposite: During the busy season mariners will poke into every space available in the coves and adjoining nooks of Prideaux Haven. Scobell Island is seen at top left in the upper, left photo. Opposite bottom: Prideaux Haven and Melanie Cove seen from Eveleigh Anchorage. Note the partially drying passage through to Prideaux Haven. Anchored in Prideaux Haven.

Above: Tenedos Bay with Bold Head on a small peninsula at its entrance, sheltering the island that occupies most of the anchorage.
Right: A quiet anchorage at Tenedos Bay in early summer.
Opposite: Heading out of Prideaux Haven during the daily shuffle. Mariners have learned that it is wise to move from anchorage to anchorage early in the day to find a good spot in the crowded bays, at the height of the season.

Above, below and right: Laura Cove, with Copplestone Point to the east of the entrance. The top photograph shows a vessel at anchor just inside the entrance of the cove. Opposite page: Exploring Tenedos Bay and several views of the bay with boats anchored in the most sheltered nooks. Stay clear of the rocks in the bay and its approaches.

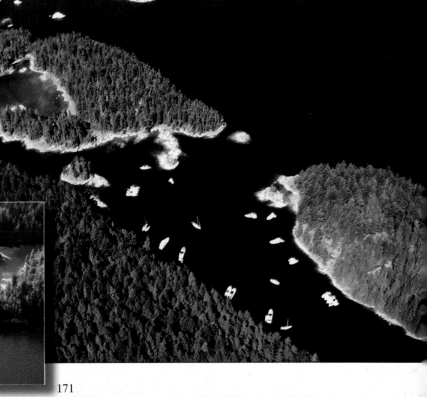

A quiet scene in Prideaux Haven.

Redonda Islands
Toba Inlet, Refuge Cove, Walsh Cove, Pendrell Sound, Teakerne Arm, Roscoe Bay

Charts 3555, 3312, 3538, 3541

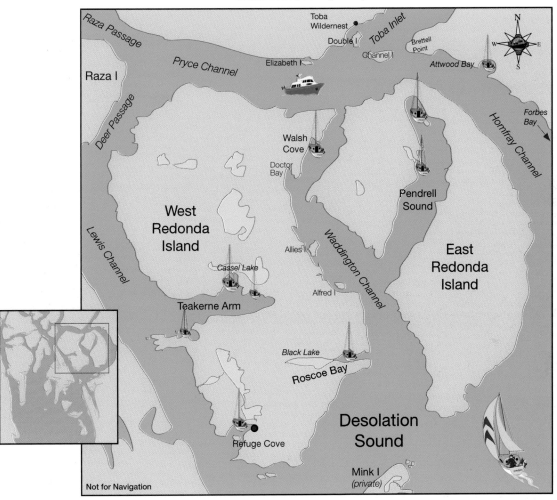

These islands are noted for their sheltered anchorages at Roscoe Bay, Walsh Cove and Teakerne Arm as well as the warm waters for bathing at Pendrell Sound.

Toba Inlet

Beyond Desolation Sound Marine Park, Homfray Channel widens to pass Forbes Bay on the mainland shore opposite East Redonda Island. It continues past Attwood Bay and links up with Pryce Channel. Here is the confluence of Toba Inlet and Waddington Channel with the anchorage at Walsh Cove on West Redonda Island nearby. This popular marine park lies just a short distance down Waddington Channel on the east side of West Redonda Island.

Anchorage at **Forbes Bay** and **Attwood Bay** is temporary.

Take shelter at Forbes Bay by anchoring stern-to in about four metres inside of Bohn Point. Attwood Bay is quite deep but fairly sheltered from wind. Anchorage is best near the shore. This bay is near the entrance to Toba Inlet. In Pryce Channel just beyond Toba Inlet, it is possible to drop anchor in about 20 metres near a waterfall behind Elizabeth Island. It is worth a temporary stop to enjoy the magnificent view.

On the shores of West Redonda Island there are several notable anchorages. The most favoured of these are Walsh

Looking up Homfray Channel from Desolation Sound. The Unwin Range towers above the waterway, with East Redonda Island to the left.

Cove, Roscoe Bay, Refuge Cove–better known for its long-established marina than the anchorage–and Teakerne Arm.

There is a marina at the confluence of Toba Inlet and Pryce Channel. It is sheltered by Double Island and has moorage and facilities for visiting mariners. Toba Wildernest marina is located not far from Walsh Cove. From here, or from Walsh Cove or Attwood Bay, it is an easy run into Toba Inlet to view the beautiful, cascading waterfalls. There is one nearby on its west shore and another a short way beyond Snout Point on the opposite side of the inlet. Opposite Snout Point, **Brem Bay** offers some shelter, while temporary anchorage is recommended near the mouth of the Brem River.

Toba Inlet ends in a delta and estuary where the Tahumming River and Toba River meet. This was the early home of the Klahoose First Nations people of Squirrel Cove. When they moved to their current Cortes Island location, they left behind only remnants of a cemetery.

Union Steamships once carried sightseers into Toba Inlet. This lasted only for a short time, while an effort was being made to influence settlers to homestead there and elsewhere in Desolation Sound. Some did try settling at the Toba River mouth but gave up after finding the area too desolate. Toba Inlet was named by the Spanish, who were surveying the area at the same time as Captain Vancouver.

Above: The view across Toba Inlet, past Double Island towards Homfray Channel and East Redonda Island.

Opposite, top: The marina at Toba Wildernest Resort accommodates boating visitors looking for moorage.

Toba Wildernest
Mouth of Toba Inlet at Double Island, Desolation Sound.
Phone 250-830-2269
tobawildernest@lincsat.com www.tobawildernest.com
There is moorage at a float for overnight or longer duration. It will take a boat up to 100 metres as space permits. Shower and washroom. Ice and some fishing supplies are available at the office. There are forest trails to a nearby waterfall which provides power for the resort. This is a nature resort offering rental cabins for boaters and fly-in guests. Those staying at the lodge have use of other facilities including a hot tub.

Walsh Cove
This anchorage with its adjacent marine park is located on the east side of Redonda Island. It is tucked in behind Butler Point in Waddington Channel. Enter the anchorage to the west of **Gorges Islands** from Waddington Channel,

Owners of Toba Wildernest, Kyle Hunter, left, his wife Andrea and their young daughter Rowan, above, have a friendly greeting for visitors to their secluded hideaway near Double Island in Toba Inlet.

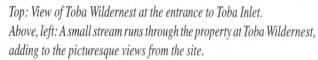

Top: View of Toba Wildernest at the entrance to Toba Inlet.
Above, left: A small stream runs through the property at Toba Wildernest,
adding to the picturesque views from the site.

approaching from the south. The anchorage may also be
entered or departed north of Gorges Islands, but great care
should be taken in this entrance, avoiding the reefs between
the islands and the bluff.

It is undeveloped, but some trails may provide a good
view of the channel and anchorage. Swimming is popular
off the Gorges Islands, but mind the sharp edged shells and
barnacles on the rocks. The water is deep for an anchorage.
Drop anchor near the shore and stern tie. A dinghy ride around
the anchorage is worthwhile. There are pictographs to be
found on the almost sheer cliffs at the north end of the cove.
Walsh Cove has walk-in campsites, picnic tables, drinking
water and toilets. A power equipped shore boat can provide
pleasant excursions, such as up to the falls in Toba Inlet.

Above, centre: Looking down Waddington Channel, Walsh Cove is
tucked in beyond Butler Point to the right.
Above: The aerial view from directly overhead shows the Gorges
Islands and some alternative anchoring spots at Walsh Cove.
Opposite page: The rock face at Butler Point in Walsh Cove.
A careful search will reveal several pictographs partially hidden
by vegetation. They were discovered in 1792 by Archibald Menzies,
botanist aboard Captain Vancouver's ships.

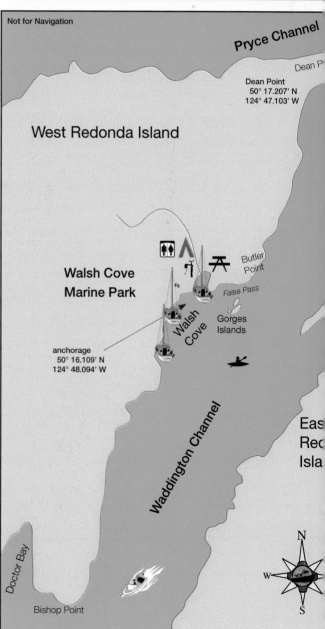

Pryce Channel

Dean P

Dean Point
50° 17.207' N
124° 47.103' W

West Redonda Island

Butler
Point

Walsh Cove
Marine Park

False Pass

Gorges
Islands

Walsh
Cove

anchorage
50° 16.109' N
124° 48.094' W

Waddington Channel

Eas
Re
Isla

Doctor Bay

Bishop Point

N
W · E
S

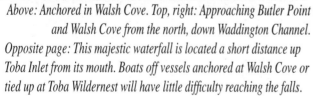

Above: Anchored in Walsh Cove. Top, right: Approaching Butler Point and Walsh Cove from the north, down Waddington Channel. Opposite page: This majestic waterfall is located a short distance up Toba Inlet from its mouth. Boats off vessels anchored at Walsh Cove or tied up at Toba Wildernest will have little difficulty reaching the falls.

Doctor Bay may provide conditional anchorage. If there is space, anchor deep inside Doctor Bay where you will be sheltered from most wind conditions, but stay clear of the aquaculture farm. The lee of Allies Island and Alfred Island are occupied by aquaculture farms but temporary, day anchorage may be found near them.

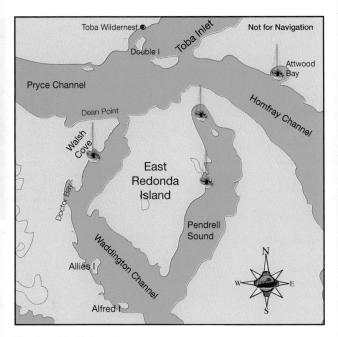

Redonda Islands

Captain Richards, who surveyed the area in 1862, named the channel between the Redonda Islands, as well as Pendrell Sound in honour of the Victoria politician and promoter of a Bute Inlet road, Alfred P. Waddington. Richards' ship, *Hecate*, was namesake for the fearsome Strait near Prince Rupert. Homfray Channel was named by Captain Pender of the surveying ship SS *Beaver*, in honour of Robert Homfray, the civil engineer who surveyed the area after Richards.

Mount Addenbroke stands high over the islands of Desolation Sound. It is located on East Redonda Island, tall and aloof, with the adjacent Homfray Channel seabed dropping steeply to a depth of about half the mountain's height.

Pendrell Sound

Pendrell Sound divides East Redonda almost into two separate islands. Because of the geography of this deep indentation into the island, the waters have a reduced tendency to flush in and out with the tide, leaving warm waters inside and especially at the head of the sound. During summer these relatively still waters warm up to provide good bathing conditions and the sound has become known for its high temperatures of 20° C or more, at and near the surface.

Many people make a regular pilgrimage to this warm water destination in summer. The best anchorage is in 5 to 10 metres in the lee of the small islet to port, adjacent to a drying inlet as you approach the end of the sound, or the bight just to the north of it. Anchor also in similar depths in the lee of the small island near the head of the sound or at the head itself. Other anchorages are at **Alfred Island** or **Allies Island** in Waddington Channel near the entrance to Pendrell Sound.

Wind conditions in the sound can be mystifying, usually

light or nonexistent while it is blowing, sometimes to extremes, elsewhere. But be cautious, as strong winds sometimes howl down the sound overnight in summer.

Oysters have a significant role in the industrial use of Pendrell Sound. Due to the warmth of the water, oyster spat is prolific, and aquaculture personnel will be found collecting the seed during summer. Oyster shells along the shore are very sharp, so wear shoes and be careful landing inflatables.

Power boats are urged to travel in Pendrell Sound at no-wake speeds. While Pendrell Sound is deep almost throughout, there are shallow shelves at the anchorages.

Above and opposite page, top: Anchorage off the lagoon in Pendrell Sound. The bottom photograph was taken from the head of the sound.

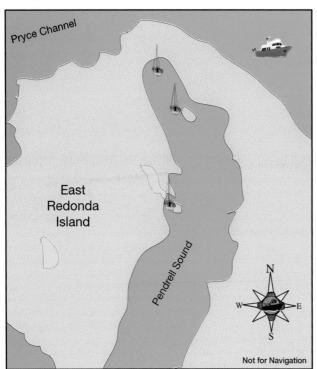

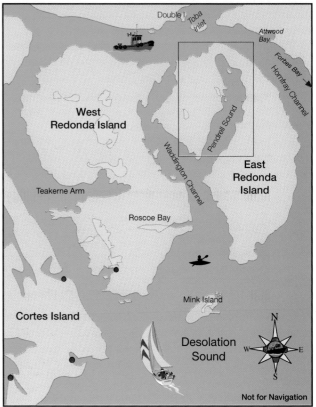

Roscoe Bay from above Black Lake.
It opens onto Waddington Channel.

Roscoe Bay

This protected bay is on the east side of West Redonda Island. It is just to the north of Marylebone Point near the junction of Waddington Channel and Homfray Channel in Desolation Sound.

The entrance to Roscoe Bay is over a drying shoal at the narrows just inside the inlet. Once you are inside, depending on the draft of your boat, you may be there until a later high tide. Plan to stay a while and leave when the shoal is well covered at high tide.

This is one of the popular anchorages in Desolation Sound. There are pit toilets and camping facilities ashore and a hiking trail to nearby Black Lake. If you want to sit in your boat for an extended period, this is the place to do it. If you want total peace and quiet, don't expect it during the height of summer, for this is a popular place for families, and children on other vessels may be noisy in their enjoyment of their vacation. Refuge Cove at the tip of West Redonda Island is the nearest centre for supplies and fuel.

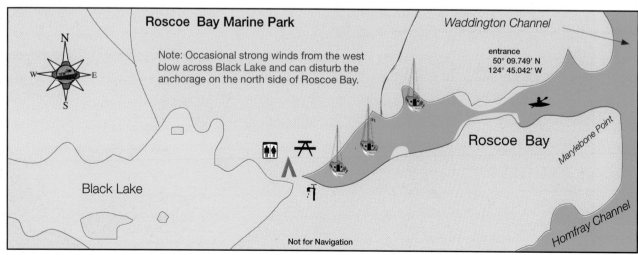

Roscoe Bay Marine Park

Waddington Channel

Note: Occasional strong winds from the west blow across Black Lake and can disturb the anchorage on the north side of Roscoe Bay.

entrance
50° 09.749' N
124° 45.042' W

Roscoe Bay

Marylebone Point

Black Lake

Homfray Channel

Not for Navigation

Roscoe Bay. The entrance is not navigable at low tide. Black Lake is good for warm bathing.

Refuge Cove lies at the entrance to Lewis Channel, on the southern tip of West Redonda Island. It is located conveniently on the route north to Stuart Island, the Broughton Islands and on to Alaska. Refuge Cove is a busy stop during the brief summer season. It affords replenishment of everything from fuels to groceries. The store is positioned high and dry above the high-water mark. It and the fuel dock are run efficiently to accommodate the heavy traffic of the short summer season and survive the balance of the year.

If the docks are crowded look for anchorage in the adjacent nook at the entrance to the lagoon. The cove is exposed to the south. Keep a weather watch for overnight southerly winds.

Refuge Cove

Refuge Cove BC V0P 1P0
Phone 250-935-6659
refcov@twincomm.ca
Refuge Cove has a fuel dock offering gas, diesel, other oils and propane. There is water and 15 amp power at some docks and nearly 400 metres of overnight moorage space. Rafting is permitted, but seldom practised at the cove. The marina has internet access. The facility offers laundry, showers and washrooms. A substantial grocery store is complete with post office, liquor agency, gifts, charts, books and a limited selection of clothing, as well as ice and fishing supplies.

The Boat Stop Cafe was anchored in Refuge Cove in 2008. Previously, for a few seasons, the restaurant-on-a-barge was found in Waddington Channel. It was open 11 am to 4 pm for breakfast and lunch and is expected to be a regular feature as part of the Refuge Cove complex in future. From time to time facilities such as this can be found in local waters, such as the bakery in nearby Squirrel Cove.

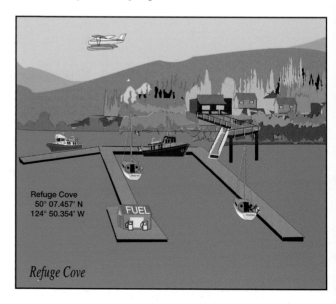

Refuge Cove
50° 07.457' N
124° 50.354' W

FUEL

Refuge Cove

Opposite page, top: The historic store building at Refuge Cove. It originally sat on a foundation that was a barge, hauled up above the tide line. Above and right: Refuge Cove, the docks, anchorage and adjacent Refuge Lagoon. It is possible to walk alongside the tidal stream up to the lagoon.

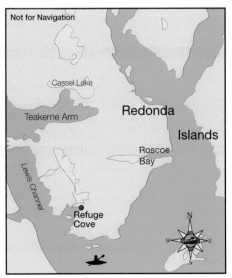

Not for Navigation

Cassel Lake

Teakerne Arm

Redonda

Islands

Roscoe Bay

Lewis Channel

Refuge Cove

N
W · E
S

Above: Refuge Cove and the store overlooking the docks. This is a central location in the Discovery Islands. It faces onto Desolation Sound and serves mariners looking for supplies, moorage and fuel. Left: Enjoying a summer's day at Refuge Cove. Left, lower: On the dining patio of The Boat Stop Cafe, a restaurant on a barge that is located at Refuge Cove. Opposite page: Anchored off the 30 metre waterfall that tumbles down from Cassel Lake at Teakerne Arm.

Teakerne Arm

This is a major attraction in Desolations Sound and it is one of the most recognized marine parks in the islands. Entrance is from Lewis Channel. Pass Joyce Point and travel the short distance eastwards to the waterfall. Anchorage is favoured near the fall and best used daytimes, preferably when there is no northwesterly wind in the forecast.

The park is undeveloped, except for the provision and maintenance by the Parks Branch of a dinghy float adjacent to the west shore on the approaches to the waterefall. This dock is meant to provide access to the trail that leads into the park. The trail leads along the waterfall up to Cassel Lake. Walk up to the waterfall and continue beyond to the lake where 20° C warm water swimming is popular during summer.

Beyond thewaterfall, a small cove opens into the north side of the east end of Teakerne Arm. This is a seldom used anchorage but suitable for perhaps one boat in most weather conditions. There is space also to anchor in nearby **Talbot Cove**, but holding is not very good. If you are planning to spend a night in the area do so only if you are absolutely certain of the wind forecast, otherwise go to the dock at Refuge Cove or anchor in another more protected place, such as Squirrel Cove or Von Donop Inlet. Teakerne Arm was once a busy logging centre.

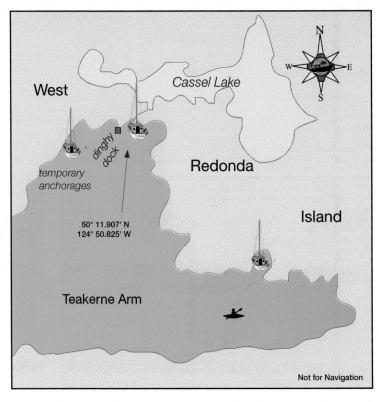

Top: The waterfall at Teakerne Arm with Cassel Lake above. The dinghy dock is to the left. There is a path from the dock to the waterfall and lake.

Above: The dogwood is the provincial flower and is used as a logo to signify marine parks in the province.

On the map: West, Cassel Lake, Redonda, Island, temporary anchorages, dinghy dock, 50° 11.907' N 124° 50.825' W, Teakerne Arm, Not for Navigation

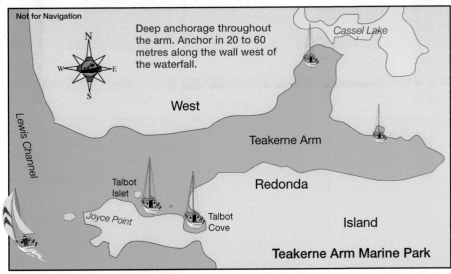

Deep anchorage throughout the arm. Anchor in 20 to 60 metres along the wall west of the waterfall.

Cassel Lake

N

W E

S

West

Teakerne Arm

Redonda

Talbot Islet

Joyce Point

Talbot Cove

Island

Lewis Channel

Teakerne Arm Marine Park

Above: Joyce Point with Talbot Cove in Teakerne Arm to the left. Anchorage is in Talbot Cove, the nook to the east of the islet off the north side of Joyce Point. Mind the rock off Talbot Cove. The south shore beyond Joyce Point follows the exposed west side of West Redonda Island to Refuge Cove. Bottom, left: The waterfall at Teakerne Arm. First come first anchored. This is a favourite spot for those in the know who arrive before the crowd. Below, right: The dinghy dock provides convenient shore access for visitors going to the lake.

Above: Looking south down Lewis Channel from above Joyce Point at the entrance to Teakerne Arm. Beyond the point on the left is Refuge Cove. Kinghorn Island is in the distance. Below: From Calm Channel, the view south down Lewis Channel includes Maurelle Island on the right, the Rendezvous Islands and Cortes Island in the centre. Raza Island and West Redonda Island are to the left.

Cortes Island
Squirrel Cove, Cortes Bay, Mansons Landing, Gorge Harbour, Von Donop Inlet

Charts 3312, 3311, 3538, 3541

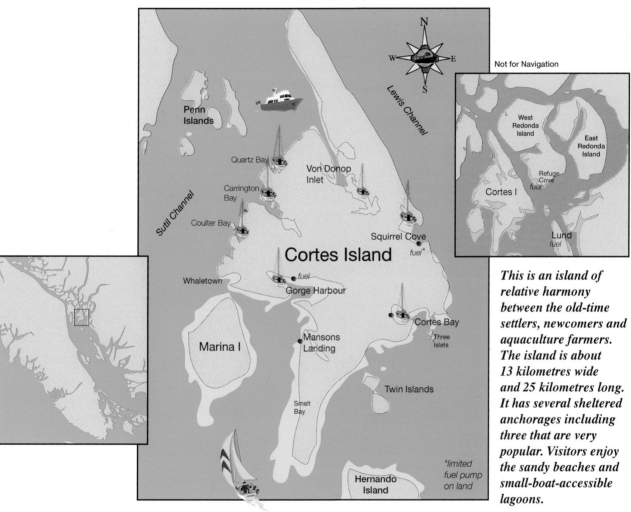

Not for Navigation

This is an island of relative harmony between the old-time settlers, newcomers and aquaculture farmers. The island is about 13 kilometres wide and 25 kilometres long. It has several sheltered anchorages including three that are very popular. Visitors enjoy the sandy beaches and small-boat-accessible lagoons.

Squirrel Cove

Across Lewis Channel from Teakerne Arm, almost directly opposite Refuge Cove on West Redonda Island, Squirrel Cove opens into Cortes Island. It is one of the first major anchorages you find in Desolation Sound when travelling up the coast beyond the Sunshine Coast. Its location is on the west side of Lewis Channel north of Cortes Bay. Overlooking the entrance to Squirrel Cove is a sign pronouncing that this is the land of the Klahoose First Nations. Their village, marked by the tall spire of a church, can be seen on the approaches across Lewis Channel. A fair amount of the adjacent shoreline is First Nations Reserve land.

Squirrel Cove has been one of the most loved and sometimes hated anchorages in all the years of pleasure boating on the British Columbia coast. It is a large cove with a convoluted shoreline featuring many nooks and corners in which to anchor.

Like Cortes Bay to the south, however, it is known to be subject to the occasional strong winds, which can cause great discomfort. In summer this is a rare event, but be cautioned, it does happen so make sure your ground tackle is truly secure and that you have lots of room to swing. Better yet, make sure that your boat is firmly stern tied to shore. Some logs or snags

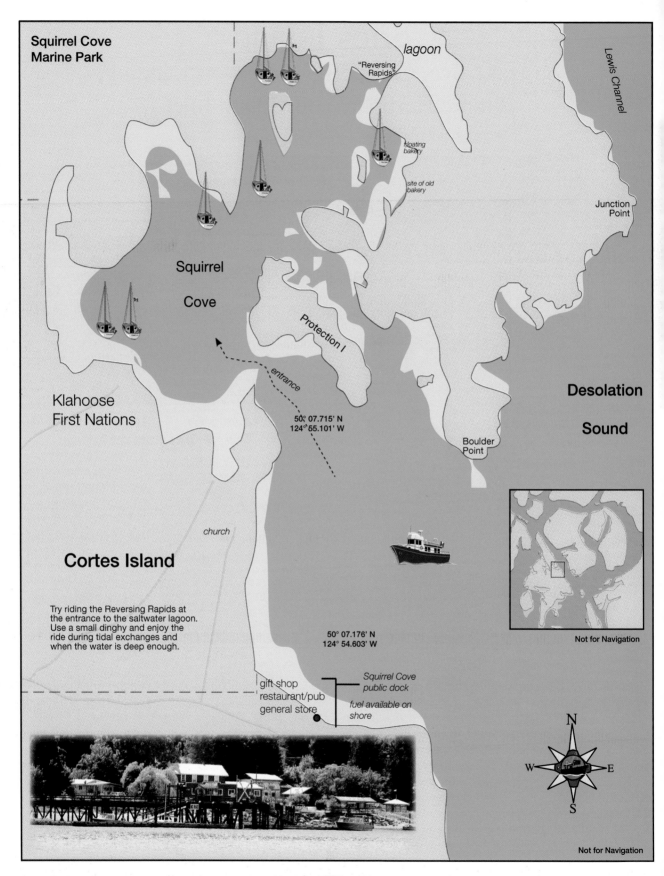

Squirrel Cove Marine Park

lagoon

"Reversing Rapids"

Lewis Channel

floating bakery

site of old bakery

Junction Point

Squirrel

Cove

Protection I

Desolation

Sound

entrance

50° 07.715' N
124° 55.101' W

Klahoose First Nations

Boulder Point

church

Cortes Island

Try riding the Reversing Rapids at the entrance to the saltwater lagoon. Use a small dinghy and enjoy the ride during tidal exchanges and when the water is deep enough.

50° 07.176' N
124° 54.603' W

gift shop
restaurant/pub
general store

Squirrel Cove public dock

fuel available on shore

Not for Navigation

N
W   E
S

Not for Navigation

194

The expansive anchorage at Squirrel Cove. It is a popular, sheltered place. Monitor forecasts, as winds can sweep through the anchorage and cause some discomfort at times. Below: A crowded Squirrel Cove in the middle of summer. The entrance is at bottom right.

Above: Landing on the island in the centre of Squirrel Cove provides an opportunity to go ashore and explore.

Below: The public dock at Squirrel Cove is outside of the cove proper. Note the small dinghy dock with its platform practically dry at low tide.

Top: The shack that was once the bakery of Bill Redel. Above left: The latest supplier of baked goods to visiting boats at anchor in Squirrel Cove. Above: Klahoose First Nations village at Squirrel Cove.

have been reported on the bottom. Monitor the overnight wind forecast. A tidal rapids flows from an adjacent lagoon into the cove, providing entertainment for those who ride them in their dinghies or inflatable watercraft.

At the head of the western arms of the cove, trails lead to Von Donop Inlet. On the east shore, north of the entrance, look for the bakery that provides goods to boats at anchor. During the 1980s and 90s, Bill Redel ran such a service in the cove. More recently it was Marilyn's Salmon Restaurant

mariners found there. Where on-the-water food services are concerned, at Squirrel Cove and at other waterways, it is a matter of 'expect it to be there if you find it there'.

Squirrel Cove General Store at the public dock in the

Squirrel Cove is a busy anchorage in mid summer.

Left and above: A sailboat lies anchored off the dock at Squirrel Cove landing. The spot is exposed but close to a quick entry of the marine park anchorage. Fuel is available on land only. The land abutting the park is Klahoose First Nations property.

outer cove has groceries and supplies as well as an adjacent restaurant and pub. Go ashore for these items and browse among the local crafts on display.

Squirrel Cove General Store

1611 Forest, Cortes Island BC V0P 1R0
Phone 250-935-6327
squirrelcovetrading@yahoo.ca
www.cortesisland.com/squirrelcove

At the adjacent beach, lying to the west of the public dock, a small landing, that almost dries at low water, serves the store as a dinghy dock. The larger Squirrel Cove public docks have power and a garbage drop. They also give access to the store and facilities at Squirrel Cove (Landing).

The store sells propane, gas and diesel fuels, available on land. It also has a post office, groceries, fresh produce, some marine supplies and hardware. Showers and laundry facilities are available. A crafts and garden store is located nearby. There is an outdoor market on Sundays.

Dine at The Cove licensed restaurant on the beach with its large patio overlooking Desolation Sound. Phone 250-935-6350.

Continuing southwards along the east shore of Cortes Island, pass around Mary Point, where temporary anchorage may be taken in the cove just west of the point.

Cortes Bay can also be approached directly from the Copeland Islands, passing Townley Island and the Powell Islets. Or from the west around Sutil Point at the south end of Cortes Island, to the west of Twin Islands. Bob Stevenson of Desolation Sound Yacht Charters says "Great caution must be taken when approaching Cortes Bay." Be aware of Central Rock, the rocks off Three Islets near the bay's entrance, and one off the point to the west of Mary Point. I am always apprehensive when using the passage north of the islets. To avoid the rocks, Stevenson offers good advice and recommends passing south of Three Islets when approaching Cortes Bay.

Twin Islands became the property of relatives of the British Royal family in the mid 1900s and were visited by the Queen during a tour of British Columbia in 1971. The islands were originally the property of an Anglican minister, who was murdered and left in his boat, anchored off the nearby rocks.

Top: The public dock at Squirrel Cove. The two pictures show the almost complete expanse of the dock, the two sections being separated by the wharf. The docks protrude into Squirrel Cove entrance off Desolation Sound at the south end of Lewis Channel.
Right: Garden centre and store at Squirrel Cove. There is a restaurant adjacent to the store. Note the gas pump on shore, the only fuel available at this stop.

Above: From the air, the anchorage at Cortes Bay is seen to be quite busy in mid summer. The Royal Vancouver Yacht Club outstation is located at the left, the public dock is in the centre left of the bay, and the Seattle Yacht Club station is in the lower, centre.

Below: Cortes Bay from the Royal Vancouver Yacht Club outstation club house. This is private property, for members only. The public dock can be seen off to the right. Note the day marker at the entrance to the bay. Keep south of it.

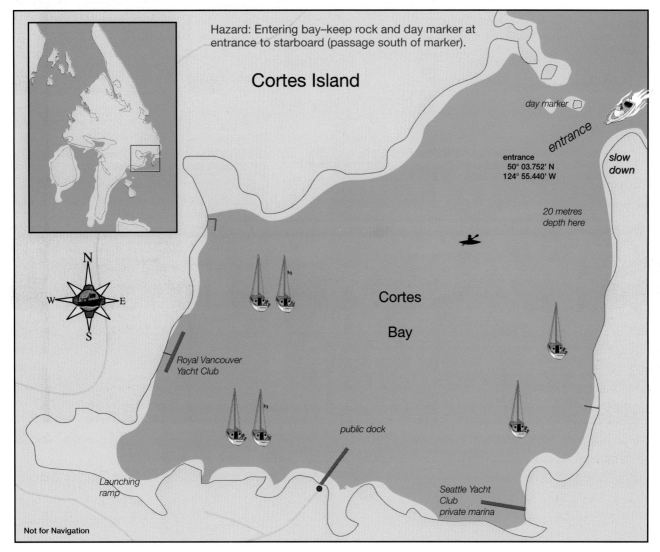

Hazard: Entering bay–keep rock and day marker at entrance to starboard (passage south of marker).

Cortes Island

day marker

entrance

entrance
50° 03.752' N
124° 55.440' W

slow
down

20 metres
depth here

N
W   E
S

Cortes

Bay

Royal Vancouver
Yacht Club

public dock

Launching
ramp

Seattle Yacht
Club
private marina

Not for Navigation

Cortes Bay

Cortes Bay is a beautiful, natural harbour located on the east side of Cortes Island.

Entering and leaving the bay, exercise caution when navigating past the rock marked by a beacon at the entrance. You must favour the south side and keep your speed to a minimum. No-wake speeds in the bay are appreciated by the many local shore-side residents who have boats at their docks.

The public dock in Cortes Bay sees a lot of pleasure traffic in summer and usually holds a full compliment of local vessels in winter. It is not secured at the deep end, but is wide, sturdy and substantial. The dock is controlled by a wharfinger and shared with local residents owning pleasure and commercial craft. Space is limited.

Many yachtsmen favour anchoring out anywhere in the bay. The public dock is available for going ashore by dinghy. Although this is a sheltered bay, occasional strong summer winds may result in discomfort overnight. Occasional blows into the bay can cause dragging anchors. If a wind does come up it is best to post a watch. We have been lucky with calm conditions in Cortes Bay, but many mariners have told us of their windy ordeals. Try to assess the wind forecasts and plan your anchoring in accordance with their direction. Allow lots of scope when anchored in the middle of the bay. Depths range between 7 and 20 metres with the greater depths occurring near the entrance.

Check with the wharfinger for island attractions such as the craft stores and the market. There are two yacht club out-stations in the bay, the Royal Vancouver and the Seattle yacht clubs. The clubs that own property in the bay reserve their docks for their own and reciprocal members.

Cortes Bay, like the island itself as well as Sutil Channel, Marina Island and Hernando Island, are named for the Spanish explorers (and their vessels) who were surveying the coast at the same time as Captain Vancouver.

The Cortes Bay dock has no piling to secure it at the deep end, but it is anchored quite securely. It is wide and spacious, with power and water, and fills up quickly in summer. The entrance can be seen in the background. Note the sign requesting that mariners slow down inside the bay.

DAMMIT--!
PLEASE
SLOW DOWN

Left: For many years the wharfingers, Bill Brown and his wife, kept the dock available for visitors, despite a predominance of local boats tied to it. It offers some space, as available, with potential for rafting. Their house on the edge of the water sat ramshackle and deteriorating quickly in 2007/8 since the passing of the elderly gentleman.

Cortes Bay public dock

Cortes Island, PO Box 243
Manson's Landing BC V0P 1K0
Phone 250-935-0180
Moorage is available at the public dock. There is about 60 metres of wide, solid dock with 20 amp power. Garbage disposal. Small boat rafting is permitted. Float planes tie-up. Cell phone reception is good. There is a launch ramp nearby.

Mansons Landing

Mansons Landing is located on the west side of Cortes Island in the centre of the Discovery Islands. Vessels travelling to Mansons Landing from Cortes Bay or Desolation Sound may arrive by way of the south end of Cortes Island. From the southwest, access is via Sutil Channel or from the northwest via Gorge Harbour and Uganda Pass at the north end of Marina Island.

Above: Boats anchor off the private docks of the Seattle Yacht Club in Cortes Bay. The outstation was formerly a popular marina which, when sold to the club, was one of those that led to a change in regulations requiring that any future marinas sold to yacht clubs maintain a portion of the available space for non-club visitors. The regulations do not apply to this one because it was sold prior to the change.
Below: The public dock at Cortes Bay.

Above: Manson Bay with Cat and Sheep Islets to the right. Mansons Lagoon opens off the bay, at left. Lovely sandy beaches and a calm lagoon with trails and picnic sites greet visitors to Mansons Landing. Note Hague Lake beyond the lagoon, and the east shore of Cortes Island. Opposite page: The photograph clearly shows the landing and the shallow lagoon with its limited boat access.

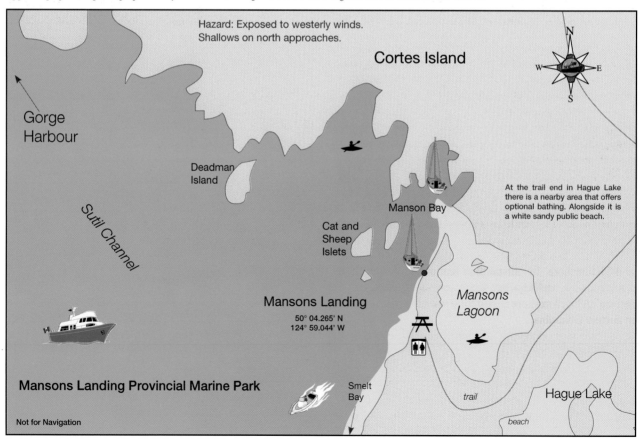

Hazard: Exposed to westerly winds.
Shallows on north approaches.

Cortes Island

N
W   E
S

Gorge
Harbour

Deadman
Island

Sutil Channel

Manson Bay

Cat and
Sheep
Islets

At the trail end in Hague Lake
there is a nearby area that offers
optional bathing. Alongside it is
a white sandy public beach.

Mansons
Lagoon

Mansons Landing

50° 04.265' N
124° 59.044' W

Mansons Landing Provincial Marine Park

Smelt
Bay

trail

Hague Lake

beach

Not for Navigation

There are extensive drying shallows at the south and west end of Cortes Island and at the south and east side of Marina Island. A drying reef extends west from the shore of Cortes Island to the south of Mansons Landing.

Smelt Bay, midway from the south tip to the landing is open and exposed and suitable only for temporary anchoring. Another anchorage can be found a short distance to the west, at Gorge Harbour.

Mansons Landing Marine Park is one of the most beautiful marine parks in local waters. It was established in 1974 and extends from Mansons Landing to Hague Lake. Its designation as a park was intended to expand the diversity of marine park attractions in the region.

The park comprises 100 hectares of which 47 is upland and 53 foreshore. Its outstanding feature is a beautiful, extensive lagoon and adjacent sandy spit and shell beach. The lagoon's white foreshore is said to be one of the finest beaches in British Columbia.

The dock at Mansons Landing provides access to the park. If you go ashore to explore, a large fish petroglyph can be found on a rock a short distance north of the bay. Within easy walking distance, there is a post office, a book store and a co-op store. Hague Lake, a mere 15 minutes walk from the landing, along a rustic pathway, has more paths and hiking trails that connect the lake with the lagoon and landing. There

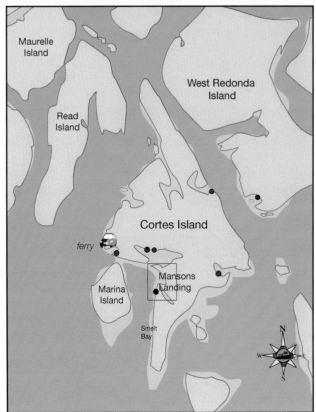

Above: Near the Mansons Landing public dock, the sandy beach is a big attraction of this designated marine park. The dock is used by locals and if there is no space for visitors, anchor out and row ashore.
Opposite: Anchor nearby in calm conditions and go ashore by dinghy. The beach is linked to adjacent trails, the lagoon and nearby roadway.
Left: Between Cortes Island and Lund is Major Islet. Scuba divers know it for its colourful marine life.

conservationist outlook that kept the landing and other areas under their influence, in a pristine condition.

Manson Bay is suitable for anchorage in conditions other than when a strong westerly or southerly wind is blowing, but Cat and Sheep Islets protect it to some extent against weather from the west.

Mansons Landing public dock and marine park

There is limited moorage at a small public dock. Groceries are available nearby at Sutil Market or at Gorge Harbour. Enjoy the ambience, paths and trails and the shallows of the adjacent beaches, lagoon and nearby Hague Lake. This is a designated marine park. Its facilities include picnic tables and toilets. There is a launching ramp on the west side of the spit at the lagoon.

is optional bathing at the lake. The lagoon is also popular for swimming, Although there are a few privately owned boats moored inside, it is shallow and not suitable for navigation other than by dinghy, or those who know the channels to their docks. The park is also accessible by road, using the car ferry from Campbell River via Quadra Island to Whaletown.

Mansons Landing was named for a Shetland Islands immigrant, Michael Manson who owned property there as well as at Hernando and Mitlenatch Islands. It was the settlers'

Above: The entrance to the lagoon at Mansons Landing. This is not a recommended passage for boats. Some locals keep their boats inside but the shallows dictate they know the channels to reach their docks at high water.

Left: A lovely beach winds along the lagoon shore at Mansons Landing. Opposite: Anchored off the beach near the dock in calm conditions. This exposed anchorage is suitable for temporary stops only.

Gorge Harbour

Entrance is through the narrow gorge from which the harbour derives its name. Mariners approach from the south and the open waters of the Strait of Georgia, passing Mitlenatch Island, or from the east around the southern tip of Cortes Island. Mind the shallows that extend a long way from the tip. Approach with caution from the west via the narrow Uganda Passage between Marina Island and Cortes Island.

As you enter through the high rock cliffs at Gorge Harbour look for the ancient rock paintings on the wall. These pictographs can be seen to the right of an arrow that points towards them.

Most vessels anchoring in Gorge Harbour choose the western portion of the bay in the far end beyond the marina, although other locations are possible. Anchor in 6 to 10 metres. Winds do cause some swinging on the hook, but seldom is there a great degree of discomfort. In the harbour there is a small, busy public dock as well as a marina with fuel, services and facilities including a restaurant that overlooks the bay. There are numerous fruit trees on the property at Gorge Harbour. These were planted by the original owners, the Allen family. There is a roadway around the island that serves to connect Gorge Harbour Marina to Whaletown. The Quadra Island to Cortes Island ferry lands near Whaletown, and many RV and camping enthusiasts arrive this way. Walking along the road between the two places provides good exercise. Nearby

This aerial photograph shows the narrow entrance to Gorge Harbour. Look for pictographs on the west rock face, but do so during slack tide as currents can run to four knots.

Mansons Landing can be reached from Gorge Harbour by passing Deadman Island either north or south of the small group of islands that include Cat and Sheep Islands, west of Mansons Bay.

Gorge Harbour Marina Resort

1374 Hunt Rd, PO Box 89
Whaletown, Cortes Island BC V0P 1Z0
Phone 250-935-6433
info@gorgeharbour.com   www.gorgeharbour.com
Gas, diesel and oil are available at the fuel dock. Moorage is extensive with many guest slips. The marina has water at the dock and 30 amp power. New docks and more power are planned. The grocery store has coffee, pastries, fishing licences, tackle, ice, books, gifts, video and DVD rentals, charts, propane and postage stamps. Internet access is available. Facilities include laundry, showers, washrooms and garbage disposal for guests. The resort has private rooms with showers. There is a picturesque gazebo for groups or casual use, and an adjoining campground. Car rentals are available. *The Floathouse* licensed restaurant, overlooking the harbour, is conveniently located on the property.

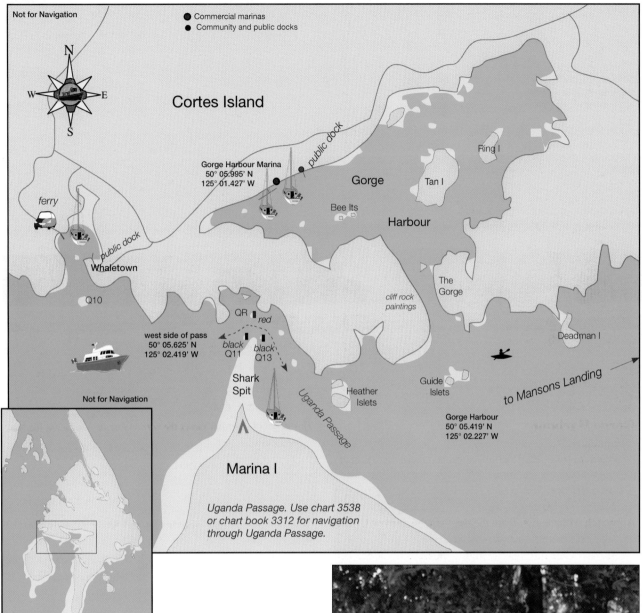

Not for Navigation

● Commercial marinas
● Community and public docks

Cortes Island

N
W · E
S

ferry

public dock

Whaletown

Q10

Gorge Harbour Marina
50° 05.995' N
125° 01.427' W

public dock

Gorge

Ring I

Tan I

Bee Its

Harbour

The
Gorge

cliff rock
paintings

Deadman I

QR   red

west side of pass
50° 05.625' N
125° 02.419' W

black
Q11   black
Q13

Shark
Spit

Uganda Passage

Heather
Islets

Guide
Islets

to Mansons Landing

Gorge Harbour
50° 05.419' N
125° 02.227' W

Not for Navigation

Marina I

Uganda Passage. Use chart 3538
or chart book 3312 for navigation
through Uganda Passage.

Walk to rustic Whaletown and visit the art gallery nearby.
The public library and the post office are located at or near
Whaletown. The ferry landing is nearby.

West of Gorge Harbour, anchorage is available on the east
side of Shark Spit on Marina Island. Instead of just going

Continued on page 218

*Managers and hard working couple, Grant Clarke and Barb Hansen. They
have been turning the marina in Gorge Harbour into a very hospitable
place and are the workforce behind major renovations and upgrades.*

Left: Gourmet food and friendly service in the Floathouse restaurant at Gorge Harbour. Below: The Floathouse restaurant in its rustic setting with a prime view of the harbour.

Top: The anchorage at Gorge Harbour.
Above: The marina at Gorge Harbour. In 2008, its floats were being rebuilt and extended, as part of overall marina improvements.

Above: Gorge Harbour entrance looking south in the direction of Mitlenatch Island. Tidal currents can be quite strong through this narrow waterway. All boats going in or out should exercise caution.

Right: An overview of Gorge Harbour looking east shows the marina with its docks, and the location of the anchorage on the west side.

Bottom: Tied up at the marina's west floats pre-2008.

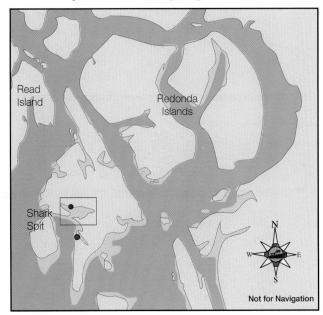

Read Island

Redonda Islands

Shark Spit

N
W E
S

Not for Navigation

Top: A tranquil day in Gorge Harbour. The harbour entrance is off to the left. There are aquaculture installations in the harbour, requiring vessels to move at no wake speeds, and observe no overboard discharge.

Above: Passing the sheer wall of the entrance and a view of the harbour from the marina. Right: Two sections of the rock face at the entrance showing some of the ancient pictographs found there.

Above: A visitor to Gorge Harbour slowly slips away from the anchorage and marina to head for more exploring of Desolation Sound.
Below: The most popular anchorage in Gorge Harbour is to the west of the marina.

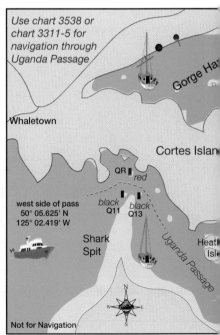

Use chart 3538 or chart 3311-5 for navigation through Uganda Passage

Gorge Ha

Whaletown

Cortes Islan

QR ■ red

west side of pass
50° 05.625' N
125° 02.419' W

black
Q11

black
Q13

Shark
Spit

Heat
Isl

Uganda Passage

Not for Navigation

from page 213

through Uganda Passage, stop and visit the lovely white sandy beach on the spit. Use the large scale chart when navigating through this passage. There are markers indicating the chan- nel. Pass to the west of the red marker QR on the rock and east of the black spar buoys Q13 and Q 11. The photographs on the adjoining pages clearly show the passage.

A vessel passing through Uganda Passage shows the route around Shark Spit on Marina Island. Many stop at the spit to play on the beach.
Opposite page: Anchored at the Spit, and a wide view showing the south end of Cortes Island and Smelt Bay, beyond.

Left: The dock at Whaletown. It is small and adjacent to shallow water. Local boats fill the space but sometimes there is room to stop. The post office is near the landing.

Left, lower: A dentist office has occupied the building at the foot of the ramp at Whaletown.

Left, bottom: For many years the building on the water's edge at the entrance to Whaletown served as a store. It is now a private home.

history of Cortes Island includes the establishment of a store and post office at the time of the earliest settlers. The store is closed now and the post office is located at a separate building nearby. The dock offers limited moorage. It is used largely by commercial and local vessels.

Whaletown was named for the extensive whaling activities in the area. The natives of Cortes Island were adept at whaling, especially at Smelt Bay, and the European newcomers proved equally efficient, producing large quantities of oil for delivery to Victoria. Despite the large number of whales in the Strait of Georgia and adjacent waterways in those days, it was not long before the whale population was decimated to such an extent that by 1872 it was all but at an end.

The route north continues through Plunger Passage or west of the Subtle Islands. The name of these islands was anglicized from Sutil Islands.

Coulter Bay (diagram page 222)

There was a sizeable logging industry on Cortes Island in the early 1900s, when there was a large sawmill operated at Coulter Bay. Walk the roadways and former logging trails that link Coulter Bay with other communities on the island.

The cove is protected by Coulter Island. It is shallow inside with most of it shoaling and drying at low tide at the south end. Anchorage may be taken in the south end of the bay. Note the drying shallows on the southeast side.

Carrington Bay (diagram page 222)

Carrington Bay is deep and not ideal for anchoring, but temporary stops may be made in the lee of Jane Islet or off the Carrington Lagoon entrance. Access to the lagoon is restricted to small boats, preferably those that can be manhandled

Whaletown

Whaletown is a fascinating place. It has a public dock and a post office but no services for mariners. Passage up Sutil Channel begins with a stop at Whaletown. Here the

Above: Whaletown was a busy whaling community in its heyday. Space is sometimes available to tie up at the dock. The Quadra Island ferry lands in the bay. Its slip is seen to the left. Below: Coulter Bay, the nearest anchorage up Sutil Channel from Whaletown. Avoid the tidal shallows when anchoring. Head for nearby Von Donop Inlet if you plan to spend extended time on the hook.

Above: Carrington Bay is the larger bay between Von Donop Inlet and Whaletown, on the west side of Cortes Island. It is mostly deep with limited, temporary anchorage, best in the lee of Jane Islet.

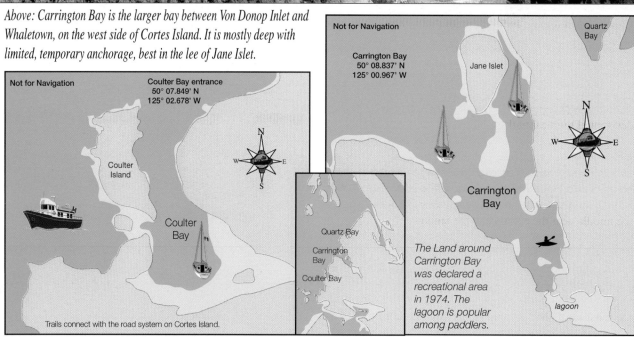

Not for Navigation

Coulter Bay entrance
50° 07.849' N
125° 02.678' W

Coulter Island

Coulter Bay

Trails connect with the road system on Cortes Island.

Quartz Bay

Carrington Bay

Coulter Bay

Not for Navigation

Quartz Bay

Carrington Bay
50° 08.837' N
125° 00.967' W

Jane Islet

Carrington Bay

The Land around Carrington Bay was declared a recreational area in 1974. The lagoon is popular among paddlers.

lagoon

Top right: Coulter Bay offers anchorage near the shallows at the far end or in the lee of the small island between Cortes Island and Coulter Island. Be careful of the exposed reef at the edge of the shallows. Lower right: Quartz Bay gives a panoramic view of vessels passing in Sutil Channel. But the bay does not offer much in the way of anchorage. It is deep almost throughout and the best place to drop the hook is in the lee of the small island, an area partially occupied by aquaculture.

across the entranceway. The land around Carrington Bay is a designated regional park.

Carrington Lagoon runs into the bay at the far south end. Jane Islet and a protruding reef fill a large portion of the entrance. Passage should be taken well over to the south shore, being mindful of a ledge shelving off into the bay. A rock with more than two metres of water over it at low tide lies in the middle near the entrance to the lagoon.

Quartz Bay

This picturesque bay with its waterfront cottages and their private docks, offers anchorage in the inner basin behind two islets on the south side. An aquaculture leaseholder occupies the most ideal shallow area of the bay. Anchor in 10 to 14 metres, to the south of the farm.

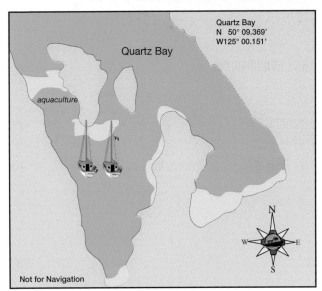

Quartz Bay
N 50° 09.369'
W125° 00.151'

Quartz Bay

aquaculture

Not for Navigation

Sailing down Sutil Channel at its northern end. The boat is coming from the direction of Drew Passage and the Rendezvous Islands.

Above: Approaching the entrance to Von Donop Inlet from the north end of Sutil Channel. Below: The popular anchorage at Von Donop Inlet Marine Park is at the end of the inlet in a large, open but protected bay. Sutil Channel lies beyond the inlet.

Von Donop Inlet

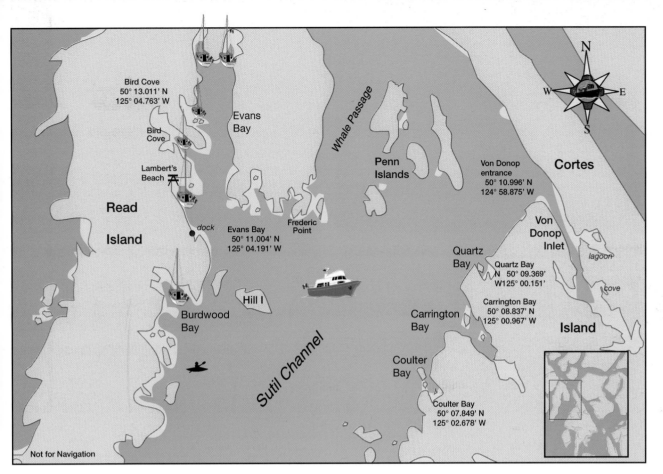

Bird Cove
50° 13.011' N
125° 04.763' W

Evans
Bay

Bird
Cove

Whale Passage

Penn
Islands

Von Donop
entrance
50° 10.996' N
124° 58.875' W

Cortes

Lambert's
Beach

Read

Island

dock

Evans Bay
50° 11.004' N
125° 04.191' W

Frederic
Point

Von
Donop
Inlet

lagoon

Quartz
Bay

Quartz Bay
N 50° 09.369'
W125° 00.151'

cove

Hill I

Burdwood
Bay

Carrington
Bay

Carrington Bay
50° 08.837' N
125° 00.967' W

Island

Sutil Channel

Coulter
Bay

Coulter Bay
50° 07.849' N
125° 02.678' W

Not for Navigation

Von Donop Inlet

Travelling north up the west side of Cortes Island or across Sutil Channel from Read Island, Von Donop Inlet's opening, facing north, is accessed after passing Whaletown, Coulter Bay, Carrington Bay and Quartz Bay. The Penn Islands lie across Sutil Channel from the entrance.

From the north, down Calm Channel, pass the Rendezvous Islands and Drew Passage into Sutil Channel and you will be facing the entrance to Von Donop Inlet. This large inlet in the west side of Cortes Island is a most beautiful place with nature all around and an anchorage that is sheltered, but not without some wind at times. Travel deep inside and anchor near or at the head of the inlet. If you have kayaks or a small portable boat, you can venture beyond the rapids at Von Donop Lagoon and explore its shallow, placid waters at high tide. Deeper into the inlet, beyond the lagoon entrance, there is a cosy nook where anchoring is suitable for a few boats.

Von Donop Creek, and hence the bay, is named for a midshipman who served on Captain Daniel Pender's ship HMS *Charybdis*. Also named by Pender was Carrington Bay. This he named in honour of a draughtsman with the Admiralty.

Captain Richards, who was surveying the coast at the time, named Sutil Channel in honour of the ship of the Spanish explorer, Captain Galiano.

A good representation of the British Columbia coastal forests of hemlock, Douglas fir, western red cedar and Sitka spruce can be found around Von Donop Inlet. Robertson Lake and Wiley Lake lie parallel to the shoreline and stream into the southern reaches of the inlet. Adjacent to these lakes and the inlet is a vast mosaic of old growth forest with undergrowth of huckleberry, Oregon grape, salal and a variety of shrubs and ferns. Harbour seals make the inlet home and during the winter it attracts northern Stellers and California sealions. Also found in the park are mink, river otters and flying squirrels. The lakes are popular for swimming and are accessible by way of a rugged trail that begins near the entrance to Von Donop Inlet.

Across Cortes Island and barely one kilometre from the lower end of the inlet is Squirrel Cove, also accessible from Von Donop by trail.

Evans Bay

Across Sutil Channel from Von Donop Inlet, Evans Bay and Burdwood Bay are on the east side of Read Island. Evans Bay has a wide entrance and several possible sheltered anchorages at its north end. These are at **Bird Cove** and in nooks along the convoluted shore. Temporary anchorage can

Above: A quiet day at Von Donop Inlet. Right: Sutil Channel with the Penn Islands. The tip of Cortes Island where it meets Lewis and Calm Channels and Raza Island are in the background. In the bottom photograph, the entrance to Evans Bay on Read Island can be seen beyond Hill Island in the middle of Sutil Channel.

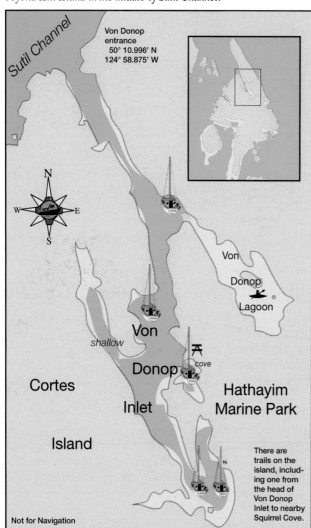

Von Donop entrance
50° 10.996' N
124° 58.875' W

Sutil Channel

Von Donop Lagoon

Von

Donop

Inlet

Cortes Island

shallow

cove

Hathayim Marine Park

There are trails on the island, including one from the head of Von Donop Inlet to nearby Squirrel Cove.

Not for Navigation

be found in 4 to 6 metres off **Lambert's Beach**, which is a regional park. A stop here affords an opportunity to go ashore and enjoy a picnic along with the outstanding view. Although Evans Bay is open to southerly winds, it offers reasonable shelter in most summer conditions.

There is a small public dock just south of the beach. This is the Read Island public wharf and is often kept busy with the coming and going of local vessels. It was a landing for the Union Steamships at one time.

Anchorage in nearby **Burdwood Bay** is best in a small nook created by a circle of islets that are linked to the shore by a drying bar. The bay is open to southerly conditions.

Burdwood Bay, at one time, was the site of a hotel and store, built in the late 1800s by a couple from New York. One of the island's early settlers claimed to have been a member of the Jessie James gang of outlaws in the Badlands of the Dakotas. He was imprisoned for life after shooting a fellow settler over an argument during a drunken binge at Evans Bay.

Another murder took place in the bay a year later. Chris Benson, a partner of the storekeeper was murdered and his wife's lover was arrested for the murder, by the famous Victoria police officer, Chief Inspector Fred Hussey, as described in *The Lawman* (Heritage House). In earlier times the bay was also the site of the landing of a group of Kwakiutl who slaughtered a band of Salish living on the island.

As noted earlier, the best nearby anchorage is at Von Donop Inlet. Carrington Bay, Quartz Bay and Coulter Bay offer short

term anchorage on the Cortes Island side of Sutil Channel, but Von Donop Inlet is by far the most protected anchorage in the area. An alternative is to continue down Sutil Channel to the anchorage at Rebecca Spit, or visit Drew Harbour where Heriot Bay offers anchorage as well as moorage, marina services, hotel, fuel and nearby stores and a public dock.

From Evans Bay or Von Donop Inlet, heading north, pass the Penn Islands either side or through them, and continue up Sutil Channel to the Rendezvous Islands in Calm Channel at the north end of Lewis Channel. Whale Passage separates the Penn Islands from Read Island.

The Rendezvous Islands, located off the north end of Cortes Island, also mark the entrance southwards to Surge Narrows by way of Whiterock Passage.

Surge Narrows
Settlers Group, Whiterock Passage, Rendezvous Islands, Lewis Channel

Charts 3312, 3537, 3539, 3538, 3541, 3543

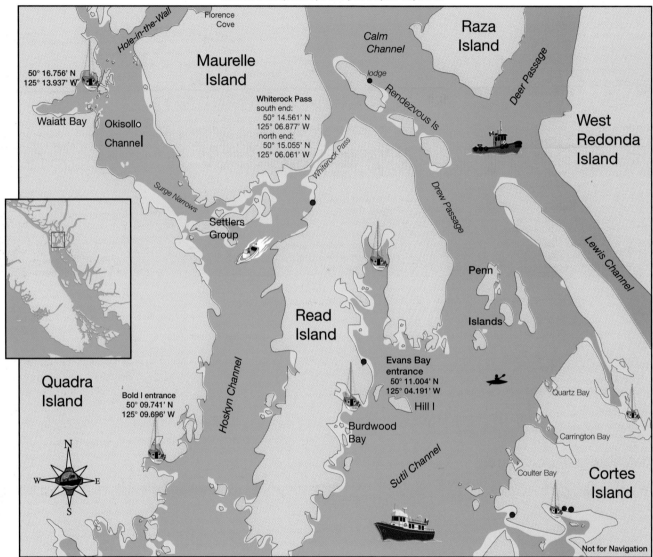

Surge Narrows and the Settlers Group is where tidal rapids lead northwards beyond the calm of the Discovery Islands.

Surge Narrows

Travelling north up Hoskyn Channel, pass the Breton Islands, Dunsterville Islet and the King Islets, sail and slow craft being mindful of the two-knot current that floods and ebbs in the channel. Pass Hjorth Bay and continue between Conville Point and Sheer Point to the Settlers Group or the dock at Surge Narrows. This is a small dock and not suitable for lengthy stays.

Robert and Margaret Tipton established a homestead at Surge Narrows in 1920. They also established the store above the dock and were instrumental in bringing other families to settle the island. The store, typically, also served as post office. In later years the post office was moved onto the dock. Fuel was available but has long since been discontinued.

Today the dock is a small float with a rock awash just off

Above: Looking across the Settlers Group from west to east. Peck Island is in the foreground. Note Tusko Rock at the entrance to Beazley Passage. Whiterock Passage is in the background. Below: Beazley Passage. Peck Island and Welsford Island are in the foreground. The tidal currents running through Beazley Passage can be seen clearly in the photo below, and along the shore, above. See diagram on page 232.

Above: South entrance to Whiterock Passage from Hoskyn Channel.
Opposite page, top: Whiterock Passage with Goepel Island of the Settlers Group near its entrance. Note the currents running in Beazley Passage (foreground). The two lower photos show a continuous view across Surge Narrows. In the left photo Peck Island is seen in the centre with Beazley Passage separating it from Sturt Island. The right hand photo shows the northeast end of Sturt Island and the edge of Goepel Island. Okisollo Channel leads off beyond to the Octopus Islands.

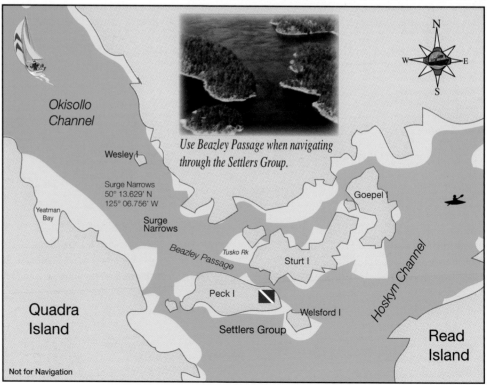

Use Beazley Passage when navigating through the Settlers Group.

Okisollo Channel

Wesley I

Surge Narrows
50° 13.629' N
125° 06.756' W

Yeatman
Bay

Surge
Narrows

Goepel I

Beazley Passage

Tusko Rk

Sturt I

Hoskyn Channel

Peck I

Welsford I

Quadra
Island

Settlers Group

Read
Island

Not for Navigation

232

its north side. After a succession of owners, the store was closed in the early 1980s but reopened later by Teresa and Doug Beyerstein until they closed it in 2007.

Passage through nearby Whiterock Pass to the Rendezvous Islands is a good alternative route to Big Bay. Check charts for depths. Reefs extend off the light at the entrance of Whiterock Passage so pass it a ways off to enter mid channel.

The close-up (large scale) inset on page 20 of the chart book 3312 provides good detail of the shallow passage. Follow the range markers and note depths.

Rendezvous Islands

There are no apparent anchorages among these islands, however it is possible to tuck in behind a couple of small islets at the north and south ends. The southernmost of the islands is a park and there is a small cove at the north end adjacent to the small islets on its west side.

The Rendezvous Lodge, on the east shore, has a dock that is used primarily for its guests or visiting boats to 38'. Visitors may dock there and stop for a meal or overnight as the limited, exposed space allows. The dock is exposed to the

Above: Powering through Beazley Passage at slack tide. Currents run to 12 knots on the flood and 10 on the ebb. Opposite page: Looking down Okisollo Channel from above the Octopus Islands. Wesley Island is seen in the distance, before Surge Narrows. Former storekeeper, Teresa Beyerstein and the dock at Surge Narrows, also shown at right in its setting with the old store.

The fabulous view in Lewis Channel, and the solitude that helps warrant the name Desolation Sound. Now, put you and your boat in the picture.

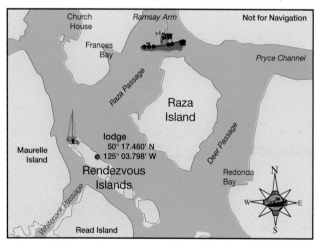

wash of vessels passing by. They are usually en route between Desolation Sound and Big Bay, heading north for the Yucultas and points beyond, or south, homebound.

Surge Narrows public dock

Moorage: 65 metres of dock space with floatplane access. The post office on the dock is used as a mail drop for local residents. Beware of the rock north of the float.

Rendezvous Lodge

PO Box 63, Surge Narrows BC V0P 1W0
Phone 250-287-0318 toll free 1-888-225-4050
info@rendezvouslodge.com www.rendezvouslodge.com
Meals: Australian 700 degrees hot stone oven food preparation. Phone for reservations.

Above: Deer Passage off Lewis Channel with Redonda Bay beyond the promontory at right on West Redonda Island.
Below: Raza Passage and the Downie Range. This was taken while passing the Rendezvous Islands in Calm Channel north of Raza Island.
Opposite: The lodge at Rendezvous Island faces onto Calm Channel. It is exposed to passing traffic but has a fairly substantial dock.

The Octopus Islands. Okisollo Channel and
Hole-in-the-Wall are in the background.

Quadra Island
Octopus Islands, Owen Bay, Hole-in-the-Wall, Drew Harbour, Heriot Bay

Charts 3537, 3312, 3539, 3538

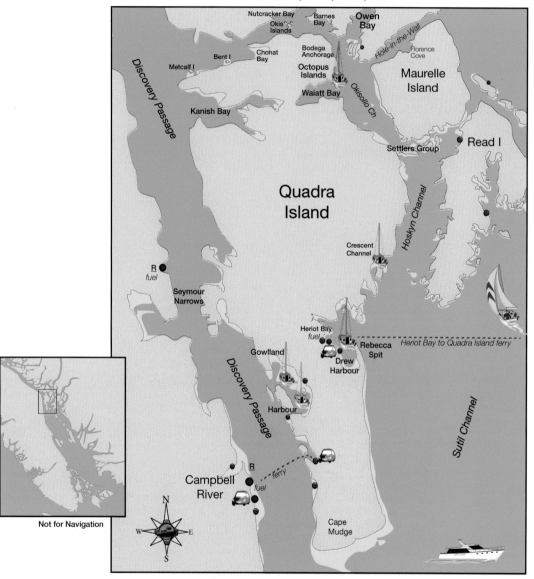

Not for Navigation

The diversity of marine activity on the east side and west side of Quadra Island is noteworthy. The west side sees lots of commercial traffic and is swept by strong tidal currents. The east side is more sedate with the beautiful Rebecca Spit Marine Park and the Octopus Islands vying for favourite destination.

Octopus Islands

From Hoskyn Channel at Surge Narrows, pass through the Settlers Group using Beazley Passage at slack tide. Continue up Okisollo Channel to Waiatt Bay. The north entrance to the Octopus Islands is from Okisollo Channel opposite the south end of Hole-in-the-Wall. From the north, Okisollo Channel opens off Discovery Passage between Sonora and Quadra Islands. Pass Barnes Bay, Owen Bay and Hole-in-the-Wall

and turn south through **Bodega Anchorage** to reach **Waiatt Bay** and the anchorage in the Octopus Islands.

Octopus Islands Marine Park is located near the northeastern tip of Quadra Island on the north shore of Waiatt Bay.

There is a vague similarity to the shape of an octopus in the outline of the waterways and groups of islands at the north and east side of Quadra Island. Locals referred to the area

Above: Hole-in-the-Wall runs into Okisollo Channel at this juncture. The current runs swiftly through the passage. Anchorage in Florence Cove offers some protection while waiting for slack tide. Note the strength of the current. In the lower picture, the currents are not as strong. Okisollo Channel widens out as it continues past Waiatt Bay towards Surge Narrows in the distance.

Above: The Octopus Islands. The narrow passage, also seen below, leads into Okisollo Channel through Bodega Anchorage and in the direction of Hole-in-the-Wall. Left: A view of Okisollo Channel, looking east from Discovery Passage. Metcalf Island lies in the foreground and Brent Island beyond, just off the south shore with Chonat Bay farther up the channel and the Okis Islands in the distance.

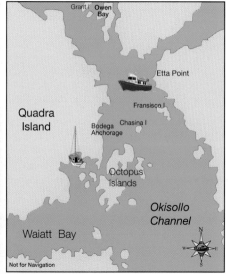

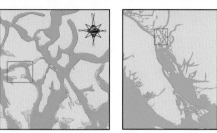

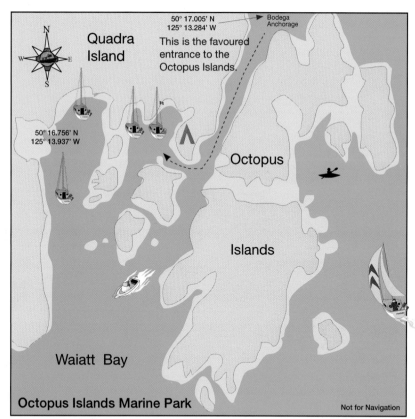

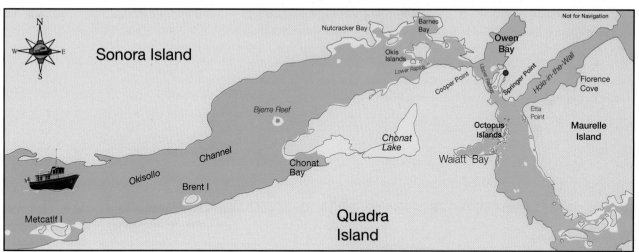

as 'the octopus' in the early days. Today the name Octopus Islands reflects the connection to that resemblance.

Many islets and coves in Octopus Islands Marine Park make it an ideal place to choose for an extended period at anchor. There are beach areas for sunbathing, swimming or scuba diving. Many visitors go ashore to picnic. The sparsely forested slopes of Quadra Island form a scenic backdrop to a group of small islands and islets near the mouth of the bay. The favoured anchorages are in the two northern coves tucked in behind the islets at the north end of Waiatt Bay.

The distance from Vancouver to the Octopus Islands is about 100 miles. It is a worthwhile trip, but make the most of it by spending a few days or more at anchor.

Owen Bay

Owen Bay entrance is on the south shore of Sonora Island, just northwest of Hole-in-the-Wall and almost opposite the entrance to the Octopus Islands. It opens off Okisollo Channel, which, along with adjacent Hole-in-the-Wall, is a very tide ripped stretch of water.

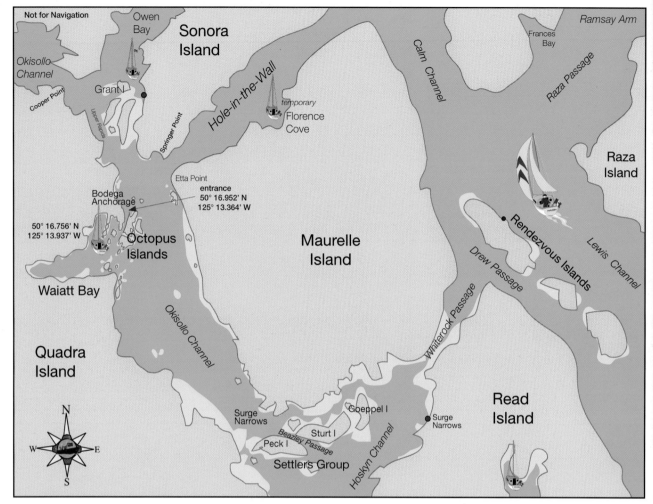

Owen Bay is a large, easy access bay where anchorage is relatively sheltered. Be mindful of tidal streams and rips in Okisollo Channel between Springer Point and Cooper Point. This is in the vicinity of an area known as Upper Rapids, where overfalls and eddies can be dangerous.

Most mariners use this peaceful bay, with a choice of places to anchor, only for short stops, some overnight. There is space for several boats in the northernmost of two coves halfway up the western shore of Owen Bay. Or anchor in 10 metres near the island opposite the small public dock on the Sonora Island shore. The dock is tucked behind **Grant Island**, but offers little if any moorage.

Liv Kennedy, in her *Coastal Villages*, tells us: The bay was named for Commander Frederick John Owen Evans of the Royal Navy Admiralty Hydrographic Service, in 1864, when it was surveyed by Captain David Pender aboard the SS *Beaver*.

The Pacific Coast and Chemainus Lumber Company set up operations in Owen Bay at the turn of the 20th century. It was one of their crew, Harry Pedersen, who remained in the bay as a homesteader when the company moved on to better pastures. It is rumoured that Owen Bay is haunted. Perhaps it is the ghost of Harry Pedersen who disappeared one day without a trace, or one of a couple who disappeared off their anchored boat in more recent years. Owen Bay is the site of an old mill and shacks left by early settlers. There have been attempts over the years to reinstate the old mill as a lodge

The public dock is tucked behind the islands to the right of the entrance of Owen Bay. Currents run between the islands and are felt near the dock.
Below: Owen Bay entrance. The islands to the right of it offer no passage. The public dock is just beyond them. Best anchorage is against the west
shore or near the public dock. Opposite page: Entrance to Octopus Islands from Bodega Anchorage in Okisollo Channel.

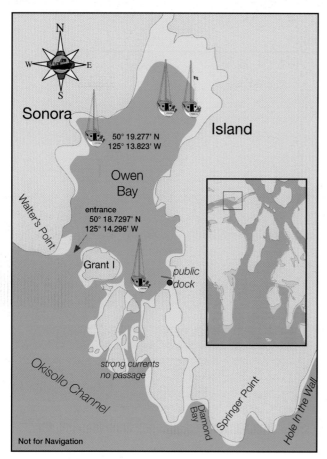

Not for Navigation

Around-Vancouver-Island cruise winds up with a restful anchorage in the lee of Grant Island in Owen Bay.

and there are likely to be new enterprises in coming years. It is believed that a meteorite struck the shore on the northeast side of the bay leaving a huge scar on the face of the cliff.

If you are venturing beyond the Octopus Islands, you will find that Okisollo Channel has no ideal anchorage west of Owen Bay. Temporary anchorages can be found in the lee of **Chonat Bay** and the **Metcalf Islands** on the north Quadra shore and in **Nutcracker Bay** west of the Okis Islands. These islands are best passed to the north to avoid the strong tidal rapids and Gypsy Shoal to their south.

Hole-in-the-Wall provides access to Stuart Island and Big Bay with its marinas and fishing lodges. Use Hole-in-the-Wall during slack or near slack tides, taking temporary anchorage at **Florence Cove**. Big Bay is at the northern extremity of Desolation Sound and is a waiting place for tide changes and safe passage through Dent and Yucalta Rapids.

Rebecca Spit

Going south, Rebecca Spit is located on the east side of Quadra Island, beyond the end of Hoskyn Channel. The spit is a long narrow strip of land that forms a splendid natural breakwater to **Drew Harbour**. The Harbour is entered from Sutil Channel off Heriot Bay. This large, fairly exposed bay is popular as an anchorage during the summer. The safest

anchorage is in 5 metres at the northwest end of the Spit. Note the shallow ledge that protrudes from the beach part way down the shore. It dries at very low tides but is shallow enough at low water for boats to touch bottom at medium low tides.

The facilities at Rebecca Spit Marine Park are extensive. It is a picturesque park with white sandy beaches lining both sides of the spit. These are backed by open uplands interspersed with stands of shrubs, grasses and second growth trees. There are many day use facilities including the availability of water, picnic tables and toilets. A boat launch ramp is located near the south end of the park. Taku Marina in Drew Harbour offers overnight moorage (see the diagram on page 252).

Heriot Bay

In Heriot Bay there is a public dock as well as a full service marina. The marina is part of the property housing the historic Heriot Bay Inn where accommodations and meals are available. Inside the pub a large poster depicts the old Canadian five dollar bill on which was portrayed a local Heriot Bay fishing boat. Near the inn are access roads to other island facilities including grocery stores and craft shops. There is sheltered anchorage in 5 to 7 metres in the lee of Heriot Island on the north side of Heriot Bay, as well as in the lee of Rebecca Spit in Drew Harbour.

Heriot Bay was the site of a major steamship landing. Today, the inter-island ferry serving Whaletown on Cortes Island leaves from Heriot Bay. Vehicles travelling across Quadra Island, land at Quathiaski Cove on the ferry out of Campbell River.

The hotel, which was built and operated initially in the 1890s, by Hosea Bull and his wife Helen, served the community

Views of Rebecca Spit and Heriot Bay. In the top photograph Gowlland Harbour and Campbell River can be seen on the other side of Quadra Island. Right and above: The sandy beaches of Rebecca Spit. Check depths before anchoring in the lee of the spit.

as an inn, a saloon and a church. When the rowdy element of the weekend wound down their drinking and carousing, the Sunday service took over. Bull and his wife kept a menagerie of exotic songbirds and, at the back of the building, a pool in which they kept a pet seal.

The original building burned to the ground in 1912 and was rebuilt to its present day style. The chimney is the only section that remained from the original hotel. Since its reconstruction the hotel and marina have been owned and operated by a number of people, notably a couple named Lyle and Angela, schoolteachers who made significant changes to the restaurant before selling it to an American couple, Tom and Julia Pearson, in the early 1990s. After Tom passed away it was sold in 2005 to Lorraine Wright who made major changes to the lounge and restaurant as well as the patio and other sections of the building. The restaurant offers fine cuisine in a warm, tasteful setting. A large chess board adorns the

front lawn overlooking the marina. The property was sold again in 2007.

Settlers at Heriot Bay included the family of Norman Dowler, one of the owners of the store at Refuge Cove. For many years there was a store on the one-time site of Hosea Bull's sawmill, adjacent to the public dock in Heriot Bay. The

Left: A late afternoon with mixed light, produced this vista from Rebecca Spit looking towards the Breton Islands and Read Island beyond.
Bottom, opposite page: Anchorage along the lee side of Rebecca Spit in Drew Harbour.
Below: Across Sutil Channel.

store was owned and operated by Norman Dowler before he moved to Refuge Cove. In 1978 the store burned to the ground and was rebuilt on the site. Later it was relocated to the small shopping centre up the hill south of the Heriot Bay Inn.

Heriot Bay public dock
Quadra Island Harbour Authority. Phone 250-285-3555
There is a launch ramp, garbage disposal and access to the island roads. Power at the dock is 15 amps.

Heriot Bay Inn and Marina
PO Box 100, Heriot Bay, Quadra Island BC V0P 1H0
Phone 250-285-3322 Toll free 1-888-605-4545
info@heriotbayinn.com www.heriotbayinn.com
The marina has a fuel dock serving gas, diesel and oil. Propane is available. The docks have 15 and 30 amp power. There is a fish cleaning station near the fuel dock. Reservations are recommended for overnight moorage at the marina.
The historic Heriot Bay Inn with private rooms, has a large pub, The Logger & The Fisherman, and a licensed restaurant with seasonal patio service. A store inside the hotel offers ice,

books, gifts and charts. Laundry, showers and washrooms are located at the Inn. Also available are internet access, fishing, sightseeing charters and whale and bear watching tours.
A water taxi service and a kayak rental service are offered. Bicycle rentals are available nearby.
Beach access is possible at nearby Rebecca Spit. The Heriot Bay Store, a liquor store, the post office and a mini shopping centre are a short walk away–delivery to boats–phone 250-285-2436. The resort includes a waterfront RV park. Heriot Bay Inn and Marina are located alongside the Quadra Island to Cortes Island ferry terminal.
The nearest, and one of the most popular anchorages on the coast, is in Drew Harbour at Rebecca Spit Marine Park.

Drew Harbour with Rebecca Spit to the right. Heriot Bay is north, to the left, with Hyacynthe Bay and Open Bay beyond to the right. Discovery Passage is seen to the west of Quadra Island in the upper left corner.

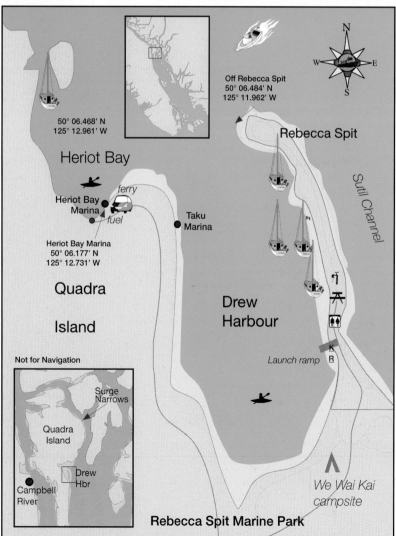

50° 06.468' N
125° 12.961' W

Off Rebecca Spit
50° 06.484' N
125° 11.962' W

N
W E
S

Rebecca Spit

Heriot Bay

Sutil Channel

ferry

Heriot Bay
Marina

fuel

Taku
Marina

Heriot Bay Marina
50° 06.177' N
125° 12.731' W

Quadra

Island

Drew
Harbour

K
R

Launch ramp

Not for Navigation

Surge
Narrows

Quadra
Island

Campbell
River

Drew
Hbr

We Wai Kai
campsite

Rebecca Spit Marine Park

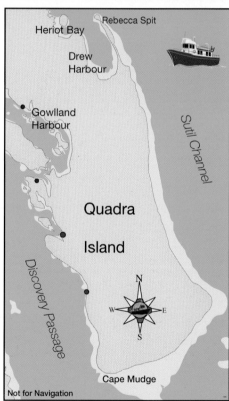

Heriot Bay

Rebecca Spit

Drew
Harbour

Gowlland
Harbour

Sutil Channel

Quadra

Island

Discovery Passage

N
W E
S

Cape Mudge

Not for Navigation

Below: The launch ramp at Rebecca Spit.

Above: Heriot Bay, Drew Harbour and Taku Resort (at the point, left).
Right: The Cortes Island ferry off Rebecca Spit. Opposite page, top: Drew Harbour from the south, Heriot Bay and its anchorage with Hyacinthe Bay off to the left. Beyond and to the right is Open Bay, Hoskyn Passage and the Breton Islands. Rebecca Spit Marine Park protrudes from the right.

Taku Resort and Marina

PO Box 1, Heriot Bay, Quadra Island BC V0P 1H0
Phone 250-285-3031 Toll free 1-877-285-8258
info@takuresort.com www.takuresort.com
Guest moorage is available on 250 metres of dock.

Power at the docks is 30 and 50 amps. Washrooms, laundry and showers are located ashore at this luxury resort. Accommodations should be arranged well in advance. Easy walking the short distance to a small shopping centre for groceries, coffee shop and other stores.

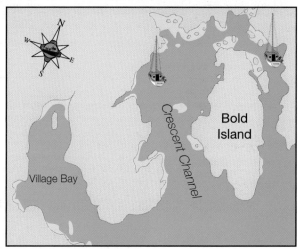

Village Bay

Crescent Channel

Bold Island

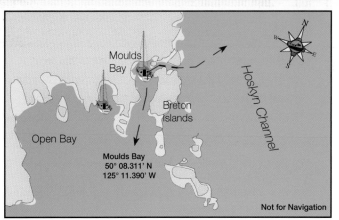

Moulds Bay

Breton Islands

Open Bay

Hoskyn Channel

Moulds Bay
50° 08.311' N
125° 11.390' W

Not for Navigation

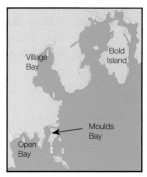

Village Bay

Bold Island

Open Bay

Moulds Bay

Top: The marina at the Heriot Bay Inn, and the ferry landing. Left: The old Heriot Bay Inn before major renovations. The diagrams show coastal features north of Heriot Bay on Quadra Island's east coast.

On Quadra Island, anchor at **Open Bay**, **Village Bay** or **Moulds Bay**, or farther north in the lee of **Bold Island** in **Crescent Channel**, but mind the rocks in this narrow passage. Stern tie in limited space.

Bold Island once had a cattle ranch. It was established by a Californian who arrived in British Columbia seeking to make his fortune in the Cariboo gold rush in the late 1800s.

Travel from Heriot Bay and Rebecca Spit north past Open Bay into Moulds Bay. This is a short cut rather than going around the Breton Islands, to reach Hoskyn Channel

Top: The newly renovated Heriot Bay Inn. The interior has been reworked and is finely finished with a tastefully appointed restaurant and lounge. The photographs above show the gift shop in the hotel, left, and the checkout at the grocery store nearby.

and Surge Narrows. The picturesque passage north out of Moulds Bay is narrow, with a sharp bend in it. Boats larger than 12 metres in length use this passage with discretion. Temporary anchorage may be taken in the bight to the west of the southern entrance.

Left: Chess is a spectator sport, especially when the board and men are so large. These young women are having fun rather than taking the game too seriously, on the lawn in front of the Heriot Bay Inn.
Bottom, left: Taku Resort marina on the west shore of Drew Harbour.
Below: Taku Resort docks.
Bottom: The anchorage in the lee of Heriot Island opposite Heriot Bay.

Discovery Passage
Kanish Bay, Seymour Narrows, Campbell River, Gowlland Harbour, Quathiaski Cove

Charts 3540, 3312, 3311, 3539, 3538, 3543

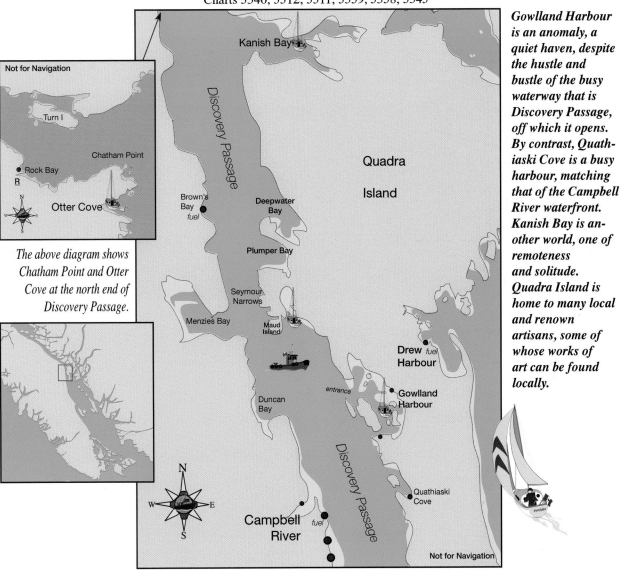

Not for Navigation

Turn I

Chatham Point

Rock Bay

R

Otter Cove

The above diagram shows Chatham Point and Otter Cove at the north end of Discovery Passage.

Kanish Bay

Discovery Passage

Quadra

Island

Brown's Bay *fuel*

Deepwater Bay

Plumper Bay

Seymour Narrows

Menzies Bay

Maud Island

Drew *fuel* Harbour

entrance

Gowlland Harbour

Duncan Bay

Discovery Passage

Quathiaski Cove

Campbell River *fuel*

Not for Navigation

N
W E
S

Gowlland Harbour is an anomaly, a quiet haven, despite the hustle and bustle of the busy waterway that is Discovery Passage, off which it opens. By contrast, Quathiaski Cove is a busy harbour, matching that of the Campbell River waterfront. Kanish Bay is another world, one of remoteness and solitude. Quadra Island is home to many local and renown artisans, some of whose works of art can be found locally.

Chatham Point

Discovery Passage and Chatham Point were, and still are, significant features of the British Columbia coast. They must have struck Captain Vancouver as being of great importance in navigating the area, considering he named them after his ship *Discovery* and her consort *Chatham*. Beaver Rock, sitting on a ledge that protrudes from shore into the waters of Johnstone Strait where it meets Discovery Passage, is named for the first steamship on the coast, SS *Beaver*, which served the Hudsons Bay Company.

Otter Cove at Chatham Point offers sheltered anchorage. This cove, just south of the light, affords shelter in the lee of Limestone Island. It is useful as an anchorage for short terms and as a means to take a small boat to the dock at the Chatham Point light. Nodales Channel shares the confluence

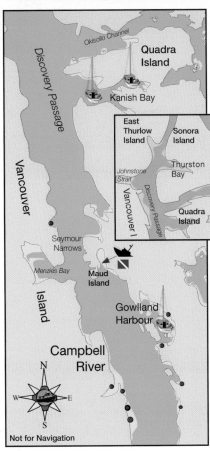

Not for Navigation

Top: Otter Cove can be seen this side of Chatham Point. Johnstone Strait lies beyond with Turn Island and Walkem Islands gracing the southern shores of East Thurlow Island.

Above: Lighthouse buildings on Chatham Point.

Opposite page, top: The Chatham Point light on Beaver Rock stands at the confluence of Discovery Passage and Johnstone Strait.

Opposite page, bottom: Otter Cove, immediately south of Chatham Point affords a place to anchor and slip ashore to visit the lighthouse at the point. A bonus is the magnificent view of tall Mount Brougham on East Thurlow Island and Discovery Mountain on Sonora Island.

of Johnstone Strait and Discovery Channel. It leads north between Sonora and East Thurlow Islands to **Thurston Bay**, **Cameleon Harbour**, and on to Cordero Channel. See the author's ***North of Desolation Sound*** for details on those destinations and beyond.

Okisollo Channel and access to the Octopus Islands, opens to the east off Discovery Passage, just north of Kanish Bay.

Kanish Bay

On the east side of Discovery Passage, Kanish Bay lies about midway between Seymour Narrows and Chatham Point. Enter from the north, south of Granite Point, or from the south after navigating through Seymour Narrows and passing Plumper Bay and Deepwater Bay. Inside Kanish Bay, there is sheltered anchorage in 5 to 10 metres in the lee of **Bodega Point** at its entrance, or at three other locations farther into

Above: Looking north towards Chatham Point from the entrance to Kanish Bay. Just north of Granite Point is the opening to Okisollo Channel with the Cinque Islands on its opposite shore. Note the tiny nook a short way into Okisollo Channel.

Left: Kanish Bay anchorage behind the Chained Islands.

Opposite page: Kanish Bay has anchorage at the entrance and at its head in Granite Bay, to the right, and in Small Bay at top, right.

the bay. At the southeast end, anchor in 8 metres in **Granite Bay**, which is well protected despite Kanish Bay being open to western exposure. Granite Bay was a thriving community at one time although there is nothing left of its former presence. It had a large population of Finnish settlers, a hotel and a landing for the Union Steamships passenger vessels.

Small Inlet is a larger anchorage but with a narrow entrance. It is well protected from all weather. Another anchorage is in a nook south of the island, marked 102 on the chart, which lies between the entrances to Granite Bay and Small Inlet.

There is an historic 1869 locomotive at the Burnaby Heritage Village near Vancouver. It ended its days of service in the logging and mining industries at Granite Bay. The locomotive had come from the Hastings Sawmill operations at Mud Bay near Bellingham, and Rock Bay in Johnstone Strait. It was originally used in San Fransisco, then during the

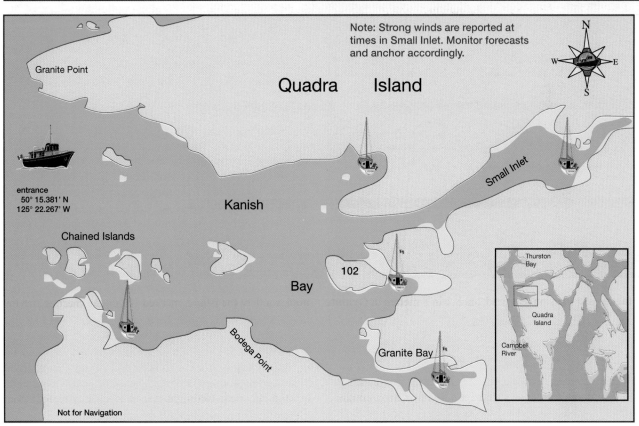

Note: Strong winds are reported at times in Small Inlet. Monitor forecasts and anchor accordingly.

N
W · E
S

Granite Point

Quadra   Island

Small Inlet

entrance
50° 15.381' N
125° 22.267' W

Kanish

Chained Islands

102

Bay

Bodega Point

Granite Bay

Thurston Bay

Quadra Island

Campbell River

Not for Navigation

261

Left, top and centre:
Two views of Brown's Bay
just north of Seymour
Narrows in Discovery
Passage.
Bottom: A tiny nook in
Discovery Passage is
bypassed as vessels make
for slack tide at Seymour
Narrows.Opposite: Sailing
up Discovery Passage.

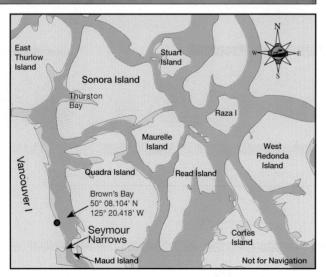

construction of the Panama Canal and later by the Canadian Pacific Railway.

In 1925 Granite Bay saw its demise when a massive forest fire destroyed a huge swath of forest down the west side of Quadra Island. It took almost everything in its path including the logging operations, hotel and store at Granite Bay and many islanders' homes.

Brown's Bay Marina

15021 Brown's Bay Rd, Campbell River BC
Phone 250-286-3135
www.brownsbayresort.com
Fuel dock with gas, diesel and oils. Enquire about available transient moorage. This is a busy fishing marina which caters mostly to trailerable boats. Water, ice and garbage disposal are available. There is a launch ramp and a seasonal licensed restaurant. Ripple Rock RV Park, nearby, has many facilities.

Seymour Narrows

Passage through Seymour Narrows should be taken at or near slack tide. This passage has a chequered history of sinkings and terrifying experiences. That is, mostly before the removal of Ripple Rock. Monolithic Ripple Rock, actually with two peaks, stood almost centre of the narrows. It was close enough to the surface to account for numerous vessels being wrecked before being leveled by a man-made explosion in 1958. About 20 large ships and some 100 smaller craft had been lost to the rock and currents in Seymour Narrows.

Among the engineers who tunneled under the narrows to reach the rock was the former owner of a boat that the author and his wife owned and used extensively in their early days of exploring the BC coast. The man who was commissioned to film the event was a neighbour of theirs in his late years. Between these two men, the author heard many tales about the blasting of Ripple Rock. The blast that cleared Ripple Rock took 1,375 tons of explosives and was the biggest man-made explosion ever at the time. It was featured on Canadian national television in the first ever live broadcast by the CBC.

The first recorded loss of a vessel to Ripple Rock was the US Navy steamer Saranac in 1875. In the ensuing years many more vessels were damaged by the notorious rock, and over 100 lives were lost. Since the rock's removal, navigation in Seymour Narrows has not been without incident. In 1984 the Bahamian registered cruise ship Sundancer struck bottom off Maud Island and limped to a dock where it later sank. The vessel was salvaged and placed back into service under new owners. Mariners are reminded of the strong tidal currents that flow in Seymour Narrows during tidal changes.

Above: Maud Island with deep anchorage in the bay to the east. Saltwater Lagoon leads off to the right in the photograph. Note how Maud Island is connected by a narrow drying strip. It was from Maud Island that engineers launched their tunnelling attack on Ripple Rock in 1958 and destroyed it with a blast larger than any other man-made explosion to date. In the photo to the left, the current is seen ripping over the now deeper peak of what was Ripple Rock. Menzies Bay lies beyond. It is not suitable for anchoring. The cove to the right of Maud Island is also not suited for anchoring. It lies just south of North Bluff, Plumper Bay and Deepwater Bay.

Bottom: The sinking of the Columbia off Maud Island. It was a major undertaking of the British Columbia Underwater Archaeological Society. The artificial reef attracts many scuba diving enthusiasts from all parts of the world. Anchor clear of markers.

Opposite page, top: Gowlland Harbour from the northwest over Gowlland Island.

Bottom: The south entrance to Gowlland Harbour, past April Point. Check your boat's draft, as well as the tides and currents before passing through.

Down Discovery Passage, past Seymour Narrows and Menzies Bay is Painter's Lodge, which is an historic resort. Shipwright Edward Painter built the lodge that today bears his name, and in so doing, started what became Campbell River's biggest tourist attraction, sport fishing. The lodge is owned today by a corporation based in Oak Bay on Vancouver Island, along with April Point Lodge on the opposite shore at the entrance to Gowlland Harbour, and Ladysmith Marina just south of Nanaimo. The present building was erected in 1986, to replace the original one that was destroyed by fire. Guests at April Point Lodge are invited to visit Painters Lodge and are transported across the passage that separates them, by the company's private launch.

Gowlland Harbour

Approach Gowlland Harbour from the south or north via Discovery Passage. The easiest and main entrance is north of Gowlland Island. It is within a very short distance of populated centres.

The harbour lies opposite the main downtown waterfront centre of Campbell River. It is a suitable place to lie at anchor in a remote wilderness despite waterfront homes and marinas. Another entrance to the harbour for smaller craft, is to the south, between April Point and Gowlland Island. Navigate this passage, with caution, during slack, high tides.

Anchorage is recommended in 2 to 9 metres between **Crow Islet** and **Fawn Island** or in the lee of **Stag Island**, or tucked in the lee of **Vigilant Islets** (see diagram page 268). Anchor elsewhere in the open areas of Gowlland Harbour subject to wind forecasts and depths. The marina at Seascape Resort in Gowlland Harbour as well as the one at April Point, offer overnight moorage. Down Discovery Passage is busy Quathiaski Cove, a short distance from Gowlland Harbour, where there are more facilities for mariners, including a cluster of stores a short way up the road from the large public marina.

Above: Anchored in Gowlland Harbour. This sailboat has dropped the hook in the lee of Crow and Fawn Islets. Beyond is the massive breakwater of Gowlland Island that protects the harbour.

Opposite page, top: Looking into the north entrance of Gowlland Harbour over Copper Cliffs and May Island. Best entry is south of Entrance Bank and Entrance Rock, past the north end of Gowlland Island and Vigilant Islets. Opposite page, lower: Close up of the Crow and Mouse Islets.

There is a large sport fishing community as well as a once busy lumber industry on the Vancouver Island shores, and a great deal of commercial and pleasure craft traffic catered to by a flourishing marine industry in Campbell River. Scuba diving has also become somewhat of an industry for the area. With the sinking in 1996 of the former destroyer escort vessel, HMCS *Columbia*, in the bay east of Maud Island at Seymour Narrows, there has been a noticeable growth of activity in that vicinity. There are strong tidal currents in Discovery Passage and it is suggested that divers use local dive operators as guides.

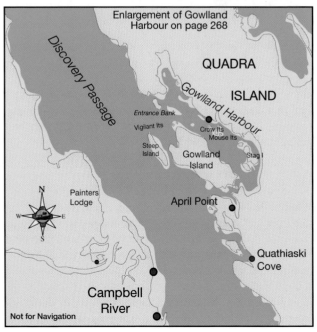

Enlargement of Gowlland Harbour on page 268

QUADRA ISLAND

Discovery Passage

Gowlland Harbour

Entrance Bank

Vigilant Its

Crow Its
Mouse Its

Steep Island

Gowlland Island

Stag I

Painters Lodge

N
W E
S

April Point

Quathiaski Cove

Campbell River

Not for Navigation

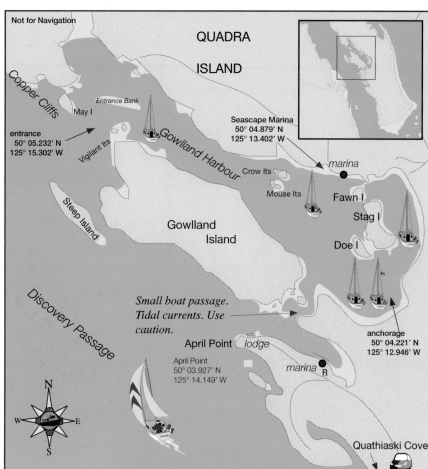

Not for Navigation

QUADRA

ISLAND

Copper Cliffs

Entrance Bank

May I

entrance
50° 05.232' N
125° 15.302' W

Vigilant Its

Gowlland Harbour

Seascape Marina
50° 04.879' N
125° 13.402' W

marina

Crow Its

Mouse Its

Fawn I

Stag I

Steep Island

Gowlland
Island

Doe I

Discovery Passage

Small boat passage.
Tidal currents. Use
caution.

anchorage
50° 04.221' N
125° 12.946' W

April Point lodge

April Point
50° 03.927' N
125° 14.149' W

marina R

N
W E
S

Quathiaski Cove

Seascape Marina

PO Box 250
Quadra Island BC V0P 1N0
Phone 250-285-3450
Toll Free 1-888-893-1626
info@seascapewaterfrontresort.com
www.seascapewaterfrontresort.com
Guest moorage is available, with reservations preferred.
Power at the dock is 15 amps. Guests are offered washrooms,
showers, laundry, ice, internet access, kayaking, power boat
rentals, sauna/hot tub, video rentals.

April Point Resort & Spa

900 April Point Rd, Quadra Island BC V0P 1N0
Phone 250-285-2222
april_point@obmg.com   www.aprilpoint.com
A large permanent marina with over 600 metres of dock space
for overnight or extended seasonal guest moorage, is located
beyond April Point. Reservations are recommended. There is
cable TV, laundry, showers, washrooms, ice, garbage drop,
launch ramp, and 15, 30 and 50 amp power at the docks.
The lodge has numerous amenities, rooms and bungalows.

Services include internet access, fishing guides and charters, a
restaurant, lounge, coffee shop, gift shop, spa and conference
rooms. Ask at the lodge for details about scuba diving arrangements and charters, scooter and kayak rentals and eco-tours.
There is a shuttle available to carry guests across Discovery
Passage to Painter's Lodge in Campbell River.

Note: Keep red channel marker close to starboard when approaching
April Point Marina, remember: red right return.

Right: Anchorage, private docks and Seascape Marina in the lee of Crow and Fawn Islets and Stag Island, in Gowlland Harbour. Below: The marina at Seascape Resort. Opposite page: The almost drying waterway between the marina and Fawn Islet and the owners of the marina and lodge, Mark and Jennifer Wanstall. The lower photograph shows a carved eagle at the resort's entrance. Like the bears in the top photo, these carvings are accompanied by more similar works in a large, spacious pavilion alongside the marina.

Campbell River

The velocity of water surging through Seymour Narrows just north of the town is dangerous. Be mindful of tides and currents, especially when venturing through the narrows or around the bottom of Quadra Island and its infamous Cape Mudge during gusty winds and swift moving tidal waters. Strong southeasterlies are particularly dangerous when the tide is in flood, so pick your weather carefully when navigating this area.

Duncan Bay, located opposite Gowlland Harbour, is the site of the Crown Zellerbach pulp mill. Its tall chimneys serve as a weather guage with winds blowing from the north indica-

tive of good weather in the offing. When entering Discovery Passage from the south, choose a slack or ebbing tide if the wind is up. Stay clear of the Wilby Shoals off Cape Mudge.

Campbell River is a busy place. You will find marinas with moorage and full boating facilities. There are all services, shopping centres, hospital, post office and airport. Charter and scheduled flights, by land and sea, fly in and out of Campbell River daily. It is a large town and the hub for many coastal destinations and communities. It is also becoming a stop for cruise ships that use Discovery Passage en route to and from Alaska.

Campbell River market and events

The Pier Street Farmers Market operartes as an open-air market every Sunday between 9 am and 2 pm, from April to September. Regular events include: Maritime Oceans Day–June. Discovery Passage Boat Rodeo–August. For more information on Campbell River events contact the Visitor Centre at *visitorcentre.ca* or phone them at 250-287-4636.

Top: April Point Lodge with its small craft docks, pavilion and accommodations. The new pavilion was added, at the point, in recent years. Mariners are accommodated at a large marina east of the point.
Left: The lobby at April Point resort has a busy gift and souvenir store. Bottom: The adjoining docks are used primarily for sport fishing guests. Marina moorage is shown on the following page.

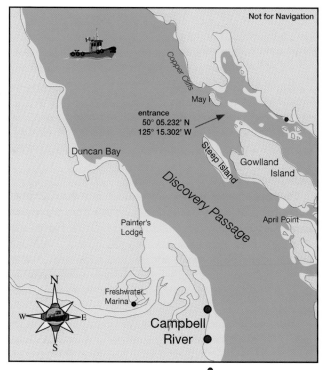

Above: The spacious and well sheltered April Point Marina, just east of April Point. Use your chart to navigate past April Point and a reef a short distance off the marina. Right: Discovery Passage from the north showing smoke from the mill at Duncan Bay. Bottom: A game of chess at the April Point lodge waterfront. From here, guests are invited to join excursions to Painters Lodge in Campbell River.

There are resorts that cater to fishermen and eco-tourists, offering guided salmon fishing and tournaments and adventure tourism. Some lodges with marinas offer no transient moorage while others have an open door to overnight boating stops.

Scuba diving in the area is outstanding and attracts visitors worldwide. Visit Quathiaski Cove where a long-time diving lodge and charter services are available. Fishing charters and boat rentals are available for excursions into the current-swept passages adjacent to the town. A water taxi service connects outlying communities.

On the west side of Discovery Passage, is the Campbell River Coast Discovery Inn and adjacent downtown shopping centre. Services, shops and restaurants are located in the city centre. Marine charts, books, fishing gear, licences and boat supplies are available at nearby marine stores.

There is a large, modern shopping centre in Campbell River adjacent to the Coast Discovery marina. Alongside the marina is the ferry landing for Quathiaski Cove on Quadra Island. Medical services are available nearby. The foreshore park with its scenic walkway connects the marinas with downtown Campbell River.

Above: Discovery Harbour Marina is a prominent and massive marina on the coast. It accommodates all sizes and is located alongside the major shopping centre and marine service facility in Campbell River.
Left: Views of Fisherman's Wharf. Bottom right: Freshwater Marina.

Freshwater Marina
2705 Island Hwy, Campbell River BC V9W 4Z9
Phone 250-286-0701. Mostly premanent moorage. Guests are not permitted to stay on board overnight.

Fisherman's Wharf
Campbell River Harbour Authority
Ph: 250-287-7931. *fishermans@telus.net*

Above: Fisherman's Wharf is usually filled with commercial vessels, but there is space for some transient craft. It is well located adjacent to downtown Campbell River. Nearest fuel is at Discovery Harbour.

Open all year, this public dock is for commercial and pleasure boats–reservations are suggested. It has three tidal grids, electric winches, garbage disposal, pumpout, 20, 30 and 50 amp power, washrooms, showers, ice, bait, tackle, seafood sales, and charts. Wireless internet access is available. Marine service, mechanic, repairs and stores are available nearby. It is located near the ferry to Quadra Island. Visit the Maritime Museum in Campbell River.

At the Discovery Marina not only will you be able to replenish your fuel and other supplies right at the marina, but also take a stroll through the adjacent large shopping centre.

There is a restaurant and pub at the landing, which provides moorage as well as a varied dinner or lunch menu for those staying over. The pub offers moorage and ocean side service with waterfront and mountain views. Seating is available in a charming interior setting or the heated ourdoor patio. A catering service is available for both on or off premises.

The large marine store in the shopping complex has an adjoining work yard complete with travel lift and full service.

Discovery Harbour Marina

392-1434 Ironwood St
Campbell River BC V9W 5T7
Phone 250-287-2614
tara@discoveryharbourmarina.com
www.discoveryharbourmarina.com
The fuel dock has gas, diesel and oils. Moorage includes 150 berths for guests, accommodating boats to 45 metres and more. Power at the docks has 20, 30, 50 and 100 amp service.
A large open-water launch ramp with no float is a short distance north of the marina.
Dockside marine service and travel lift can be arranged. The marina provides internet access, laundry, showers, ice, bait, and garbage disposal.
House of Treasure native art gallery is located on shore next to the Discovery Harbour Marina entrance.

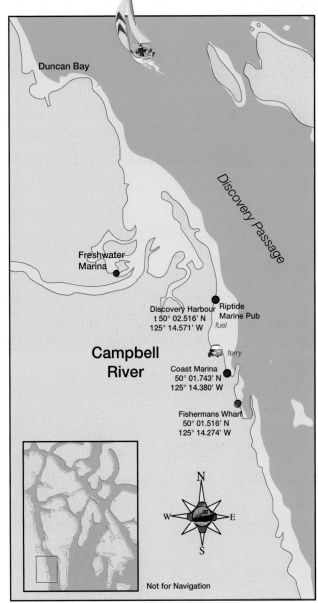

Duncan Bay

Discovery Passage

Freshwater Marina

Discovery Harbour t 50° 02.516' N 125° 14.571' W

Riptide Marine Pub
fuel

Campbell River

ferry

Coast Marina
50° 01.743' N
125° 14.380' W

Fishermans Wharf
50° 01.516' N
125° 14.274' W

N
W E
S

Not for Navigation

Above: Tyee spit. The Campbell River flows into Discovery Channel around the Spit. The launch ramp is located just north of the jetty immediately north of Discovery Harbour. Left: Discovery Marina's floating office is located on the dock.

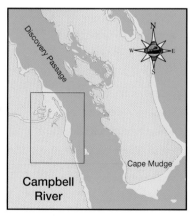

Left: Native structure on display near the Quadra Island ferry terminal.

Above: The Coast Discovery Campbell River Inn and Marina dock alongside the ferry landing in Campbell River. The hotel's fine amenities are available to mooring customers. The close proximity of the ferry landing makes foot passenger excursions to Quadra Island convenient. Right: The hotel's marina has overnight moorage and facilities for visiting mariners. A fish and chips restaurant is conveniently located in the harbour.

Enjoying the sunshine at the Coast Discovery Inn and Marina, located off Discovery Passage alongside the Quadra Island ferry terminal.

Coast Marina
50° 01.743' N
125° 14.380' W

Restaurant

Ferry terminal

Coast Discovery Marina

The River

For those who wish to venture up the Campbell River estuary it is necessary to round the end of the spit north of the large, exposed launch ramp on Discovery Passage and travel upstream. A waterway opens to port, with several seaplane floats lining the lee shore. The channel takes small boats up river as far as a bridge over the Island Highway. Turning off the channel before the bridge, a slough opens up to accommodate a small-boat marina. We have been as far up the river as this marina in a 21 foot outboard propelled boat and found the river to have adequate depth. Care must be taken not to stray from the marked channel. Paddlers find their way farther up the river, reaching all the way to the Elk Falls Provincial Park. Use caution in estuaries and even the marked channels, because by the nature of things, changes to channel depths are ongoing.

Riptide Marine Pub and Grill

1340 Island Hwy
Campbell River BC V9W 8C9
Phone 250-830-0044
riptide@connected.bc.ca www.riptide.homestead.com
Some moorage, laundromat, shower facilities. Adjacent, *Ocean Pacific Marine Supply* offers all yacht repairs and services.

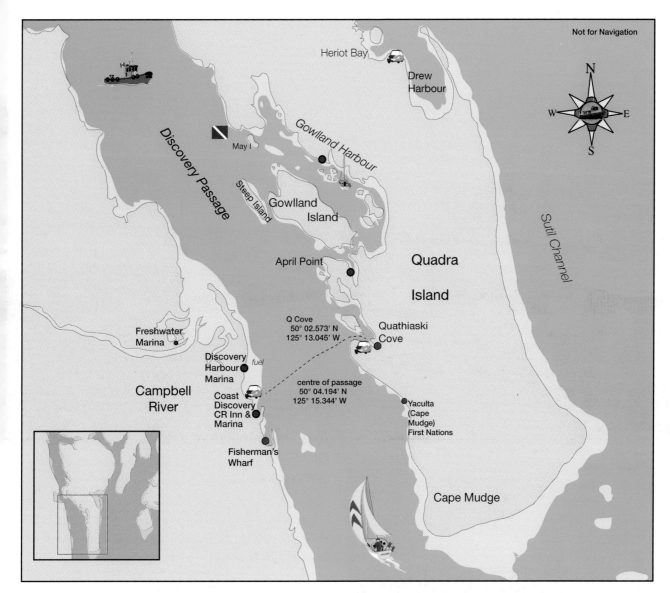

Heriot Bay

Drew Harbour

Discovery Passage

May I

Gowlland Harbour

Steep Island

Gowlland Island

N
W   E
S

Sutil Channel

April Point

Quadra

Island

Q Cove
50° 02.573' N
125° 13.045' W

Quathiaski Cove

Freshwater Marina

Discovery Harbour Marina   *fuel*

Campbell River

Coast Discovery CR Inn & Marina

centre of passage
50° 04.194' N
125° 15.344' W

Yaculta (Cape Mudge) First Nations

Fisherman's Wharf

Cape Mudge

Coast Discovery C.R. Inn & Marina

975 Shoppers Row
Campbell River BC V9W 2C4
Phone 250-287-7455 *www.coasthotels.com*
Moorage is available on 1,900 feet of docks, which can take boats to 50 metres. Power is 30, 50 and 100 amp service. Fish and chips, water taxi, dive shop at the marina and an on-site liquor store. Other facilities include garbage disposal, showers, ice, bait, washrooms, restaurant and lounge.

Take on fuel at Campbell River or just beyond Seymour Narrows at Brown's Bay, because you may not find fuel too conveniently if you are heading north up Johnstone Strait. There is fuel at Blind Channel or at Refuge Cove in Desolation Sound. It is also available at Heriot Bay on the east side of Quadra Island as well as at Gorge Harbour on Cortes Island.

The private docks of a complex south of Campbell River.

Above: This broad view across Quathiaski Cove shows Grouse Island, Gowlland Harbour and Drew Harbour beyond. Sutil Channel continues past the east sides of Quadra Island and Read Island, upper right. Left: The dock at Quathiaski Cove is mostly filled with local and commercial vessels. Short visits to the cove may be made conveniently via ferry from Campbell River.

Quathiaski Cove

The south end of Quadra Island was settled and developed even before Campbell River. It was a busy community, with stores, logging operations, hotel, mission, school and jailhouse. Quathiaski Cove was the landing for travellers between Vancouver Island and Quadra. Canoes were the original means of crossing Discovery Passage, but it was not long before a couple of settlers put their power launches into service to taxi people across. Later a more formal ferry service came into operation, followed by a larger vessel being put into service. Eventually BC Ferries included the crossing in their fleet operations.

Passage around Grouse Island is mostly unrestricted. Unkak Cove, opening off the north end of Quathiaski Cove is shallow and dries completely at low tide. Sheltered anchorage is best in Gowlland Harbour.

Above: From Quathiaski Cove, looking northwest over Grouse Island, Tyee spit can be seen guarding the mouth of the Campbell River. The mill at Duncan Bay is at the upper right corner. Right and below: The ferry to Campbell River leaves the landing at Quathiaski Cove.

Quathiaski Cove public dock

Quadra Island Harbour Authority public dock (DFO)
Ph: 250-285-3622

The marina lies alongside the ferry terminal for Campbell River. Fuel is available at Campbell River or at Heriot Bay–phone 250-285-3212. There are 195 metres of float at this busy local dock. Much of the dock space is taken by permanent mooring vessels. Alongside there is a launch ramp. Garbage is accepted for a fee. Amenities include showers, washrooms and laundry. Shops are located a short walk up the hill from the waterfront.

Above: Looking over Grouse Island in Quathiaski Cove. Beyond lower Quadra Island and Sutil Channel lie Marina Island and Cortes Island.
Below: Busy docks at Quathiaski Cove leave little room for visitors. Rafting up alongside other vessels is permitted.

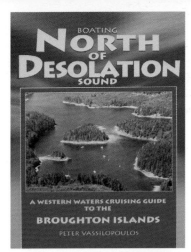

Cruising Guide Series

North of Desolation Sound–Volume 1
ISBN 0-919317-32-4 2004. $46.95
North of Desolation Sound– a coffee table styled full colour, Illustrated guide-book. This companion book to the Gulf Islands Cruising Guide is a comprehensive reference book/guide to the Broughton Islands area and routes from Stuart Island to Seymour Inlet. Filled with full colour photos, aerial pictures and diagrams. A must for serious mariners cruising the BC inland coast. Available at all marine stores and book sellers.

More guides and books from
Pacific Marine Publishing
PO Box 1310 Delta BC V4M 3Y8.
PO Box 984 Point Roberts WA 98281.

Gulf Islands Cruising Guide–Volume 2
ISBN 0-919317-38-3.2006 $46.95
The Gulf Islands Cruising Guide is a colourful refere4nce book to the Gulf Islands Archipelago. It features all of the islands and adjacent Vancouver Island anchorages and marinas, passages, coves and routes. The pages are packed with information accompanied by full colour aerial and ambient photographs of the islands. It includes the south end of Vancouver Island from Sook to Victoria as well as the southeast coast of Vancouver Island to Comox and the adjacent Northern Gulf Islands. Tidal Rapids in the Gulf Islands by Kevin Monahan, author of *Local Knowledge*.

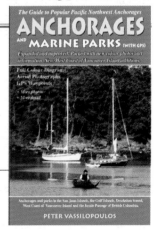

Directory Series

Anchorages and Marine Parks (Second edition)
ISBN 0919317-24-3 2000 b/w $19.95

A companion to Docks and Destinations, this book is a complete coastal guide to marine parks and anchorages. It covers the area from the San Juan Islands to Ketchikan following the coast in geographical sequence from south to north, returning down the west coast of Vancouver Island in a north to south progression. The guide is loaded with aerial and ambient photographs and concise diagrams clearly depicting location of anchorages and parks. Foreword by Captain Ken Burton, RCMP, Marine Division.

Docks and Destinations (Seventh edition)
ISBN 0-919317-36-7 2005 $29.95.
With GPS and Golf Course phone numbers.
Full colour throughout.
This is a complete guide to marinas on the coast of British Columbia and Puget Sound, Washington. It covers the inside passage to Ketchikan, Alaska from Olympia in Washington state in geographical sequence. The west coast of Vancouver Island is included from north to south. The book is filled with hundreds of aerial and ambient photographs and concise diagrams with pertinent information on marina services and facilities.
GPS Waypoints have been included for all entries in this popular marine guide.

Author Peter Vassilopoulos has travelled extensively throughout the entire area during nearly 35 years of boating in the Pacific Northwest, and provides up-to-date information on where to go, what to look for and why to visit the destinations included.

INDEX

This index provides primary and some secondary references to names of anchorages, marinas, passages, islands and features of the coast deemed to be notable. Most are found as headings, titles, subtitles and in bold typeface. Some appear only on the diagrams and/or in plain reference in the text. They may appear also elsewhere in the guide, not indexed as such, in a secondary context.

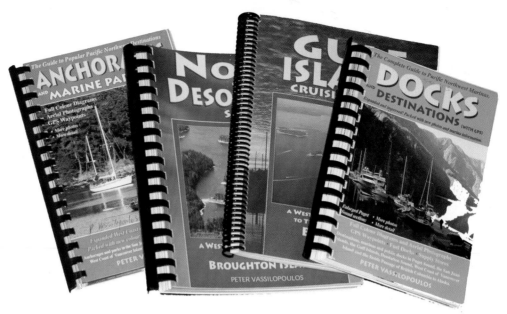

Keep them together.

Thank you for choosing this marine guide. It has been printed and bound to high standards and should last for many years of normal use.

Wear and tear on the binding can be minimized by not pressing the open spreads flat. Doing so can result in cracking the glue that binds the individual pages or sections together. If you choose to flatten the open book and the pages break away from the binding, it is recommended that you take the book to your local office supply store or instant copy printer, where, for a small fee, it can be rebound using a spiral type of binding. Many people who purchase books such as these guides have them bound this way right from the outset.

There are two popular types of binding: regular plastic coil spiral or a flat form of ring binding known as Cerlox. Ask your supplier to show you samples.

Recommended reading and marine books on the areas covered in this guide

151 Dives in theProtected Waters of British Columbia and Washington State. Betty Pratt-Johnson. 2007.

Anchorages and Marine Parks: Guide to anchorages and marine parks in British Columbia and the San Juan Islands. Peter Vassilopoulos. Seagraphic Publications. 2008.

Best Anchorages of the Inland Sea: Anne Vipond. Ocean Cruise Guides. 2007

BC Marine Parks Guide: The official guide to BC's coastal marine parks. OP Publishing. 2005.

Birds of Southwestern British Columbia. Cannings, Aversa and Opperman. Heritage House. 2006.

Cruising Guide to British Columbia: Vol. 2 Desolation Sound. Bill Wolferstan. Whitecap Books. 1980.

Cruising Guide to British Columbia: Vol. 3 Sunshine Coast. Bill Wolferstan. Whitecap Books. 1982.

Canadian Tide and Current Tables: Vol. 5 Juan de Fuca Strait & Strait of Georgia. Canadian Hydrographic Service.

Desolation Sound: A History: Heather Harbord. Heritage House. 2007.

Docks and Destinations: A guide to marinas in British Columbia and Puget Sound, Wash. GPS coordinates included. Peter Vassilopoulos. Pacific Marine Publishing. 2007.

Evergreen Pacific Cruising Atlas: Olympia to Queen Charlottes. Evergreen Pacific.

Exploring the South Coast of British Columbia: Gulf Islands and Desolation Sound to Broughton Archipelago and Blunden Harbour. Don Douglass, Reanne Hemingway-Douglass. Fine Edge.

Dreamspeaker Guide: Vol. 2 Desolation Sound. Anne & Laurence Yeadon-Jones. Fine Edge.

Dreamspeaker Guide: Vol. 3 Vancouver, Howe Sound, & the Sunshine Coast. Yeadon-Jones. Fine Edge.

Edible Seashore: Pacific Shores Cookbook and Guide. Rick Harbo. Hancock House. 2005.

Following the Curve of Time: Cathy Converse. Touch-Wood Editions. 2008.

High Boats: A Century of Salmon Remembered. Pat Wastell Norris. Harbour Publishing. 2003.

Islands in the Salish Sea: A Community Atlas. Edited by Sheila Harrington and Judi Stevenson. TouchWood. 2005.

Journeys Through the Inside Passage: Seafaring Adventures along the Coast of British Columbia and Alaska. Joe Upton. 1998.

Local Knowledge: The Skipper's Reference-Tacoma to Ketchikan. Kevin Monahan. Fine Edge.

Marine Weather Hazards Manual: Local forecasts and conditions for the West Coast. Environment Canada.

Naturally Salty: Coastal Characters of the Pacific Northwest. Marianne Scott. TouchWood. 2003.

Navigating the Coast: A History of the Union Steamship Company. Edited by Peter Chapman. 1977.

Oceanography of the British Columbia Coast: Richard E. Thomson. Canadian Special Publication of Fisheries and Aquatic Sciences. 1981.

Pacific Reef & Shore: Marine Life of the Pacific Northwest. Rick Harbo. Harbour Publishing. 2003.

Ports and Passes: Tides, currents and charts. Olympia to Prince Rupert. Chyna Sea Ventures. Annual.

Proven Cruising Routes: Vol. 1. Precise courses to steer Seattle to Ketchikan. Kevin Monahan. Fine Edge.

Sailing Directions: Pacific Coast, General Information. Fisheries and Oceans Canada.

Sea Kayak Desolation Sound and the Sunshine Coast: Heather harbord. Rocky Mountain Books. 2005.

Seven Knot Summers: Beth Hill. Horsdal & Schubart. 1994.

Shorelines: Edited by Jocelyn Reekie & Annette Yourk. Kingfisher Publishing, Quadra Island. 1995.

Spilsbury's Coast: Jim Spilsbury & Howard White. Harbour Publishing. 1991.

The Curve of Time: M. Wylie Blanchet. Whitecap Books. 1997.

The Lawman: Lynne Stonier-Newman. Heritage House. 2007.

The Radar Book: Effective Navigation and Collision Avoidance. Kevin Monahan. Fine Edge.

Tidal Passages: Jeanette Taylor. Harbour Publishing 2008.

Tidepool & Reef: Marine life Guide to the Pacific Northwest Coast. Rick Harbo. Hancock House.

Upcoast Summers: Beth Hill. Horsdal & Schubart. 1985.

Waggoner Cruising Guide: Puget Sound to Prince Rupert. Robert Hale. Weatherly Press. Annual.

Weatherly Waypoint Guides: Vol. 2 Gulf of Georgia, includes Gulf Islands, Jervis Inlet, & Princess Louisa Inlet. Weatherly Press.

Whelks to Whales: Coastal Marine Life of the Pacific Northwest. Rick M. Harbo. Harbour Publishing. 1999.

Pacific Yachting

Pacific Yachting Magazine is the magazine of choice for regular articles on the cruising areas covered in this book. Visit their website at *www.pacificyachting.com*

My wife Carla and I have cruised the area this guide covers for more than 35 years. We have visited all areas described in the book and have stopped at or anchored in most anchorages. There are numerous books on cruising the coast and these along with your charts and reference books should enable you to extend your cruising range substantially and safely.

Safe and happy boating–Peter Vassilopoulos.